HISTORY OF
ENGLISH HUMOUR

Alfred Guy Kingan L'estrange

Author of "The Life of the Rev. William Harness,"
"From the Thames to the Tamar," Etc.

HISTORY OF
ENGLISH HUMOUR

With an Introduction upon Ancient Humour.

In Two Volumes.
Vol. I.

BIBLIOBAZAAR

HISTORY OF
ENGLISH HUMOUR

CONTENTS OF THE FIRST VOLUME.

PART III.
ROMAN HUMOUR.

ENGLISH HUMOUR.

CHAPTER I.
MIDDLE AGES.

CHAPTER II.

CHAPTER III.

CHAPTER IV.

CHAPTER V.

CHAPTER VI.

CHAPTER VII.

CHAPTER VIII.

CHAPTER IX.

CHAPTER X.

CHAPTER XI.

PRELIMINARY OBSERVATIONS.

Subjective Character of the Ludicrous—The Subject little
  Studied—Obstacles to the Investigation—Evanescence—
  Mental Character of the Ludicrous—Distinction between
  Humour and the Ludicrous.

The ludicrous is in its character so elusive and protean, and the
field over which it extends is so vast, that few have ever undertaken
the task of examining it systematically. Many philosophers and literary
men have made passing observations upon it, but most writers are
content to set it down as one of those things which cannot be understood,
and care not to study and grapple with a subject which promises small
results in return for considerable toil. Moreover, the inquiry does not
seem sufficiently important to warrant the expenditure of much time
upon it, and there has always been a great tendency among learned
men to underrate the emotional feelings of our nature. Thus it comes
to pass that a much larger amount of our labour has been expended
upon inquiring into physical and intellectual constitution than upon the
inner workings of our passions and sentiments, for our knowledge of
which, though affecting our daily conduct, we are mostly indebted to
the representations of poets and novelists. Beattie well observes that
nothing is below the attention of a philosopher which the Author of
Nature has been pleased to establish. Investigations of this kind would
not be unrewarded, nor devoid of a certain amount of interest; and I
think that in the present subject we can, by perseverance, penetrate a
little distance into an almost untrodden and apparently barren region,
and if we cannot reach the source from whence the bright waters
spring, can at least obtain some more accurate information about
the surrounding country.

  Notwithstanding all the obstructions and discouragements in
the way of this investigation a few great men have given it a certain

amount of attention. Aristotle informs us in his "Rhetoric" that he has dealt fully with the subject in his Poetics, and although the treatise is unfortunately lost, some annotations remain which show that it was of a comprehensive character. Cicero and Quintilian in their instructions in Oratory, made the study of humour a necessary part of the course, and in modern days many ingenious definitions and descriptions of it are found among the pages of general literature. Most philosophers have touched the subject timidly and partially, unwilling to devote much time to it, and have rather stated what they thought ought to be in accordance with some pet theories of their own, than drawn deductions from careful analysis. They generally only looked at one phase of the ludicrous, at one kind of humour, and had not a sufficient number of examples before them—probably from the difficulty of recalling slight turns of thought in widely scattered subjects. Add to this, that many of them—constantly immersed in study—would have had some little difficulty in deciding what did and did not deserve the name of humour. Most of their definitions are far too wide, and often in supporting a theory they make remarks which tend to refute it. The imperfect treatment, which the subject had received, led Dugald Stewart to observe that it was far from being exhausted.

The two principal publications which have appeared on humour, are Flögel's "Geschichte der Komischen Litteratur" (1786), and Léon Dumont's "Les Causes du Rire." The former is voluminous, but scarcely touches on philosophy, without which such a work can have but little coherence. The latter shows considerable psychological knowledge, but is written to support a somewhat narrow and incomplete view. Mr. Wright's excellent book on "The Grotesque in Literature and Art," is, as the name suggests, principally concerned with broad humour, and does not so much trace its source as the effects it has produced upon mankind. Mr. Cowden Clark's contributions on the subject to the "Gentleman's Magazine," are mostly interesting from their biographical notices.

To analyse and classify all the vagaries of the human imagination which may be comprehended under the denomination of humour, is no easy task, and as it is multiform we may stray into devious paths in pursuing it. But vast and various as the subject seems to be, there cannot be much doubt that there are some laws which govern it, and that it can be brought approximately under certain heads. It seems to be as generally admitted that there are different kinds of humour as that some observations possess none at all. Moreover, when remarks of a certain kind are made, especially such as show confusion or exaggeration, we often seem to detect some conditions of humour, and by a little change are able to make something, which has more or less the character of a jest.

There is in this investigation a very formidable "Dweller on the Threshold." We contend with great disadvantages in any attempts to examine our mental constitution. When we turn the mind in upon itself, and make it our object, the very act of earnest reflection obscures the idea, or destroys the emotion we desire to contemplate. This is especially the case in the present instance. The ludicrous, when we attempt to grasp it, shows off its gay and motley garb, and appears in grave attire. It is only by abstracting our mind from the inquiry, and throwing it into lighter considerations, that we can at all retain the illusion. A clever sally appears brilliant when it breaks suddenly upon the mental vision, but when it is brought forward for close examination it loses half its lustre, and seems to melt into unsubstantial air. Humour may be compared to a delicate scent, which we only perceive at the first moment, or to evanescent beauty—

> "For every touch that wooed its stay
> Has brushed its brightest hues away."

This last simile is especially in point here, and the quotations in this book will scarcely be found humorous, so long as they are regarded as mere illustrations of the nature of humour.

We need not—taking these matters into consideration—feel much surprised that some people say the ludicrous cannot be defined; as for instance, Buckingham,

> "True wit is everlasting like the sun,
> Describing all men, but described by none;"

and Addison:—"It is much easier to decide what is not humorous than what is, and very difficult to define it otherwise than Cowley has done, by negatives"—the only meaning of which is that the subject is surrounded with rather more than the usual difficulties attending moral and psychological researches. Similar obstacles would be encountered in answering the question, "What is poetry?" or "What is love?" We can only say that even here there must be some surroundings by which we can increase our knowledge.

Humour is the offspring of man—it comes forth like Minerva fully armed from the brain. Our sense of the ludicrous is produced by our peculiar mental constitution, and not by external objects, in which there is nothing either absurd or serious. As when the action of our mind is imperceptible—for instance, in hearing and seeing with our "bodily" senses—we think what we notice is something in the external world, although it is only so far dependent upon it that it could not exist without some kind of outer influence, so the result of our not recognising the amusing action of the mind in the ludicrous is that we regard it as a quality resident in the persons and things we contemplate.[1] But it does not belong to these things, and is totally different from them in kind. Thus, the rose is formed of certain combinations of earth, air, and water; yet none of these dull elements possess the fragrance or beauty of the flower. These properties come from some attractive and constructive power. Not only are there no types or patterns in things of our emotions, but there are none even of our sensations; heat and cold, red or blue, are such only for our constitution. This truth is beautifully set forth by Addison in a passage in which, as Dugald Stewart justly remarks, "We are at a loss whether most to admire the author's depth and refinement of thought, or the singular felicity of fancy displayed in its illustration." "Things," he observes, "would make but a poor appearance to the eye, if we saw them only in their proper figures and motions. And what reason can we assign for their exciting in us many of those ideas which are different from anything that exists in the objects themselves (for such are light and colours) were it not to add supernumerary ornaments to the universe, and make it more agreeable to the imagination? We are everywhere entertained with pleasing shows and apparitions. We discover imaginary glories in the heavens and on the earth, and see some of this visionary beauty poured out over the whole creation. But what a rough, unsightly sketch of Nature should we be entertained with, did all her colouring disappear, and the several distinctions of light and shade vanish! In short, our souls are delightfully lost and bewildered in a pleasing delusion, and we walk about like the enchanted hero of a romance, who sees beautiful castles, woods, and meadows, and at the same time hears the warbling of birds and the purling of streams; but upon the finishing of some secret spell, the fantastic scene breaks up, and the disconsolate knight finds himself on a barren heath, or in a solitary desert."

I have introduced these considerations, because it is very difficult for us to realize that what we behold is merely phenomenal, that

"Things are not what they seem;"

but that we are looking into the mirror of Nature at our own likeness. When we speak of a ludicrous occurrence, we cannot avoid thinking that the external events themselves contain something of that character. Thus, the ludicrous has come in our ideas and language to be separated from the sense in which alone it exists, and it is desirable that we should clearly understand that the distinction is only logical and not real.

When the cause of our laughter—be it mind, matter, or imaginary circumstance—is merely regarded as something incongruous and amusing, we name it the ludicrous, and a man is called ludicrous as faulty or contemptible. But when the cause of it is viewed as something more than this, as coming from some conscious power or tendency within us—a valuable gift and an element in our mental constitution—we call it humour, a term applied only to human beings and their productions; and a man is called humorous as worthy of commendation. Both are in truth feelings—we might say one feeling—and although we can conceive humour to exist apart from the ludicrous, and to be a power within us creating it, there is a difficulty in following out the distinction. The difference between them is in our regard.

As soon as in course of time it became plainly evident that gay creations might emanate from man, and not only from the outer world, the fact was marked by the formation of a distinctive name, and by degrees several names—among which the most comprehensive in English is Humour. This kind of gift became gradually known as more or less possessed by all, and when the operations of the mind came to be recognised, we were more enlightened on the subject, and acknowledged it to be a mental and creative power.

Such admissions would not be made by men in general without some very strong evidence, and therefore a humorous man was not merely one who had an internal sense of the ludicrous, but one who employed it for the delectation of others. Hence, also, though there is no consciousness of being amusing in the man who is ludicrous, there is in one that is humorous. A wit must always be pleasant intentionally. A man who in sober seriousness recounts something which makes us laugh is not humorous, although his want of discrimination may not be sufficient to make him ludicrous. Children are not regarded as humorous, for, although they enjoy such simple humour as toys afford, they very seldom notice what is merely ludicrous, and do not reproduce it in any way; and the same may be said of many grown persons, who require to be fed as it were, and although they can enjoy what is embellished by others, have no original observation. Thus, although Herbert Mayo is substantially correct in saying that "humour is the sentiment of the ludicrous," he might have added that there is a difference between the two in our knowledge of them. In the former, the creative mind is more marked, and, a man though he laughs much, if he be dull in words is only considered to have mirth, *i.e.*, joyousness or a sense of the ludicrous, not humour. The gift can only be brought prominently forward in speech or writing, and thus humour comes to be often regarded as a kind of ingredient or seasoning in a speech or book, if not actually synonymous with certain sentences or expressions. Still we always confine the name to human productions, as, for instance, gestures, sayings, writings, pictures, and plays.

The recognition of the mental character of humour did not necessarily imply any knowledge as to the authority, instability, or constancy of the feeling—that could only be acquired by philosophical investigation. Nor have we yet so far ascertained its character as to be able to form humorous fancies upon any fixed principle. We are guided by some sense of the ludicrous which we cannot analyse; or we introduce into new and similar cases relationships in things which we have observed to be amusing. Some forms are so general that they will produce a vast number of jests, and we thus seem to have some insight into the influences that awaken humour, but we see only approximately and superficially, and can merely produce good results occasionally—rather by an accident than with any certainty.

INTRODUCTION.

PART I.

ORIGIN OF HUMOUR.

Pleasure in Humour—What is Laughter?—Sympathy—First Phases—Gradual Development—Emotional Phase—Laughter of Pleasure—Hostile Laughter—Is there any sense of the Ludicrous in the Lower Animals?—Samson—David—Solomon—Proverbs—Fables.

Few of the blessings we enjoy are of greater value than the gift of humour. The pleasure attendant upon it attracts us together, forms an incentive, and gives a charm to social intercourse, and, unlike the concentrating power of love, scatters bright rays in every direction. That humour is generally associated with enjoyment might be concluded from the fact that the genial and good-natured are generally the most mirthful, and we all have so much personal experience of the gratification it affords, that it seems superfluous to adduce any proofs upon the subject. "Glad" is from the Greek word for laughter, and the word "jocund" comes from a Latin term signifying "pleasant." But we can trace the results of this connection in our daily observation. How comes it to pass that many a man who is the life and soul of social gatherings, and keeps his friends in delighted applause, sits, when alone in his study, grave and sedate, and seldom, if ever, smiles in reading or meditation? Is it not because humour is a source of pleasure? We are not joyously disposed when alone, whereas in society we are ready to give and receive whatever is bright and cheering.

The first question which now presents itself is what is laughter? and our answer must be that it is a change of countenance accompanied by a spasmodic intermittent sound—a modification of the voice—but that we cannot trace its physical origin farther than to attribute it to some effect produced upon the sympathetic nerve, or rather the system of nerves termed respiratory. These communicate with every organ affected in mirth, but the ultimate connection between mind and body is hidden from our view.

In all laughter there is more or less pleasure, except in that of hysteria, when by a sudden shock the course of Nature is reversed, and excessive grief will produce the signs of joy, as extravagant delight will sometimes exhibit those of sorrow. We should also exclude the laughter caused by inhalation of gas, and that of maniacs, which arising from some strange and unaccountable feeling is abnormal and imperfect, and known by a hollow sound peculiar to itself. None of these kinds of laughter are primary, they are but imperfect reflections of our usual modes of expression, and, excepting such cases, we may agree that M. Paffe is correct in observing that "Joy is an indispensable condition of laughter." Dr. Darwin refers to the laughter of idiots to prove that it may be occasioned by pleasure alone. Strangely enough, he quotes as an instance in point the fact of an idiot boy having laughed at receiving a black eye.

Proceeding onwards, we next come to inquire why the sense of humour is expressed by voice and countenance, and does not merely afford a silent and secret delight? The answer may be given, that one object, at least, is to increase social communication and multiply pleasure. The well-being of the animal world largely depends upon the power of each member of it to communicate with others of the same species. They all do so by sound and gesture, probably to a larger extent than we generally imagine. A celebrated physician lately observed to me that "all animals have some language." How far mere signs deserve so high a name may be questioned. But man has great powers of intercourse, and it is much owing to his superior faculties in this respect that he holds his place so high above the rest of creation. Orators, who make it their study to be impressive, give full importance to every kind of expression, and say that a man should be able to make his meaning understood, even when his voice is inaudible. It has been lately discovered that the mere movement of the lips alone, without sound, is sufficient to convey information.[2] Facial expression has been given us as a means of assisting communication, and smiles and laughter have become the distinctive manifestations of humour. Thus the electric spark passes from one to another, and the flashing eye and wreathed lip lights up the world. Profit also accrues—fear of being laughed at leads us to avoid numerous small errors, and by laughing at others we are enabled to detect shortcomings in ourselves.

Sympathetic laughter does not arise from any contemplation of ludicrous circumstances, but is only a sort of reflection of the feelings of others. There seems to be little intelligence in it, but something almost physical, just as yawning is infectious, or as on seeing a person wounded in a limb we instinctively shrink ourselves in the same part of the body. Even a picture of a man laughing will have some effect upon us, and so have those songs in which exuberant mirth is imitated. Thus we often laugh without feeling just cause, as we often feel cause without laughing. All exhibitions of emotion are infectious. We feel sad at seeing a man in grief, although the source of his sorrow is unknown to us; and we are inclined to be joyous when surrounded by the votaries of mirth. Not unfrequently we find a number of persons laughing, when the greater part of them have no idea what is the cause of the merriment. Sometimes we cannot entirely resist the impulse, even when we ourselves are the object of it, so much are we inclined to enter into the feelings and views of those who surround us. In this, as well as in many other cases, the sight and proximity of others exercise over us a great influence, and sometimes almost a fascination.

To this sympathy we are largely indebted for the diffusion of high spirits. It is pleasant to laugh and see others laughing, and thus the one leads to the other. "Laugh and be fat," is a proverb, and it has been well observed that "we like those who make us laugh," because they give us pleasure. We may add that we like to see others joyous, because we feel that we are surrounded by kindly natures. A gallant writer tells us that he hopes to be rewarded for his labours in the field of literature by "the sweetest of all sounds in nature—the laughter of fair women." Macready, speaking of this influence, says:

"The words of Milman would have applied well to Mrs. Jordan, 'Oh, the words laughed on her lips!' Mrs. Nesbitt, the charming actress of a late day, had a fascinating power in the sweetly-ringing notes of her hearty mirth; but Mrs. Jordan's laugh was so rich, so apparently irrepressible, so deliciously self-enjoying, as to be at all times irresistible."

The agreeable influence of smiles is so well known that many are tempted to counterfeit them, and assume an expression in which the eye and lip are in unhappy conflict.[3] On the other hand, painful thoughts are inimical to mirth. No sally of humour will brighten the countenance of a man who has lately suffered a severe loss, and even mental reflection will extinguish every sparkle. But the bed of sickness can often be better cheered by some gay efflorescence, some happy turn of thought, than by expressions of condolence. Galen says that Æsculapius wrote comic songs to promote circulation in his patients; and Hippocrates tells us that "a physician should have a certain ready humour, for austerity is repulsive both to well and ill." The late Sir Charles Clark recognised this so far that one of his patients told me that his visits were like a bottle of Champagne; and Sir John Byles observes, "Cheerfulness eminently conduces to health both of body and mind; it is one of the great physicians of nature.

> "Il y a trois médecins qui ne se trompent pas,
> La gaité, le doux exercice, et le modeste repas.

Every hour redeemed from despondency and melancholy, and bathed in the sunshine of cheerfulness, is an hour of true life gained."

Our views with regard to the first appearance of laughter depend on whether we consider that man was gradually developed from the primeval oyster, or that he came into the world much in the same condition as that in which we find him now. If we adopt the former opinion, we must consider that no outward expressions of feeling originally existed; if the latter, that they were from the first almost as perfect as they are at present. But I think that we shall be on tolerably safe ground, and have the support of probability and history, if we say that, in his earliest condition, the mental endowments of man were of the very humblest description, but that he had always a tendency to progress and improve. This view obtains some little corroboration from the fact that the sounds animals utter in the early stages of their lives are not fully developed, and that the children of the poor are graver and more silent than those of the educated classes. But a certain predisposition to laughter there always was, for what animal has ever produced any but its own characteristic sound? Has not everyone its own natural mode of expression? Does not the dog show its pleasure by wagging its tail, and the cat by purring? We never find one animal adopting the vocal sounds of another—a bird never mews, and a cat never sings. Some men have been called cynics from their whelpish ill-temper, but none of them have ever adopted a real canine snarl, though it might express their feelings better than human language. Laughter, so far as we can judge, could not have been obtained by any mere mental exercise, nor would it have come from imitation, for it is only found in man, the yelping of a hyena being as different from it as the barking of a dog, or the cackling of a goose. We may, however, suppose that the first sounds uttered by man were demonstrative of pain or pleasure, marking a great primary distinction, which we make in common with all animals. But our next expression showed superior sensibility and organism: it denoted a very peculiar perception of the intermingling of pain and pleasure, a combination of opposite feelings not possessed by other animals, or not distinct enough in them to have a specific utterance. There might seem to be something almost physical in the sensation, as it can be excited by tickling, or the inhalation of gas. Similar results may be produced by other bodily causes. Homer speaks of the chiefs laughing after a sumptuous banquet, and of a man "laughing sweetly" when drunk. Bacon's term *titillatio*, would seem very appropriate in such cases. There was an idea, in olden times, that laughter emanated from a particular part of the body. Tasso, in "Jerusalem Delivered," describing the death of Ardonio, who was slain by a lance, says that it

> "Pierced him through the vein
> Where laughter has her fountain and her seat,
> So that (a dreadful bane)
> He laughed for pain, and laughed himself to death."

This idea probably arose from observing the spasmodic power of laughter, which was greater formerly than now, and to the same origin we may attribute the stories of the fatal consequences it has, at times, produced; of Zeuxis, the painter, having expired in a fit brought on by contemplating a caricature he had made of an old woman, and of Franciscus Cosalinus, a learned logician, having thus broken a blood-vessel, which led to his dying of consumption. Wolfius relates "that a country bumpkin, called Brunsellius, by chance seeing a woman asleep at a sermon fall off her seat, was so taken that he laughed for three days, which weakened him so that he continued for a long time afterwards in an infirm state."

We must suppose that laughter has always existed in man, at least as long as he has been physically constituted as he is now, for it might always have been produced by tickling the papillæ of the nerves, which are said to be more exposed in man than in other animals. When we have stated the possibility of this pleasurable sensation being awakened under such circumstances, we have, in fact, asserted that it was in course of time thus called into existence. But the enjoyment might have been limited to this low phase, for the mind might have been so vacant, so deficient in emotion and intelligence that the moral and intellectual conditions necessary for a higher kind of laughter might have been wanting. This seems to be the case among some savages at the present day, such as the New Zealanders and North American Indians. The earliest laughter did not arise from what we call the ludicrous, but from something apparently physical—such as touch—though it does not follow that it would never otherwise have existed at all, for, as the mind more fully developed itself, facial expressions would flow from superior and more numerous causes. Nor can we consider that what is properly called mirth was shown in this primitive physical laughter, which was such as may be supposed to have existed when darkness was on the face of the intellectual world. How great, and of what continuance, was this primeval stagnation must be for ever unknown to us, but it was not destined to prevail. Light gradually dawned upon the mental wastes, and they became productive of beauty and order. As greater sensibility developed itself, emotion began to be expressed; first, probably at an adult period of life, by the sounds belonging to the corresponding feelings in the bodily constitution. Tears and cries betoken mental as well as physical anguish, and laughter denoted a mixed pleasurable feeling either in mind or body. There is a remarkable instance of this transference from the senses to the emotional feelings in the case of what is called sardonic laughter, in which a similar contortion of countenance to that caused by the pungency of a Sardinian herb is considered to denote a certain moral acerbity. Here there is an analogy established between the senses and emotions in their outward manifestation, just as there is in language in the double meaning of such terms as bitter and sweet.

When we consider the fact that matter is that which gives, and mind that which receives impressions, or that our perceptions do not teach the nature of external things, but that of our own constitution, we shall admit that there is not such a fundamental difference between feelings derived from the sense of touch, and those coming through our other senses. But we must observe that there is a great practical difference between them, inasmuch as the one sense remains in its original primitive state, and is not cultivated as are the others. Physical laughter requires no previous experience, no exercise of judgment, and therefore has no connection with the intellectual powers of the mind. The lowest boor may laugh on being tickled, but a man must have intelligence to be amused by wit. The senses which are the least discriminating are the least productive of humour, little is derived from that of smell or of taste, though we may talk sometimes of an educated palate and an acquired taste. The finer organs of sight and hearing are the chief mediums of humour, but the sense of touch might by education be rendered exquisitely sensitive, and Dickens mentions the case of a girl he met in Switzerland who was blind, deaf, and dumb, but who was constantly laughing. Among infants, also, where very slight complication is required, the sense of humour can be excited by touch. Thus nurses will sing, "Brow brinky, eye winkey, nose noppy, cheek cherry, mouth merry," and greatly increase the little one's appreciation by, at the same time, touching the features named. Contact with other bodies occasions a sensation, and might, by degrees, awaken an emotion; and we might thus have such a sense of the ludicrous as that obtained through eye and ear, which is sometimes almost intuitive, and but slightly derived from reflection or experience. Of this kind is that aroused by the rapid changes of form and colour of the kaleidoscope, and those pantomimic representations which amuse the young and uneducated, and others who live mostly in the senses.

We have now arrived at the emotional phase of laughter, that in which emotion far exceeds intellectual action. At this stage, we have a kind of laughter which we may call that of pleasure, inasmuch as it is the first that deserves a distinct name. This laughter of pleasure required very little complication of thought, contained no unamiable feeling, and expressed the mildest sense of the ludicrous. At the same time, it did not flow from any mere constitutional joyousness, but only arose upon certain occasions, in consequence of some remarkable and unusual occurrence—such as the reception of glad tidings, or the sudden acquisition of some good fortune. This ancient laughter, now no longer existing, is alluded to in early writings.

Thus we read in Gen. xxi. 6, that Sarah, on the birth of Isaac, said "God hath made me to laugh, so that all that hear will laugh with me," and in Ps. cxxvi., "When the Lord turned again the captivity of Zion, we were like them that dream. Then was our mouth filled with laughter, and our tongue with singing." And in Proverbs we find, "There is a time to weep, and a time to laugh," contrasting the expression of sorrow with that of pleasure. Passing into Greek literature, we find laughter constantly termed "sweet." In Iliad xxi, "Saturn smiled sweetly at seeing his daughter;" in xxiii. "The chiefs arose to throw the shield, and the Greeks laughed, *i.e.*, with joy." In Odyssey, xx. 390, they prepare the banquet with laughter. Od. xxii., 542, Penelope laughs at Telemachus sneezing, when she is talking of Ulysses' return; she takes it for a good omen. And in the Homeric Hymns, which, although inferior in date to the old Bard, are still among the earliest specimens of literature, we find, in that to Mercury, that the god laughs on beholding a tortoise, "thinking that he will make a beautiful lyre out of its shell;" and a little further on, Apollo laughs at hearing the sound of the lyre. In the hymn to Aphrodite, the laughter-loving Venus laughed sweetly when she thought of men and mortals being intermarried. The fact that this and the preceding kinds of laughter were not necessarily regarded as intellectual, is evident from the ancient poets attributing them to vegetable and inorganic life. Considerable licence in personification must no doubt be conceded to those who went so far as to deify the elements, and to imagine a sort of soul in the universe, and no doubt language as well as feeling was not at the time strictly limited. But it must be remarked that, while they rarely attribute laughter to the lower animals, they also never ascribe any other sign of emotion, nor even that in its higher kinds, to insensate matter. In all these passages it is of a physical, or merely pleasurable description. In Iliad xiv. 362, speaking of the Grecian host, Homer says that "the gleam of their armour was reflected to heaven, and all the earth around laughed at the brazen refulgence."

In Hesiod's Theogony, v. 40, we read that when the Muses are singing "the palace of loud-thundering Jove laughs (with delight) at their lily voice;" and in the Hymn to Ceres we find Proserpine beholding a Narcissus, from the root of which a hundred heads sprang forth "and the whole heavens were scented with its fragrance, and the whole earth laughed and the briny wave of the sea." Theognis writes that Delos, when Apollo was born, "was filled with the ambrosial odour, and the huge earth laughed." The poets seemed scarcely to have advanced beyond such a bold similitude, and we may conclude that while they saw in laughter something above the powers of the brute creation, they did not consider that it necessarily expressed the smallest exercise of intellect.

This laughter of pleasure, which cheered the early centuries of the world, now no longer exists except perhaps in childhood. It belongs to simpler if not happier natures than our own. If a man were now to say that his friends laughed on hearing of some good fortune having come to him, we should suppose that they disbelieved it, or thought there was something ridiculous in the occurrence. In these less emotional ages, in which the manifestations of joy and sorrow are more subdued, it is mute, and has subsided into a smile. It is difficult to say when the change took place, but our finding smiles mentioned in Homer, though not in Scripture, might suggest their Greek origin, if they were at first merely a modification of the early laughter of pleasure, betokening little more than kindly or joyous emotions. Although not always now genial, the smile continues to be used for the symbol of pleasure, even in reference to inanimate Nature, as where Milton writes "Old Ocean smiled." The smile may have preceded laughter, as the bud comes before the blossom, but it may, on the other hand, have been a reduction of something more demonstrative.

We have still a kind of laughter approaching very nearly to that of pleasure, which contains little reflection, but cannot be regarded as simply physical. This description seems to be that alluded to in the Book of Ecclesiastes, "I said of laughter, it is mad, and of mirth, what good doeth it?" Of the same nature is that to which some excitable and joyous persons are constitutionally inclined. Their perpetual merriment seems to us childish and silly. Thus Steele observes to an hilarious friend, "Sir, you never laughed in your life," and farther on he remarks, "Some men laugh from mere benevolence."

The pleasure accompanying the perception of the ludicrous has been by some attributed to the exercise of certain muscles in the face, and by others to the acquisition of new ideas. But we may safely discard both theories, for the former derives the enjoyment from physical instead of mental sources, and the latter gives us credit for too great a delight in knowledge, even were it thus generally obtained. The enjoyment seems partly to arise from stimulation and activity of mind, excitement being generally agreeable, whereas inaction is monotonous and wearisome. But it seems also partly to be derived from sources which are, or appear to be, collateral. Thus, in the early laughter of pleasure, some solid advantage or gratification, present or future, was always in view, and from men being delighted at their own success, which must often have been obtained at the expense of others, it was an easy transition to rejoice at the failure of rivals. In those primitive times, when people felt themselves insecure, and one tribe was constantly at war with another, there was nothing that gave them so much joy as the misfortunes of their enemies. They exhibited their exultation by indulging in extravagant transports, in shouting, in singing and dancing, and when there appeared some strangeness or peculiarity, something sudden or unaccountable in such disasters, laughter broke forth of that rude and hostile character which we may occasionally still hear among the uneducated classes. It accorded with the age in which it prevailed—a period when men were highly emotional and passionate, while their intellectual powers were feeble and inactive.

The two early phases of the ludicrous—those of pleasure and of hostility—containing small complexity, and a large proportion of emotion, are to a certain extent felt by the lower animals. Dr. Darwin has observed an approximation to the laughter of pleasure in monkeys, but he does not connect it with intelligence, and would not, I believe, claim for them any sense of the ludicrous. I have, however, seen a dog, on suddenly meeting a friend, not only wag his tail, but curl up the corners of his lips, and show his teeth, as if delighted and amused. We may also have observed a very roguish expression sometimes in the face of a small dog when he is barking at a large one, just as a cat evidently finds some fun in tormenting and playing with a captured mouse. I have even heard of a monkey who, for his amusement, put a live cat into a pot of boiling water on the fire. These animals are those most nearly allied to man, but the perception of the ludicrous is not strong enough in them to occasion laughter. The opinion of Vives that animals do not laugh because the muscles of their countenances do not allow them, can scarcely be regarded as philosophical. Milton tells us that,

> "Smiles from reason flow,
> To brutes denied;"

a statement which may be taken as generally correct, although we admit that there may be some approximation to smiling among the lower animals, and that it does not always necessarily proceed from reason.

The pleasure found in hostile laughter soon led to practical jokes. Although now discountenanced, they were anciently very common, and formed the first link between humour and the ludicrous. They were not imitative, and did not show any actual power to invent what was humorous, but a desire to amuse by doing something which might cause some ludicrous action or scene, just as people unable to speak would point to things they wish to designate. These early jokes had severer objects coupled with amusement, and were what we should call no joke at all. The first character in the records of antiquity that seems to have had anything quaint or droll about it is that of Samson. Standing out amid the confusion of legendary times, he gives us good specimens of the fierce and wild kind of merriment relished in ancient days; and was fond of making very sanguinary "sport for the Philistines." He was an exaggeration of a not very uncommon type of man, in which brute strength is joined to loose morals and whimsical fancy. People were more inclined to laugh at sufferings formerly, because they were not keenly sensitive to pain, and also had less feeling and consideration for others. That Samson found some malicious kind of pleasure and diversion in his reprisals on his enemies, and made their misfortunes minister to his amusement, is evident from the strange character of his exploits. "He caught three hundred foxes, and took fire-brands, and turned tail to tail, and put a fire-brand in the midst between two tails, and when he had set the brands on fire, he let them go into the standing corn of the Philistines, and burnt up both the shocks and also the standing corn of the Philistines, with the vineyards and olives." On another occasion he allowed himself to be bound with cords, and thus apparently delivered powerless into the hands of his enemies; he then broke his bonds "like flax that was burnt with fire," and taking the *jaw-bone of an ass*, which he found, slew a thousand men with it. His account of this massacre shows that he regarded it in a humorous light: "With the jaw-bone of an ass heaps upon heaps, with the jaw of an ass I have slain a thousand men." We might also refer to his carrying away the gates of Gaza to the top of a hill that is before Hebron, and to his duping Delilah about the seven green withes.

In the above instances it will be observed that destruction or disappointment of enemies was the primary, and amusement the secondary object. It must be admitted that all such jokes are of a very poor and severe description. They have not the undesigned coincidence of the ludicrous nor the fanciful invention of true humour. Samson was evidently regarded as a droll fellow in his day, but beyond his jokes the only venture of his on record is a riddle, which showed very little ingenuity, and can not be regarded as humorous now, even if it were so then.

It would, perhaps, be going too far to assert that no laughter of a better kind existed before the age at which we are now arrived; some minds are always in advance of their time, as others are behind it, but they are few. The only place in which there is any approach in early times to what may be called critical laughter is recorded where Abraham and Sarah were informed of the approaching birth of Isaac. Perhaps this laughter was mostly that of pleasure. Sarah denied that she laughed, and Abraham was not rebuked when guilty of the same levity.[4]

With the exception of the above-mentioned riddle, and rough pranks of Samson, we have no trace of humour until after the commencement of the Monarchy. The reigns of David and Solomon seemed to have formed the brightest period in the literary history of the Jews. The sweet Psalmist of Israel was partly the pioneer to deeper thought, partly the representative of the age in which he lived. It is the charm of his poetry that it is very rich and recondite—a mine of gold, which the farther it is worked, the more precious its yield becomes. But it everywhere bears the stamp of passion and religious ardour, and does not bespeak the critical incisiveness of a highly civilised age. Argumentative acumen would have been as much below the poetic mind of David in one respect as it was above it in another, and while his rapturous language of admiration and faith seems above the range of human genius; his bitter denunciations of his enemies remind us of his date, and the circumstances by which he was surrounded. Such immaturity would be sufficient to account for the non-existence of humour. It may be urged that David had no tendency in that direction. His thoughts were turned towards the sublime, and his religious character, his royal estate, and the vicissitudes of his early life, all inclined him to serious reflection. But we do not find that David was invariably grave and solemn. He indulged in laughter at the misfortunes of his adversaries, as we may conclude from a passage in Psalm lii, 6. "God shall likewise destroy thee for ever; he shall take thee away and pluck thee out of thy dwelling-place, and root thee out of the land of the living. Selah. The righteous also shall see and fear, and shall laugh at him."

He also considered that, in turn, his enemies would deride him, if he were unsuccessful. Psalm xxii, 7—"All they that see me laugh me to scorn; they shoot out the lip and shake the head, saying, 'He trusted in the Lord.'"

He evidently thought there was nothing wrong in such laughter, for he even considers it compatible with Divine attributes,[5] Psalm ii, 4, "He that sitteth in Heaven shall laugh; the Lord shall have them in derision;" and Psalm xxxvii, 13, "The Lord shall laugh at him, for he seeth that his day is coming."

Nothing can make it more certain than such expressions that the prophets interpreted the intimations they received from above by clothing them with their own mundane similitudes.

On the other hand, although David laughed at his enemies, he never seems to have done so at anything else. He frequently mentions fools, but always with detestation. To him the term did not convey any idea of frivolity or eccentricity, but of crime and wickedness. All these considerations tend to convince us that we can see in the writings of David a fairly good reflection of the mirth common in his day. Add to this that there is no trace in any contemporary work of an attempt beyond the emotional phases of the ludicrous, and we do not at this time read of any performance of Jewish plays, or of any kind of amusing representations.

A more advanced, but less faithful age is represented by another man. The soldier-king passed away to make room for one educated under milder influences. He inherited not the piety or warlike virtues of his father, but turned the same greatness of mind into a more luxurious and learned channel. In his writings we find little that approaches the sublime, but much that implies analytical depth and complexity of thought. His tone bespeaks a settled and civilized period favourable to art and philosophy, in which subtlety was appreciated, while the old feelings of acerbity had become greatly softened.

In the intellectual and moral state at this date, there were many conditions favourable to the development of humour. But we do not find it yet actually existing, although we must suppose that a mind capable of forming proverbs could not have been entirely insensible to it. We may define a proverb to be a moral statement, instructive in object, and epigrammatically expressed. It is always somewhat controversial, and when it approaches a truism scarcely deserves the name.

A great many of Solomon's proverbs may be regarded in two lights, and I think a comparison between some of them will show that he was aware of the fact, and if so he could scarcely have avoided feeling some sense of the ludicrous, and even of having a slight idea of humour in its higher phases. I shall allude in illustration of this to a proverb often quoted ironically at the present day. "In the multitude of counsellors there is wisdom," and which we have combated and answered by a common domestic adage.

Again Solomon is rather hard upon the failings of the ladies, "The contentions of a wife," he says, "are a continual dropping." "It is better to dwell in the corner of a housetop than with a brawling woman in a wide house." "It is better to dwell in the wilderness than with a contentious and angry woman." The meaning of all these sayings must be that women are of a very irritable and vexatious character. But did Solomon really believe in the strong terms he used towards them. We should say not to judge by his life, for he had "seven hundred wives, and three hundred concubines;" and although he says that, "as a jewel of gold in a swine's snout, so is a fair woman that is without discretion"—a very strong comparison—we may be sure that he had a great many of these despicable creatures domiciled in his own palace.

Solomon's strictures with regard to money may also be regarded as of somewhat uncertain value:—"How much better is it to get wisdom than gold," sounds very well, although Solomon must have known that many men would prefer the latter, and history seems to say that he was not averse from it himself. "He that is despised and hath a servant is better than he that honoureth himself, and lacketh bread," shows at least some appreciation of the usefulness of wealth. Ecclesiastes makes a more decided statement. "Money answereth all things." I should imagine Solomon was as much alive to the two sides of the question, as was the Greek who on being asked scoffingly "why philosophers followed rich men, but rich men never followed philosophers," replied, "Because philosophers know what they want, but rich men do not."

In one place Solomon shows his consciousness that his proverbs may be viewed as true or false. He gives two opposite propositions—"Answer not a fool according to his folly, lest thou also be like unto him," and, "Answer a fool according to his folly, lest he be wise in his own conceit." Shortly afterwards, he observes, as if the idea of perverting and turning proverbs was in his mind, "The legs of a lame man are not equal, so is a parable in the mouth of fools."

There was another form besides that of Proverbs, in which during earlier ages moral and political teachings were expressed. One of the first comparisons man learned to draw was that between himself and the lower animals; and the separation between reason and instinct would not appear to be at first so clearly defined as it is at present. Before the growth of cities, and the increased intercourse and accumulated experience resulting from their formation, the mental development of man was so small as not to offer any very strong contrast to the sagacity of other animals. The greatest men of ancient times were merely nomad chiefs living on the wild pasture plains, often tending their own flocks, and, no doubt, like the Arabs of the present day, making companions of their camels and horses. By the rivers and in the jungles, they often encountered beasts of prey, became familiar with their habits, and formed a higher opinion of their intelligence than we generally hold. At that time, when strength was more esteemed than intellectual gifts, there was sometimes a tendency to consider them as rather above than below the human race. The lion, the eagle, and the stag possessed qualities to which it was man's highest ambition to aspire, and, in some cases, he even went so far as to worship them. In the ancient civilisation of Egypt we find the most numerous traces of this culture and feeling—gods, kings, rulers, and disembodied spirits being represented entirely or partially under the forms of what we call the lower animals. The strange allegorical figures found at Nineveh may also be considered illustrations in point. There was evidently no caricature intended in these representations, and it is worthy of notice that such as are grotesque are not earlier than Roman times.

It is unnecessary to recapitulate the beautiful comparisons of this character which are profusely scattered through Holy Writ, but we should especially notice the blessing given by Jacob to his sons on his death-bed; in which we seem almost to discover the first origin of heraldry. Another remarkable comparison is that of Nathan, aptly made, and likely to sink with weight into the heart of the Shepherd-King. The same respect for animals survived in the time of the earliest Greek writers.

Homer in his solemn epic has numerous instances of it:— Hector in "Iliad" xi, 297, is setting the Trojans on "like dogs at a wild boar or lion." In xi, 557, Ajax retreating slowly from the Trojans is compared to an ass who has gone to feed in a field, and whom the boys find great difficulty in driving out, "though they belabour him well with cudgels." Agamemnon is compared to a bull, Sarpedon and Patroclus in deadly combat to two vultures, and Diomed and Ulysses pursue Dolon as two fleet hounds chase a hare. All these were evidently intended to be most poetical, if not elevating similes; their dignity would have been lost could they possibly have been regarded as humorous.

Simonides of Amorgos in the seventh century B.C., is remarkable for this kind of illustration. After some lamentations about human life, he observes that nothing is better than a good wife, or worse than a bad one, and he proceeds to compare women to various animals. He is also evidently very serious over the subject, and regards it as no joke at all. Perhaps there was also something to be said on the other side, for he remarks that a gadding wife cannot be cured, even if you "knock out her teeth with a stone." He likens them to pigs and polecats, horses and apes; and only praises the descendant of the bee. In a passage undoubtedly of early date, and attributed to Xenophanes, the founder of the Eleatic school of philosophy, (540-500) the writer enumerates the various ways, in which other animals are superior to man. "If by the will of God there were an equality and community in life, so that the herald of the Olympian games should not only call men to the contest, but also bid all animals to come, no man would carry off a prize; for in the long race the horse would be the best; the hare would win the short race; the deer would be best in the double race. No man's fleetness would count for anything, and no one since Hercules would seem to have been stronger than the elephant or lion; the bull would carry off the crown in striking, and the ass in kicking, and history would record that an ass conquered men in wrestling and boxing."

But the light in which the lower animals were regarded, produced other fanciful combinations. Not only were men given the attributes of animals, but animals were endowed with the gifts peculiar to man. All things were then possible. Standing as he seemed in the centre of a plain of indefinite or interminable extent, how could any man limit the productions or vagaries of Nature, even if he possessed far more than the narrow experience of those days? Moreover, the boundary lines were vague between the natural and supernatural, and the latter was supposed to be constantly interposing in the ordinary affairs of life. Among other beliefs then prevalent, was one in the existence of a kind of half nature, such as that in Centaurs, dragons, and griffins. In the Assyrian cuneiform inscriptions lately deciphered, we read, of one Heabani, a semi-bovine hermit, supposed to have lived 2,200 B.C. Thus the accounts in Scripture of the serpent accosting Eve, and of Balaam arguing with his ass, would not have seemed so remarkable then as they do to us. In an Egyptian novel—the oldest extant, cir. 1,400 B.C.—a cow tells Bata that his elder brother is standing before him with his dagger ready to kill him. He understood, we are told, the language of animals, and was afterwards transformed into a bull. Greek tradition as recorded by Plato, Xenophon, Babrius, and others, speaks of an early golden age in which men and animals held colloquies together "as in our fables;" whence we should conclude this much—that there was a time when poets very commonly introduced them as holding conversations, and when philosophers illustrated their doctrines from the animal world.

The fable, we are told, was "an invention of ancient Assyrian men in the days of Ninus and Belus," and in confirmation of its Eastern origin, we may observe that the apologues of Lokman are of Indian derivation. He is supposed, by Arabian writers, to have been either a nephew of Abraham or Job, or a counsellor of David or Solomon.

The first specimen we have of an ordinary fable, *i.e.*, of one in which the interlocutors are lower animals, is found in Hesiod, who is placed about a century after Homer. It runs thus:—

"Now I will tell the kings a fable, which they will understand of themselves. Thus spake the hawk to the nightingale, whom he was carrying in his talons high in air, 'Foolish creature! why dost thou cry out? One much stronger than thou hath seized thee, though thou art a songster. I can tear thee to pieces, or let thee go at my pleasure.'"

But fables do not come fully under our view until they are connected with the name of Æsop, who is said to have introduced them into Greece. In general his fables pretend to nothing more than an illustration of proverbial wisdom, but in some cases they proceed a step farther, and show the losses and disappointments which result from a neglect of prudent considerations. It cannot be denied that there is something fanciful and amusing in these fables, still there is not much in them to excite laughter—they are not sufficiently direct or pungent for that. The losses or disappointments mentioned, or implied, give a certain exercise to the feelings of opposition in the human breast, and if they are supposed to be such as could not easily have been foreseen, we should regard the narratives as humorous. But this is scarcely the case; the mishaps arise simply and directly from the situations, and are related with a view to the inculcation of truth, rather than the exhibition of error. Hence the basis is different from that in genuine humour, and the complication is small. Still the object evidently was to allure men into the paths of wisdom through the pleasure grounds of imagination.

Addison has justly observed that fables were the first kind of humour. As the days of Athenian civilization advanced, their light chaff was thought more of than their solid matter. Two hundred years of progress in man caused the animals to be truly considered "lower," natural distinctions were better appreciated, and there seemed to be something absurd in the idea of their thinking or talking. Hence Æsop's fables are spoken of by Aristophanes as something laughable, and the fabulist came to be regarded as a humorist. This feeling gained ground so much afterwards that Lucian makes Æsop act the part of a buffoon in "The Isles of the Blessed." Such views no doubt influenced the traditions with regard to the condition and characteristics of their composer. There was the more field for this, inasmuch as even the fables were only handed down orally. Some biographer, formerly supposed to have been Planudes the monk, seems to have fertilized with his own inventive genius many tales which had themselves no better foundation than the conjectures derived from the tone and nature of the fables. Æsop was represented as droll, as a sort of wit, and by a development of the connection in the mind between humour and the ludicrous, they gave him an infirm body, hesitating speech, and servile condition. Improving the story, they said his figure frightened the servants of the merchant who bought him. At the same time many clever tricks and speeches were attributed to him. What we really glean from such stories is, that animal fables soon came to be regarded as humorous. It is probable that some fabulist of the name of Æsop at one time existed, but we know nothing with certainty about his life, and many of the fables attributed to him were perhaps of older date.

The advance in the direction of humour, which was manifested in Æsop's fictions, was also found in the opulent Ionian Sybaris. This city, situated on the lovely Bay of Tarentum, was now at the height of its fame, the acknowledged centre of Greek luxury and civilization. A reflection of oriental splendour seems to have been cast upon it, and we read of all kinds of extravagant and curious arrangements for the indulgence of ease and indolence. Amid all this luxury and leisure, fancy was not unemployed. We find that, like the former leaders of fashion in this country, they kept a goodly train of monkeys,[6] and anticipated our circus performances by teaching their horses to dance on their hind legs, an advance above practical joking and below pictorial caricature. Moreover, intellectual entertainment was required at their sumptuous feasts, and genius was tasked to find something light and racy, maxims of deep significance interwoven with gay and fanciful creations. There was not sufficient subtlety about these inventions to entitle them to the name of humour in our modern sense of the word; much complication was not then required, nor much laughter expected. The "fables" of Sybaris seem to have been of a similarly philosophical cast to those of Æsop. The following specimen is given in the Vespæ, 1427.

"A man of Sybaris fell from a chariot, and, as it happened, had his head broken—for he was not well acquainted with driving—and a friend who stood by, said, 'Let every man practise the craft, which he understands.'"

We observe that these fables are not carried on through the assistance of our four-footed friends. At Sybaris, conversation between men and the lower animals had begun to appear not only absurd, but to be improved upon and made with the evident intention of being humorous. Hence, inanimate things were sometimes made to speak, and in succeeding fictions birds and beasts were given such special characteristics and requirements of men as could least have belonged to them. As an example of this, we may refer to the Batrachomyomachia—a production called Homeric but proved by the very length of its name to belong to a later date. It is ascribed by Plutarch to Pigres, the brother of the Halicarnassian Queen, Artemisia, contemporary with the Persian War. This poem, which is a parody on Homer, reminds us, in its microscopic representation of human affairs, of the travels of Gulliver in Lilliput. A frog offers to give a mouse a ride across the water on his back. Unfortunately, a water-snake lifts up its head when they are in the middle passage, and the frog diving to avoid the danger, the mouse is drowned. From this trifling cause there arises a mighty war between the frogs and the mice. The contest is carried on in true Homeric style; the mice-warriors are armed with bean-pods for greaves, lamp-bosses for shields, nutshells for helmets, and long needles for spears. The frogs have leaves of willow on their legs, cabbage leaves for shields, cockle-shells for helmets, and bulrushes for spears. Their names are suggestive, as in a modern pantomime. Among the mice we have Crumb-stealer, Cheese-scooper, and Lick-dish; among the frogs, Puff-cheeks, Loud-croaker, Muddyman, Lovemarsh, &c.

PART II.

GREEK HUMOUR.

Birth of Humour—Personalities—Story of Hippocleides—
Origin of Comedy—Archilochus—Hipponax—
Democritus, the Laughing Philosopher—Aristophanes—
Humour of the Senses—Indelicacy—Enfeeblement of the
Drama—Humorous Games—Parasites, their Position and
Jests—Philoxenus—Diogenes—Court of Humour—
Riddles—Silli.

There is every reason to suppose that a very considerable
period elapsed before any progress was made in advance of the
ludicrous, but at length by those who appreciated it strongly, and
saw it in things in which it did not appear to others, humorous
devices were invented from a growing desire to multiply the
occasions for enjoyment. Observation and our power of imitation
provided the means, and men of humour employed themselves in
reproducing some ludicrous situations; and thus, instead of things
derided being as previously wholly separate from those who derided
them, a man could laugh, and yet be the cause of laughter to others.
This discovery was soon improved upon, and by aid of imagination
and memory, as opportunities offered, certain connections and
appearances were represented under a great variety of forms. As
the mind enlarged, the exciting causes of laughter were not mainly
physical or emotional, but assumed a higher and more rational
character.

At the period at which we have now arrived, we find humour
dawning through various channels. We have traced approximations
towards it in proverbs and fables, and, in a coarse form, in practical

jokes; and as from historical evidences we are ready to admit that civilization had an Eastern origin, so we shall feel little difficulty in assigning Greece as the birthplace of humour. A greater activity of mind now begins to prevail, reflection has gradually given distinctness to emotion, and the ludicrous is not only recognised as a source of pleasure, but intentionally represented in literature.

Before the time of Æsop, though not perhaps of his fables, Homer related a few laughable occurrences of so simple a character as to require little ingenuity. In this respect he is not much better than a man who recounts some absurd incident he has witnessed without adding sufficient to it to show that he has a humorous imagination. His mirth, except when merely that of pleasure, is of the old hostile character. In Iliad, xi, 378, Paris, having hit Diomed, from behind a pillar with an arrow in the foot, springs forth from his concealment and laughs at him, saying he wished he had killed him. In Iliad, xxi, 407, where the gods descend into the battle, Minerva laughs at Mars when she has struck him with a huge stone so that he fell, his hair was draggled in the dust, and his armour clanged around him. In the Odyssey, Ulysses speaks of his heart laughing within him after he had put out Polyphemus' eye with a burning stick without being discovered. And in Book xviii, Ulysses strikes Irus under the ear and breaks his head, so that blood pours from his mouth, and he falls gnashing and struggling on the ground, at which, we are told, the suitors "die with laughter."

From this hostile phase the transition was easy to ridiculing personal defects, and so Homer tells us that when the gods at their banquet saw Vulcan, who was acting as butler, "stumping about on his lame leg," they fell into "unextinguishable laughter."

Thersites is described as "squint-eyed, lame-legged, with bent shoulders pinched over his chest, a pointed head, and very little hair on it." Homer may merely have intended to represent the reviler of kings as odious and despicable, but there seems to be some humour intended. Ridicule of personal defects must always be of an inferior kind, being a matter of sight, and of small complexity. As the first advance of the ludicrous was from the hostile to the personal, so the beginning of humour seems to have been the representation of personal defects.[7]

In accordance with this, we find that the only mention of laughter made by Simonides of Amorgos is where he says that some women may be compared to apes, and then gives a very rude description of their persons. This subservience to the eye can also be observed in the appreciation of monkeys and dancing horses, already mentioned, the latter forming a humorous exhibition, as the animals were trained with a view to amuse. We have marks of the same optical tendencies in the appreciation of antics and contortions of the body, either as representing personal deformity, or as a kind of puzzling and disorderly action. A little contemporary story related by Herodotus shows that these pantomimic performances were now becoming fashionable in Athens. Cleisthenes, tyrant of Sicyon, was even at this date so much in favour of competitive examinations, that he determined to give his daughter to the most proficient and accomplished man. On the appointed day the suitors came to the examination from every quarter, for the fair Agariste was heiress to great possessions. Among them was one Hippocleides, an Athenian, who proved himself far superior to all the rest in music and dissertation. Afterwards, when the trial was over, desiring to indulge his feelings of triumph and show his skill, he called for a piper, and then for a table, upon which he danced, finishing up by standing on his head and kicking his legs about. Cleisthenes, who was apparently one of the "old school," and did not appreciate the manners and customs of young Athens, was much offended by this undignified performance of his would-be son-in-law, and when he at last saw him standing on his head, could no longer contain himself, but cried out, "Son of Tisander, thou hast danced away thy marriage." To which the other replied with characteristic unconcern: "It's all the same to Hippocleides,"— an expression which became proverbial. In this story we see the new conception of humour, though of a rude kind, coming into collision with the old philosophic contests of ingenuity, which it was destined to survive if not to supersede.

We have another curious instance about this date of an earnest-minded man being above the humour of the day, (which, no doubt, consisted principally of gesticulation), and he was probably voted an unsociable, old-fashioned fellow. Anacharsis, the great Scythian philosopher, when jesters were introduced into his company maintained his gravity, but when afterwards a monkey was brought in, he burst into a fit of laughter, and said, "Now this is laughable by Nature; the other by Art." That amusement should be thus excited by natural objects denotes a very eccentric or primitive perception of the ludicrous, seldom now found among mature persons, but it is such as Diodorus, quoting no doubt from earlier histories, attributed to Osiris—"to whom," he says, "when in Ethiopia, they brought Satyrs, (who have hair on their backs,) for he was fond of what was laughable."

But a further development of humour was in progress. As people were at that time easily induced to regard sufferings as ludicrous, the idea suggested itself of creating mirth by administering punishment, or by indulging in threats and gross aspersions. A very slight amount of invention or complexity was here necessary. The origin of the comic drama furnishes an illustration of this. It commenced in the harvest homes of Greece and Sicily—in the festivals of the grape-gatherers at the completion of the vintage. They paraded the villages, crowned with vine-leaves, carrying poles and branches, and smeared with the juice of grapes. Their aim was to provoke general merriment by dancing, singing, and grotesque attitudes, and by giving rein to their coarse and pugnacious propensities. Spectators and passers by were assailed with invectives, pelted with missiles, and treated to all that hostile humour which is associated with practical joking. So vile was their language and conduct that "comedy" came to signify abuse and vilification. As the taste for music and rhythm became general in that sunny clime, even these rioters adopted a kind of verse, by which rustic genius could give additional point to scurrility. Thus arose the Iambic measure used at the festivals of Ceres and Bacchus, and afterwards fabled to have been invented by Iambe, the daughter of the King of Eleusis. Hence, also, came the jesting used in celebrating the rites of Ceres in Sicily, and the custom for people to post themselves on the bridge leading to Eleusis in Attica, and to banter and abuse those going to the festivals. The story of Iambe only marks the rural origin of the metre, and its connection with Ceres, the Goddess of Harvest. Eleusis was her chosen abode, and next in her favour was Paros; and here we accordingly find the first improvement made upon these uncouth and virulent effusions. About the commencement of the 7th century, Archilochus, a native of this place, harnessed his ribaldries better, and put them into a "light horse gallop." He raised the Iambic style and metre so as to obtain the unenviable notoriety of having been the first to dip his pen in viper's gall. Good cause had he for his complaints, for a young lady's father, one Lycambes, refused to give him his daughter's hand. There was apparently some difficulty about the marriage gifts—the poet having nothing to give but himself. Rejected, he took to writing defamatory verses on Lycambes and his daughters, and composed them with so much skill and point that the whole family hanged themselves. Allusions, which led to such a catastrophe, could not now be regarded as pleasantries; but at that time he obtained a high reputation, and perhaps the suicide of the wretched Lycambes was considered the best joke of all.[8] The fragments which remain to us of Archilochus' productions seem melancholy enough, and the only place where he speaks of laughter is where he calls Charilaus "a thing to be laughed at,"—an expression which would seem to point to some personal deformity—we are told, however, by later writers, that he was a glutton. In another remaining passage Archilochus says that "he is not fond of a tall general walking with his legs apart, with his hair carefully arranged, and his chin well shaven;" where we still detect the same kind of caricature, and in default of any adequate specimen of his "gall," we may perhaps be excused for borrowing an illustration from Alcæus, who lived slightly later; and who, speaking of his political opponent Pittacus, calls him a "bloated paunch-belly," and a "filthy splay-footed, crack-footed, night fellow."

Archilochus lived in the fable age, and the most perfect of the small fragments remaining of his works are of that allegorical description. But he may be regarded as a representative of the dull and bitter humour of his time—a large proportion of which, as in his writings, and those of Simonides and Hesiod, was ungallantly directed against the "girls of the period."[9]

But Archilochus' humour, though rude and simple, opened a new mine of wealth, and if it was not at first very rich, it was enough to indicate the golden treasure beneath. Sonorous narratives about heroes and demi-gods were to be gradually supplanted by the bright contrasts of real life. Archilochus' ingenuity had introduced light metres suited for flippant and pointed allusions. The conceit was generally approved, and though the new form could not exactly be called humorous, it occurred to Hipponax, in the next century, that he could make it so by a slight alteration. Perhaps this "Father of Parody" intended to mimic Archilochus; at any rate, by means of a change in termination, he manufactured "limping" Iambics. We must suppose that he produced something better than this, but look in vain into his lines for any instances of real pungency. He was a sort of Greek Samson, his best jokes seem to have been connected with great strength, and to judge from what remains of his works, we should conclude that he was more justly famous for "tossing an oil cruise" than for producing anything which we should call humour. But, were we asked whether in that age his sayings would have been amusing, we may reply in the affirmative; they certainly had severity, for his figure having been caricatured by the sculptors of Chios, Bupalus and Anthermus, he repaid them so well in their own coin, that they also duly hanged themselves. It must be admitted that the fact of the same kind of death having been chosen by them, and by the objects of Archilochus' derision, does not increase greatly the credibility of the stories.

We now come to consider what we may call a serious source of humour. Already we have noticed the tendency in ancient times to exercises of ingenuity in answering hard questions. These led to deeper thought, to the aphoristic wisdom of the seven wise men, and the speculations of those who were in due time to raise laughter at the follies of mankind.

This introduces the era of the philosophers—a remarkable class of men, who grew up in the mercurial atmosphere of Greece. One of the most distinguished of them was Democritus, born 460 B.C. He came of noble descent, and belonged to so wealthy a family of Abdera that his father was able to entertain Xerxes on his return to Asia. The King left some Chaldean Magi to instruct his son, who, early in life, evinced a great desire for the acquisition of knowledge, and after studying under Leucippus, travelled to Egypt, Persia, and Babylon. He almost seemed a compound of two different characters, uniting the intellectual energy of the sage with the social feelings of a man of the world. Living in ease and opulence, he was not inclined to be censorious or morose; having mingled much in society, he was not very emotional or sympathetic; not tempted to think life a melancholy scene of suffering, but callous enough to find amusement in the ills he could not prevent. He regarded man, generally, as a curious study, as remarkable for not exercising the intellect with which he was endowed—not so much from censurable causes as from some obliquity in mental vision. Not that he regarded him as unaccountable—a fool in the ordinary acceptation of the word, is always a responsible being, and not synonymous with an idiot.

The humour of this laughing sage, grounded upon deep philosophy, was so little understood in his day that none were able to join in his merriment, nor did he expect that they should be; if he was humorous to himself, he was not so, and did not aim at being so, to others. On the contrary, he was thought to be mad, and Hippocrates was directed to inquire into his disorder, but the learned physician returned answer that not he, but his opponents were deranged. Whether this story be a fabrication or not, we may regard it as a testimony that wise men saw much truth in his philosophy. Montaigne, in his Essay on Democritus and Heraclitus, gives his preference to the former, "Because," he observes, "men are more to be laughed at than hated," showing that he regarded him as imputing folly to men rather than vice.

Even Socrates, whom we are accustomed to regard as the most earnest of philosophers was by no means a melancholy man. Fully aware of the influence exercised by humour, he often put his teachings into an indirect form, and he seems to have first thus generally attracted attention. He introduced what is called irony[10]— the using expressions which literally mean exactly the opposite to what is intended. A man may be either praised or blamed in this way, but Socrates' intention was always sarcastic. He put questions to men, as if merely desiring some information they could easily give him, while he knew that his inquiries could not be answered, without overthrowing the theories of those he addressed. Thus, he gave instruction whilst he seemed to solicit it. In various other ways he enlivened and recommended his doctrines by humorous illustration. It is said that he even went to the theatre to see himself caricatured, laughed as heartily as any, and stood up to show the audience how correctly his ill-favoured countenance had been reproduced. This story may be questioned, and it has been observed that he was not insensible to ridicule, for he said shortly before his death that no one would deride him any longer. We are told that he spent some of his last days in versifying the fables of Æsop.

We now return from theoretical to practical life, from the philosophers to the public. Nothing exhibits more forcibly the variable character of humour than that, while philosophers in their "thinking shops" were laughing at the follies of the world, the populace in the theatre were shaking their sides at the absurdities of sages. Ordinary men did not appreciate abstract views, nor understand abstruse philosophic humour, indeed it died out almost as soon as it appeared, and was only contemporary with a certain epoch in the mental history of Greece. Every popular man is to a great extent a reflection of the age in which he lives, "a boat borne up by a billow;" and what, in this respect is true generally, is especially so with regard to the humorist, who seeks a present reward, and must be in unison with the characters of those he has to amuse. He depends much on hitting the current fancies of men by small and subtle allusions, and he must have a natural perception of fitness, of the direction in which he must go, and the limits he must not transgress. The literature of an epoch exhibits the taste of the readers, as well as that of the authors.

We shall thus be prepared to find that the mind of Aristophanes, although his views were aristocratic, harmonized in tone with that of the people, and that his humour bears the stamp of the ancient era in which he lived. The illustrations from the animal world in which he constantly indulges remind us of the conceits of old times, when marvellous stories were as much admired as the monstrous figures upon the Persian tapestry. Would any man at the present day produce comedies with such names as "The Wasps," "The Frogs," and "The Birds."[11] But we here meet with our feathered and four-footed companions at every corner. The building of the bird's city is a good illustration of this. Thirty thousand cranes brought stones for the foundations from Libya, and ten thousand storks made bricks, the ducks with aprons on carried the bricks, and the swallows flew with trowels behind them like little boys, and with mortar in their beaks.

We also notice in Aristophanes a simple and rude form of the ludicrous, scarcely to be called humour, much in favour with his immediate predecessors. I refer to throwing fruits and sweatmeats among the audience. Trygæus (Vintner), celebrating a joyous country festival in honour of the return of peace and plenty, takes occasion to throw barley among the spectators. In another place Dicæpolis, also upon pacific deeds intent, establishes a public treat, and calls out, "Let some one bring in figs for the little pigs. How they squeak! will they eat them? (throws some) Bless me! how they do munch them! from what place do they come? I should say from Eaton."

In this scrambling fun there would be good and bad fortune, and much laughter would be occasioned, but mostly of an emotional character. Some of the jokes of Hegemon, who first introduced dramatic parody, were of a similar description, but more unpleasant. On one occasion he came into the theatre with his robe full of stones, and began to throw them into the orchestra, saying, "These are stones, and let those who will throw them." Aristophanes makes great use of that humour which is dependent upon awakening hostile and combative feelings. Personal violence and threats are with him common stage devices. We have here as much "fist sauce," and shaking of sticks, and as many pommellings, boxings of ears, and threats of assault and battery as in any modern harlequinade.

Next in order, we come to consider some of the many instances in Aristophanes of what may be called optical humour—that in which the point principally depends upon the eye. Thus he makes Hercules say he cannot restrain his laughter on seeing Bacchus wearing a lion's skin over a saffron robe. A Megarian reduced to extremities, determines to sell his little daughters as pigs, and disguises them accordingly.[12] In the Thesmophoriazusæ, there is a shaving scene, in which the man performed upon has his face cut, and runs away, "looking ridiculous with only one side of his face shaven." In another play where the ladies have stolen the gentlemen's clothes, the latter come on the stage in the most ludicrous attire, wearing saffron-coloured robes, kerchiefs, and Persian slippers. In another, the chorus is composed of men representing wasps, with waists pinched in, bodies striped with black and yellow, and long stings behind. The piece ends with three boys disguised as crabs, dancing a furious breakdown, while the chorus encourages them with, "Come now, let us all make room for them, that they may twirl themselves about. Come, oh famous offsprings of your briny father!—skip along the sandy shore of the barren sea, ye brothers of shrimps. Twirl, whirl round your foot swiftly, and fling up your heels in the air like Phrynicus, until the spectators shout aloud! Spin like a top, pass along in circle, punch yourself in the stomach, and fling your leg to the sky, for the King himself, who rules the sea, approaches, delighted with his children!"

The greater the optical element in humour, the lower and more simple it becomes, the complexity being more that of the senses than of intellect. It may be said there is always some appeal to both, but not in any equal proportions, and there is manifestly a great difference between the humour of a plough-boy grinning through a horse-collar, and of a sage observing that "when the poor man makes the rich a present, he is unkind to him." Caricature drawings produce little effect upon educated people, unless assisted by a description on which the humour largely depends. We can see in a picture that a man has a grotesque figure, or is made to represent some other animal; by gesticulation we can understand when a person is angry or pleased, or hungry or thirsty; but what we gain merely through the senses is not so very far superior to that which is obtained by savages or even the lower animals, except where there has been special education.

Next to optical humour may be placed acoustic—that of sound—another inferior kind. The ear gives less information than the eye. In music there is not so much conveyed to the mind as in painting, and although it may be lively, it cannot in itself be humorous. We cannot judge of the range of hearing by the vast store of information brought by words written or spoken, because these are conventional signs, and have no optical or acoustic connection with the thing signified. We can understand this when we listen to a foreign language.

Hipponax seems to have been the first man who introduced acoustic humour by the abrupt variation in his metre. Exclamations and strange sounds were found very effective on the stage, and were now frequently introduced, especially emanating from slaves to amuse the audience. Aristophanes commences the knights with a howling duet between two slaves who have been flogged,

"Oh, oh—Oh, oh—Oh, oh—Oh, oh—"

In another play, there is a constant chorus of frogs croaking from the infernal marshes.

"Brekekekex, coax, coax, brekekekex, coax, coax."

In "The Birds," the songsters of the woods are frequently heard trilling their lays. As they were only befeathered men, this must have been a somewhat comic performance. The king of birds, transformed from Tereus, King of Thrace, twitters in the following style.

"Epopopopopopopopopopoi! io! io! come, come, come, come, come. Tio, tio, tio, tio, tio, tio, tio! trioto, trioto, totobrix! Torotorotorotorolix! Ciccabau, ciccabau! Torotorotorotorotililix."

Rapidity of utterance was also aimed at in some parts of the choruses, and sometimes very long words had to be pronounced without pause—such as green-grocery-market-woman, and garlic-bread-selling-hostesses. At the end of the Ecclesiazusæ, there is a word of twenty-seven syllables—a receipt for a mixture—as multifarious in its contents as a Yorkshire pie.

We may conclude that there was a humour in tone as well as of rhythm in fashion before the time of Aristophanes, and we read that there was a certain ventriloquist named Eurycles; but Aristophanes must be content to bear the reproach of having been the first to introduce punning. He probably had accomplices among his contemporaries, but they have been lost in obscurity. Playing with words seems to have commenced very early. The organs of speech are not able to produce any great number of entirely different sounds, as is proved by the paucity of the vowels and consonants we possess. To increase the vocabulary, syllables are grouped together by rapid utterance, and distinctions of time were made. Similarities in the length and flow of words began soon to be noticed, and hence arose the idea of parallelism, that is of poetry—a similarity of measure. A likeness in the tone of words, in the vowel and consonant sounds, was afterwards observed, and became the foundation of punning. The difference between rhythm and puns is partly that of degree—and the latter were originally regarded as poetical. Simonides of Ceos called Jupiter Aristarchus, *i.e.*, the best of rulers; and Æschylus spoke of Helen as a "hell,"[13] but neither of them intended to be facetious. Aristotle ranked such conceits among the ornaments of style; and we do not until much later times find them regarded as ludicrous.

With Aristophanes they are humorous, and his ingenuity in representing things as the same because their names were so, would not have been unworthy of a modern burlesque writer. They, perhaps, were more appreciated at that time from their appearing less common and less easily made. But there is a worse direction than any above mentioned, in which Aristophanes truckled to the low taste of his day. The modern reader is shocked and astounded at the immense amount of indelicacy contained in his works. It ranges from the mild impropriety of saying that a girl dances as nimbly as a flea in a sheepskin, or of naming those other industrious little creatures he euphemistically calls "Corinthians," to a grand exhibition of the blessings of Peace under the form of a young lady, the liberal display of whose charms would have petrified a modern Chamberlain. In one place, Trygæus is riding to heaven on a dung-beetle, and of course a large fund of amusement is obtained from the literal and metaphorical manipulation of its food. Socrates' disciples are discovered in a kneeling posture, with their heads on the ground. "What are they doing?" inquires the visitor. "They are in search of things below the earth." "And why are their backs up in the air?" "With them they are studying astronomy."

These passages will give some faint idea, though not an adequate one, of the coarseness of Aristophanes' humour. The primitive character of it is marked by the fact that the greater portion has no reference to the sexes.

It is a crumb of comfort to know that women were not generally present at performances of comedies, and Aristotle says that young men should not be allowed to attend them until they are old enough to sit at table and get drunk. Moreover, to be humorous the comedian must necessarily have exceeded the bounds of ordinary usage. Aristophanes occasionally deplores the degeneracy of his times,—the youth of the period making "rude jests," but his own writings are the principal evidence of this depravity. His allusions are not excusable on the ground of ignorance; they are intentionally impure. There was once an age of innocence—still reflected in childhood, and among some unprogressive races— in which a sort of natural darkness hung over the thoughts and actions of men,—but it was in reality an age of ignorance. When light broke forth delicacy sprang up, and when by degrees one thing after another had been forbidden and veiled from sight by the common consent of society, there was a large borderland formed outside immorality upon which the trespasser could enter and sport; and much could be said which was objectionable without giving serious offence. Before the days of Aristophanes and the comic performances for which he wrote, very little genius or enterprise was directed into the paths of humour, but now every part of them was explored. Indelicacy would here afford great assistance, from the attraction it possesses for many people and the ease with which it is understood. Something perhaps is due to the fact that Greece had now reached the highest point of her prosperity, and that a certain amount of lawlessness prevailed as her brilliancy began to tremble and fade. From whatever cause it arose, Aristophanes stands before us as one of the first to introduce this base ornamentation. The most remarkable circumstance connected with it is that he assigns a large part of his coarse language to women. His object was to amuse a not very refined audience, and one that relished something preposterous.

Thus Aristophanes lowered his style to the level of his audience, but in his brighter moments, forgetting his failings and exigencies, he disowns expedients unworthy of the comic art. He says he has not like "Phrynicus, Lycis, and Amisias" introduced slaves groaning beneath their burdens, or yelping from their stripes; he comes away, "a year older from hearing such stage tricks." "It is not becoming," he observes in another place for a dramatic poet to throw figs and sweetmeats to the spectators to force a laugh, and "we have not two slaves throwing nuts from a basket." In *his* plays "the old man does not belabour the person next him with a stick." He claims that he has made his rivals give up scoffing at rags and lice, and that he does not indulge in what I have termed optical humour. He has not, like some of his contemporaries, "jeered at the bald head," and not danced the Cordax. He seems in the following passage even to despise animal illustrations—

> *Bdelycleon.* Tell me no fables, but domestic stories about men.
> *Philocleon.* Then I know that very domestic story, "Once on a time there was a mouse and a weazel."
> *Bdel.* "Oh, thou lubberly and ignorant fellow," as Theogenes said when he was abusing the scavenger. Are you going to tell a story of mice and weazels among men?
> Like most humorists he blames in one place what he adopts in another.

Plato had so high an opinion of Aristophanes that, in reply to Dionysius of Syracuse, he sent him a copy of his plays as affording the best picture of the commonwealth of Athens. This philosopher is also said to have introduced mimes—a sort of minor comedy—from Sicily, and to have esteemed their composer Sophron so highly that he kept a copy of his works under his pillow. Plato appreciated humour, was fond of writing little amatory couplets, and among the epigrams attributed to him is the following dedication of a mirror by a fading beauty, thus rendered by Prior:—

> "Venus, take this votive glass,
> Since I am not what I was!
> What I shall hereafter be,
> Venus, let me never see!"

Plato objected to violent laughter as indicative of an impulsive and ill-regulated temper, observing "that it is not suitable for men of worth, much less for the gods," the first part of which remark shows that he was not emotional, and the second that a great improvement in critical taste had taken place since the early centuries of Homer and David.

As youth is romantic, and old age humorous, so in history sentiment precedes criticism and poetry attained a high degree of excellence, while humour was in its infancy. Comedy is said to have been produced first in Sicily by Susarion in 564 B.C., but we have only two or three lines by which to judge of his work, and they are on the old favourite topic. "A wife is an evil, but you can't live in a house without one." As it is said his wife left him, it must be considered doubtful whether this was not meant seriously. He was succeeded by Epicharmus, whose humour seems to have been of a very poor description. His subjects were mostly mythological, and he was fond of representing the gluttony of Hercules, and Bacchus making Vulcan drunk. In the more intellectual direction his taste was entirely philosophical, so much so that Plato adopted many of his views. We may safely assert that no comic performance worthy of the name took place until towards the end of the fifth century,[14] though in the meantime the tragic drama had reached its highest point of excellence. One *Satyric* play, so called because the chorus was formed of Satyrs, was put on the stage with three tragedies by those competing for the dramatic prize. It seems to have been mythological and grotesque rather than comic, but in the Cyclops of Euripides, the only specimen extant, we have feasting and wine drinking, the chorus tells Polyphemus he may swallow any milk he pleases so that he does not swallow them—which the Cyclops says he would not do because they might be dancing in his stomach—and Silenus recommends the Cyclops to eat Ulysses' tongue, as it will make him a clever talker.

After the time of Aristophanes, the literary, and, we may say, the social humour of Greece altered. It grew less political as liberty became more restricted, and men's minds were gradually diverted by business and foreign trade from that philosophical and artistic industry, which had made Athens the centre of the world. The brighter part of the country's genius descended to effeminate pursuits, and employed itself in the development of amorous fancies. In the comedies which came into favour, the dramatis personæ represented a strange society of opulent old men, spendthrift sons, intriguing slaves, and courtezans. If we did not know what temptation there is to make literary capital out of the tender passion, we might suppose that the youth of that day were entirely occupied in clandestine amours, and in buying and selling women as if they were dogs and parrots. No wonder that "to live like the Greeks" became a by-word and reproach. Beyond this, the authors throw the whole force of their genius into the construction of the plot, upon the strength and intricacy of which their success depends; and the management of the various threads of the story so as to meet together in the conclusion, shows a great improvement in art since the days of Aristophanes. Advancing time seems also to have brought a greater refinement in language. The indelicacy we now meet with is almost entirely of an amatory character, and not quite of so low a description as that previously in use. But in quantity it was greater. Philemon, who is said to have died from a fit of laughter caused by seeing an ass eat figs, wrote much that was objectionable; and Diphilus was probably little better. Philemon found coarseness answer, and was more often crowned, and a greater favourite than Menander, who is reported to have said to him, "Do you not blush to conquer me?" but it may be doubted whether even the latter was as free from indelicacy as is generally supposed. Plautus and Terence both complain that they cannot find a really chaste Greek play.

The age of Greek fables, that is the period when they were in common use in writing and conversation, was now drawing to a close. A few remain in Callimachus, and Suidas quotes some of perhaps the same date. At this time Demetrius Phalareus made a prose collection of what were called Æsop's Fables—as we seek to perpetuate the memory of that which is passing away. Babrius, also, who performed the same charitable office in "halting iambics," like those of Hipponax, may be supposed to have flourished about this period, although it has been contended that he was a Roman and lived in the Augustan age. However this may be, fabular illustrations began to drop out of fashion soon after this time, and by degrees were so far disallowed, that the man, who would have related such stories, would have been regarded as ludicrous rather than humorous. Although Phædrus Romanized Æsop's Fables, and gave them a poetical meaning, he never gained any fame or popularity by them. Martial calls him "improbus," *i.e.*, a rascal.

In these and earlier days, besides the humour exhibited in comedies, a considerable amount was displayed at public festivals and private entertainments. In the Homeric hymn to Mercury, we read that the god extemporized a song, "just as when young men at banquets slily twit each other." When the cups flowed, and the conversation sparkled, men indulged in repartee, or capped each other in verses. One man, for instance, would quote or compose a line beginning and ending with a certain letter, and another person was called upon for a similar one to complete the couplet. Sometimes the line commenced with the first syllable of a word, and ended with the last, and a corresponding conceit was to be formed to answer it. The successful competitors at these games were to be kissed and crowned with flowers; the unsuccessful to drink a bowl of brine. These verbal devices were too simple and far-fetched to be humorous, but were, to a certain extent, amusing, and no doubt the forfeits and rewards occasioned some merriment.

A coarser kind of humour originated in the market-place, where professed wags of a low class were wont to congregate, and amuse themselves by chaffing and insulting passers-by. Such men are mentioned centuries afterwards by St. Paul as "lewd fellows of the baser sort,"—an expression which would be more properly rendered "men of the market-place." Such centres of trade do not seem to have been improving to the manners, for we read of people "railing like bread-women," and of the "rude jests" of the young men of the market.[15] Lysistratus was one of these fellows in Aristophanes' days, and his condition seems to have been as miserable as his humour, for his garment had "shed its leaves,"[16] and he was shivering and starving "more than thirty days in the month."

By degrees, as wealth increased, there came a greater demand for amusement. Jesters obtained patrons, and a distinct class of men grew up, who, having more humour than means were glad to barter their pleasantries for something more substantial. Wit has as little tendency to enrich its possessor as genius—the mind being turned to gay and idle rather than remunerative pursuits, and into a destructive rather than a constructive channel. Talent does not imply industry, and where the stock in trade consists of luxuries of small money value, men make but a precarious livelihood. One of them says that he will give as a fortune to his daughter "six hundred *bon mots*—all pure Attic," which seems to suggest that they were to be puns. No doubt it was the demand that led to the supply, for jesters were in request at convivial meetings, and the jealousy of their equally poor, but less amusing neighbours, not improbably led to some of the ill-natured reflections upon them. Society was to blame for encouraging the parasite, who seems to have become an institution in Greece. He is not mentioned by Aristophanes, but figures constantly in the plays of later writers, where he is a smooth-tongued witty varlet, whose aim is to make himself agreeable, and who is ready to submit to any humiliation in order to live at other people's expense. Thus Gelasimus—so called, as he avers, because his mother was a droll—laments the changed times. He liked the old forms of expression, "Come to dinner—make no excuse;" but now it is always, "I'd invite you, only I'm engaged myself." In another place a parasite's stomach is called a "bottomless pit," and they are said to "live on their juices" while their patrons are away in the country. Their servility was, of course, exaggerated in comedy to make humorous capital, but as they were poor and of inferior social standing to those with whom they consorted, they were sure occasionally to suffer indignities varying in proportion to the bad taste and insolence of their patrons. Thus we read that they not only sat on benches at the lower end of the table, but sometimes had their faces daubed and their ears boxed. In the ambiguous position they occupied, they were no doubt exposed to temptations, but we are not to suppose that they were generally guilty of such short-sighted treachery as that attributed to them by the dramatists. Still, they certainly were in bad repute in their generation, and hence we are enabled to understand Aristotle's observation that he who is deficient in humour is a boor, but he who is in culpable excess is a *bomolochos*, or thorough scoundrel. He would connect the idea of great jocosity with unprincipled designs.

Philoxenus, had a more independent spirit than most parasites, and the history of his sojourn in Syracuse gives us an amusing insight into the state of Court life in Sicily 400 years B.C. He was an Athenian dithyrambic poet and musician; and as Dionysius affected literature, he was welcomed at his palace, where he wrote a poem entitled "The Banquet," containing an account of the luxurious style of living there adopted. Philoxenus was probably the least esteemed guest at these feasts, of which, but for him no record would survive. He was a man of humour, and some instances of his quaintness remain. On one occasion, when supping with the tyrant, a small mullet was placed before him, and a large one before Dionysius. He thereupon took up his fish and placed it to his ear. Dionysius asked him why he did so, to which he replied that he was writing a poem, called "Galatæa," and wanted to hear some news from the kingdom of Nereus. "The fish given to him," he added, "knew nothing about it, because it had been caught so young; but no doubt that set before Dionysius would know everything." The tyrant, we are told, laughed and sent him his mullet. As might have been anticipated, he soon greatly offended Dionysius, who actually sent him to work in the stone-quarries; but the cause of his misfortune is uncertain. Athenæus attributes it to his falling in love with a favourite "flute-girl" of Dionysius, and says that in his "Galatæa," he caricatured his rival as the Cyclops. According to another account, his disgrace was owing to his having, when asked to revise one of Dionysius' poetical compositions, crossed out the whole of it from beginning to end. He was, however, restored to favour, and seated once more at the royal table; but, unfortunately, the tyrant had again been perpetrating poetry, and recited some of his verses, which were loudly applauded by all the courtiers. Philoxenus was called upon to join in the commendation, but instead of complying, he cried out to the guards, "Take me back to the quarries." Dionysius, took the joke and pardoned him. He afterwards left the Syracusan Court, and went to his native place, Cythera; and it was characteristic of his bluntness and wit, that, on being invited by the tyrant to return, he replied by only one letter of the alphabet signifying "NO."

And now a most grotesque figure stands before us—it is that of Diogenes, who was a youth at the time of Aristophanes' successes, and was, no doubt by many, classed with those rude idlers of the market-place of whom we have already spoken. Some people have questioned his claim to be regarded as a philosopher. He does not appear to have been learned, or deeply read; but he was meditative and observant, and that which in an anchorite, or hermit, would have been a mere sentiment, and in an ordinary man a vague and occasional reflection, expanded in his mind into a general and practical view of life. Observing that the things we covet are not only difficult of attainment, but unsatisfactory in possession, he thought to solve the problem of life by substituting contempt for admiration. He was, probably, somewhat influenced by his own condition in this vain attempt to draw sweetness from sour grapes. He was poor, and we find that this despiser of the goods of this world, who considered money to be the "metropolis of all evils"—in his youth coined false money, and was banished to Sinope in consequence. Among his recorded sayings, he expresses his surprise that the slaves attending at banquets could keep their hands off their master's dainties.

But we should be doing Diogenes an injustice, if we set him down as a mere discontented misanthrope. In giving due weight to unworthy motives, we have looked only at one side—and that the worst—of his character. His mind was of an inquiring speculative cast, and in youth he aspired to join the disciples of Zeno. So persistent indeed was he that the stoic, unwilling to have such a questionable pupil, one day forgot his serene philosophy, and set upon him with a cudgel. Such arguments did not tend to soften Diogenes' disposition, and although he accused man of folly rather than malignity, he went so far to say that a man should have "reason or a rope." He probably thought it easier than Democritus to follow wisdom, because he did not see quite so far. Still he showed that he took an interest in social life, and had he been less of a moralist, he would have had better claims to be regarded as a "wit" than any other character in Grecian history. Many examples could be adduced in which his principal object was evidently to be amusing:—

Entering a school in which he saw many statues of the Muses, but few pupils, "You have many scholars among the gods," he said to the master. On being asked at what time it was proper to dine, "If you are rich, when you will; if poor, when you can," he replied, perhaps a little sadly; and to "What wine do you like to drink?" he quickly responded "Another man's." Meeting one, Anaximenes, a very fat man, he called out, "Give us poor fellows some of your stomach; it will be a great relief to you, and an advantage to us."

That Diogenes recognised humour as a means of drawing attention and impressing the memory, is shown by the story that on one occasion, when he was speaking seriously and found no one attending, he began to imitate the singing of birds, and when he had thus collected a crowd, told them they were ready to hear folly but not wisdom. There was also, probably, in adopting this form a desire to preclude the possibility of his being contradicted. He was thus proof against criticism—if his statements were said to be false—well, they were intended to be so; while, if they raised a laugh, there was an admission that they contained some seeds of truth. The following are examples of his disguised wisdom:—

On being asked when a man should marry, "A young man not yet; an old man not at all," he replied. "Why men gave money to beggars and not to philosophers?" "Because they think they may themselves become blind and lame, but never philosophers." When Perdiccas threatened that unless he came to him he would kill him, "You would do no great thing," he replied, "even a beetle or a spider could do that."

We can scarcely suppose that all the sayings attributed to Diogenes are genuine. There has always been a tendency to attribute to great men observations made in accordance with their manner.

Philosophers have generally been to a certain extent destructive, and seldom spared the religion of their times. Diogenes, who was called "Socrates gone mad," was no exception to this rule. Humour, which is seasoned with profanity, is most telling when there is not too large an amount either of faith or scepticism; very few could find any amusement in the sneers of an utter infidel. Diogenes was almost as deficient in ordinary religious belief as in most other kinds of veneration. Sometimes he may have had the good effect of checking the abuse of sacerdotal power, as when he observed to some who were admiring the thank offerings at Samothracia, "There would have been many more, had those made them, who had not been cured." He also said that the Dionysian festival was a great sight for fools, and that when he heard prophets and interpreters of dreams, he thought nothing was so silly as man. His blaming men for making prayers, because they asked not that which was good, but only what seemed desirable to them, may be taken in a favourable sense.

Before the end of Diogenes' life fanciful conceits became so much appreciated in Greece, that a regular "Court of Humour" was held at Heracleum, a village near Athens, and it is to be feared that many of the racy sayings attributed to eminent men, originated in the sessions of this jocund assembly. It was composed of sixty members, and their sayings came forth with the stamp of "The Sixty" upon them. Their reputation became so great, that Philip of Macedon gave them a talent to write out their jokes, and send them to him. He was himself fond of gaiety, invented some musical instruments, and kept professed jesters.

Soon after this time, we read of amateur jesters or rather practical jesters called *planoi*. Chrysippus, who was not only a philosopher, but a man of humour—a union we are not surprised to find common at that date—and who is said, perhaps with equal truth, to have died like Philemon in a fit of laughter, on seeing an ass eat figs off a silver plate—mentions a genius of this kind, one Pantaleon, who, when at the point of death told each of his sons separately that he confided to him alone the place where he had buried his gold. When he was dead, they all betook themselves to the same spot, where they laboured for some time, before discovering that they had all been deceived.

From this period we are mostly indebted to epigrams for any knowledge of Greek humour. They originated in inscriptions or offerings in temples; afterwards came to be principally epitaphial or sarcastic; and grew into a branch of literature.

We can scarcely understand some of the fancies indulged in at the time, which contain no salt at all—"Sports," Hephæstio calls them. Of these devices may be mentioned the "Wings of Love" by Simmias, a Rhodian, who lived before 300 B.C. The verses are graduated so as to form a pair of wings. "The first altar," written by Dosiadas of Rhodes, is the earliest instance of a Greek acrostic, or of any one which formed words. An acrostic is a play upon spelling, as a pun is upon sound; and in both cases the complication is too slight for real humour. They are rather to be considered as ingenious works of fancy. The first specimens are those in the Psalms—twelve of which have twenty-two verses beginning with the twenty-two letters of the Hebrew alphabet. The 119th Psalm is a curious specimen of this conceit; it is divided into twenty-two stanzas, and a letter of the alphabet in regular order begins each of them. The initial letters of "The First Altar" of Dosiadas of Rhodes, form four words, and seem to be addressed to some "Olympian," who, the dedicator hopes "may live to offer sacrifice for many years." The altar states that it is not stained with the blood of victims, nor perfumed with frankincense, that it is not made of gold and silver; but formed by the hand of the Graces and the Muses. In the "Second Altar," also usually attributed to Dosiadas of Rhodes, we find not only a fanciful outline formed by long and short verses, but also a studious avoidance of proper names. Not one is mentioned, although thirteen persons are designated. It is evident that this "Altar" was a work of ingenuity, and intended to be enigmatical. Probably the substitutions were also considered to be somewhat playful and amusing, as in Antiphanes—a comic poet, said to have died from an apple falling on his head—we read,

A. Shall I speak of rosy sweat
From Bacchic spring?

B. I'd rather you'd say wine.

A. Or shall I speak of dusky dewy drops?

B. No such long periphrasis—say plainly water.

A. Or shall I praise the cassia breathing fragrance
That scents the air.

B. No, call it myrrh.

Another conceit in the form of a Sphinx or Pandean pipe has been attributed to Theocritus—perhaps without good foundation.

In the "Egg" there is not only the form of the lines, which gradually expand and then taper downwards, but there is also a great amount of similitude—the literary egg being compared to a real egg, and the poet to the nightingale that laid it. There is also a remarkable involution in form—the last line succeeding the first, and so on; and this alternation of the verses is compared to the leaping of fawns. The Axe or Hatchet is apparently a sort of double axe, being nearly in the form of wings; and is supposed to be a dedicatory inscription written to Minerva on the axe of Epeus, who made the wooden horse by which Troy was taken.

The ancient riddles seem to have been generally of a descriptive character, and not to have turned upon quibbles of words, like those of the present day. They more corresponded to our enigmas—being emblematic—and in general were small tests of ingenuity, some being very simple, others obscure from requiring special knowledge or from being a mere vague description of things. Of the learned kind were doubtless those hard questions with which the Queen of Sheba proved Solomon, and those with which, on the authority of Dius and Menander, Josephus states Solomon to have contended with Hiram. The riddle of Samson also required special information; and the same characteristics which marked the early riddles of Asia, where the conceit seems to have originated, is also found in those of Greece. Who could have guessed the following "Griphus" from Simonides of Ceos, without local knowledge, or with it, could have failed,

> "I say that he who does not like to win
> The grasshopper's prize, will give a mighty feast,
> To the Panopeiadean Epeus."

This means, we are told, that when Simonides was at Carthea he used to train choruses, and there was an ass to fetch water for them. He called the ass "Epeus," after the water-carrier of the Atridae; and if any member of the chorus was not present to sing, *i.e.*, to win the grasshopper's prize, he was to give a choenix of barley to the ass. Well might Clearchus say "the investigation of riddles is not unconnected with philosophy, for the ancients used to display their erudition in such things."

Somewhat of the same character is found in the following from Aristophanes.

People. How is a trireme a "dog fox?"
Sausage Seller. Because the trireme and the dog are swift.
   People. But why fox?
Sausage Seller. The soldiers are little foxes, for they eat up the
   grapes in the farms.

The simplicity of some of the ancient riddles may be conjectured from the fact that the same word "griphus" included such conceits as verses beginning and ending with a certain letter or syllable.

An instance of the emblematic character of early riddles is seen in that proposed by the Sphinx to OEdipus. "What is that which goes on four legs in the morning, on two in the middle of the day, and on three in the evening?" And in the riddle of Cleobulus, one of the seven wise men:

"There was a father, and he had twelve daughters; each of his daughters had thirty children; some were white and others black, and though immortal they all taste of death."

Also in the following griphi, which are capable of receiving more than one answer.

The first two are respectively by Eubulus and Alexis—writers of the "New Comedy"—who flourished in the first half of the 4th century, B.C.

"I know a thing, which while it's young is heavy,
But when it's old, though void of wings, can fly,
With lightest motion out of sight of earth.

"It is not mortal or immortal either
But as it were compounded of the two,
So that it neither lives the life of man
Nor yet of god, but is incessantly
New born again, and then again
Of this its present life invisible,
Yet it is known and recognised by all."

From Hermippus:—

> "There are two sisters, one of whom brings forth,
> The other and in turn becomes her daughter."

Diphilus, in his Theseus, says, there were once three Samian damsels, who on the day of the festival of Adonis delighted themselves with riddles. One of them proposed, "What is the strongest of all things?" Another answered, "Iron, because it is that with which men dig and cut." The third said, "The blacksmith, for he bends and fashions the iron." But the first replied, "Love, for it can subdue the blacksmith himself."

The following is from Theadectes, a pupil of Isocrates, who lived about 300 B.C., and wrote fifty tragedies—none of which survive.

> "Nothing which earth or sea produces,
> Nought among mortals hath so great increase.
> In its first birth the largest it appears,
> Small in its prime, and in old age again,
> In form and size it far surpasses all."[17]

To make a riddle, that is a real test of ingenuity for all, and which but one answer satisfies, shows an advanced stage of the art. The ancient riddles were almost invariably symbolical, and either too vague or too learned. They seem to us not to have sufficient point to be humorous, but no doubt they were thought so in their day.

It may not be out of place here to advert to those light compositions called Silli, about which we have no clear information, even with regard to the meaning of the name. From the fragments of them extant, we find that they were written in verse, and contained a considerable amount of poetical sentiment; indeed, all that has come down to us of Xenophanes, the first sillographer, is of this character. We are told that he used parody, but his pleasantry, probably, consisted much of after-dinner jests and stories, for we find that although he praises wisdom, and despises the fashionable athletic games, he rejoiced in sumptuous banquets, and said that the water should first be poured into the cup, then the wine. But the most celebrated sillographer was Timon the Phliasian—intimate with Antigonus and Ptolemy Philadelphus—who wrote three books of Silli, two in dialogues, and one in continuous narrative. He was a philosopher, and the principal object of his work was to bring other sects into ridicule and discredit. A few reflections of general application are scattered through it, but they are in general quite subsidiary and suggested by the subject matter.

PART III.

ROMAN HUMOUR.

Roman   Comedy—Plautus—Acerbity—Terence—Satire—
Lucilius—Horace—Humour of the Cæsar Family—
Cicero—Augustus—Persius—Petronius—Juvenal—
Martial—Epigrammatist—Lucian—Apuleius—Julian
the Apostate—The Misopogon—Symposius' Enigmas—
Macrobius—Hierocles and Philagrius.

The light of genius which shone in Greece was to some
extent reflected upon Rome, where there was never an equal
brilliancy. As for humour, such as was indigenous in the country, it
was only represented by a few Saturnian snatches, some Fescennine
banterings at weddings and harvest-homes, and rude pantomimic
performances also originating in Etruria. Intellectual pleasantry was
unknown, except as an exotic, and flourished almost exclusively
among those who were imbued with the literature of Greece.

About the date at which we arrived at the end of the last
chapter—the middle of the third century, B.C.—the first regular
play was introduced at Rome by Livius Andronicus. He was a Greek
slave, having been taken prisoner at the capture of Tarentum.
Scarcely anything remains by which to judge of his writings, but we
know that he copied from Greek originals. His plays were, no doubt,
mostly appreciated by the better educated classes of the audience.
He had a rival in Noevius, a Campanian by birth, who also copied
from the Greek, but retained something of the Fescennine licence,
or rather, we should say, had much of the hostile humour common
to the earlier periods of Greece and Rome. So violent were his
attacks upon the leading men of the day, that he was imprisoned,

and finally died in exile at Utica. This early connection of comedy with abuse and buffoonery was probably one cause of professional actors being held in contempt in Rome. We read that they were frequently slaves, who were whipped if they came late. At the same time native scurrility was allowed. Freeborn Romans might act for amusement in the Atellane plays, which were considered to be Italian, and were accompanied by broad "Exodia" or pantomimic interludes containing regular characters such as Maccus the clown, Buccones the chatterers, Pappus the pantaloon, and Simus, the ape. But these productions came from Campania, and it is probable that the better parts of them were Greek in spirit, though not in form.

Some fifty years later brings us to Plautus—the most remarkable of the Roman comic writers. Little is known of his origin, except that he was born in Umbria. There is a story that at one time he was in so humble a position that he was employed in grinding corn for a baker; but, if so, he must have possessed extraordinary ability and perseverance to acquire such a thorough knowledge of Greek and Latin. The fact of his adopting the stage as a profession, and acting in his own dramas, proves that he was not encumbered with rank or wealth. His plays were numbered among the classics, and were produced upon the stage till the time of Diocletian, five hundred years after his death; he generally copied from the Greek, often naming the author to whom he was indebted.

Plautus is interesting, not only as giving us an insight into the Greek mode of life before his time, and preserving many of the works of Philemon, Diphilus, and others, but as being the only Latin writer of his date whose productions have survived. He wrote one hundred and thirty plays, of which thirty are extant, and show an orthography very different from that of the Augustan age. His style was forcible, and like that of all the Latin comic writers, highly complex. He sometimes coins words, (such as Trifurcifur, gugga,[18] parenticida,) and he is constantly giving new metaphorical senses to those already in use—as when he speaks of a man being a "hell of elms," *i.e.*, severely flogged with elm-rods—calls cooks "briars," because they take fast hold of everything they touch, and threatens a slave with "memorials of oxen," *i.e.*, a thrashing that will make him remember the thong.

We may possibly trace the Greek original in a few references to conversations of animals—although no plays are now called after them—and the names, places, and money he introduces are generally Greek. Still, we cannot regard him as a mere servile imitator—much of his own genius is doubtless preserved in the plays. In some, we can clearly recognise his hand, as where he alludes to Roman customs, or indulges in puns. For instance, where a man speaks of the blessing of having children, (liberi,) another observes he would rather be *free* (liber). In "The Churl," we read that it is better to fight with minæ than with menaces, and a lover says that Phronesium has expelled her own name (wisdom) from his breast.

An old man says he has begun to go to school again, and learn his letters. "I know three already," he continues, "What three?" is asked, "A M O."

While we are glad to mark an advancement in less pleasures being derived from personal threats and conflicts on the stage, we are pained to find such an entire want of sympathy with the sufferings of those in a servile condition. The severity with which slaves were treated in previous times was not mitigated under the Roman rule, and at the present day it is difficult to realise the moral state of those who could derive amusement from hearing men threatened with bull-hidings, and flogged on the stage. Such terms as "whip-knave" became stale from repetition, and so many jokes were made even about crucifixion, that we might suppose it to be a very trifling punishment. Chrysalus, a slave, facetiously observes, that when his master discovers he has spent his gold, he will make him "cruscisalus" *i.e.* "cross jumper." In "The Haunted House," Tranio, who, certainly seems to have been a great scamp, soliloquises as follows on hearing of his master's return:—

"Is there any one, who would like to gain a little money, who could endure this day to take my place in being tortured? Who are those fellows hardened to a flogging, who wear out iron chains, or those who for three didrachmas[19] would get beneath besieging towers, where they might have their bodies pierced with fifteen spears? I'll give a talent to that man who shall be the first to run to the cross for me, but on condition that his feet and arms are doubly fastened there. When that is done, then ask the money of me."

Acoustic humour appears not only in puns, but under the form of long names of which Plautus was especially fond,

Periplecomenus, Polymacharoplagides, and Thesaurochrysonicocræ are specimens of his inventive genius in this direction.

In the "Three Coins," Charmides asks the sharper's name.

Sh. You demand an arduous task.
Charmides. How so?
Sh. Because if you were to begin before daylight at the first part of my name 'twould be dead of night before you could reach the end of it. I have another somewhat less, about the size of a wine cask.

In the "Persian," Toxilus gives his name as follows,

"Vaniloquidorus Virginisvendonides
Nugipolyloquides Argentiexterebronides
Tedigniloquides Nummorumexpalponides
Quodsemelarripides
Nunquampostereddides."

There are a few other cases in which there is a playing upon sound, as where Demipho remarks that if he had such a good-looking girl as Pasicompsa for a servant, all the people would be "staring, gazing, nodding, winking, hissing, twitching, crying, annoying, and serenading."

The failings of the fair seems always to have been a favourite subject for men's attack, but reflections of this kind have decreased in number and acerbity since the days of Aristophanes. We find, however, some in Plautus, such as the following:—

"Love is a fawning flatterer. For he that is in love, soon as ever he has been smitten with the kisses of the object he loves, forthwith his substance vanishes out of doors, and melts away. 'Give me this, my honey, if you love me.' And then Gudgeon says, 'Oh apple of my eye, both that and still more, if you wish.' He who plunges into love perishes more dreadfully than if he leapt from a rock. Away with you, Love, if you please."

He is fully alive to the power of this destructive passion. In one place Philolaches half mad with love and jealousy sees his mistress looking into a mirror. "Ah, wretched me," he exclaims passionately, "she gave the mirror a kiss. I wish I had a stone to break the head of that mirror."[20]

The love of money has always been a stock subject with humorists. This common weakness of human nature can be played upon even by those who can produce no other wit, and many worse jokes have been made on it than the following,—

Calidorus asks his servant, Pseudolus, to lend him a drachma.

P. What for?
C. To buy a rope to hang myself.
P. Who then will pay me back? Do you wish to hang yourself
   to cheat me out of my drachma?

The "Concealed Treasure" turns on an old man having found a pot of gold. He conceals it, and his nervousness lest some one should discover it is brought out with excellent humour. He drives the cooks out of the place with his stick. He has a battle-royal with a dunghill cock, who, he imagines is trying to scratch for it, then thinks Strobilus has stolen it, and calls on him to show one hand, and the other, and then the third.

We are the more inclined to lament the utter destruction of ancient African literature on finding that the most refined Roman dramas were placed upon the stage by a Carthaginian, when Plautus, whose enterprize and perseverance had given the great impetus to Latin comedy, was approaching the end of his long life. Terence was born the last, and as some think the greatest master in this branch of Art. He was at one time a slave, but his literary talent was so remarkable that his master set him free, and he became the friend of distinguished men, especially of Scipio the younger. It must seem strange that this brilliancy should have flashed up for a moment, and then been for ever quenched, but it was derived from Greece and not in its nature enduring. The genius of Menander fed the flame of Terence, as that of Diphilus and others gave power to Plautus, and it may well be supposed that men of their talent appropriated all that was most excellent, and left their successors to draw from inferior sources. It may, moreover, be doubted, whether the regular drama was ever popular among the lower classes in Rome, who preferred the more exciting scenes of the circus. Such plays as were intended for them were coarser and more sensational.

Terence has not the rough power and drollery of Plautus; his whole attraction lies in the subtlety of his amorous intrigues. Steele, speaking of one of the plays, "The Self-Tormentor," observes, "It is from the beginning to the end a perfect picture of human life, but I did not observe in the whole one passage that could possibly raise a laugh." It was for this reason, no doubt, that Cæsar spoke of him as only "half a Menander," and as deficient in comic force. Ingenious complexity is so exclusively his aim, that we have neither the coarseness nor the sparkle of earlier writers. He was the first to introduce Comedies, which were not comic, and whatever humour he introduces is that of situation.

We now come to consider a kind of humour of which the Romans claim to have been the originators, and which they certainly developed into a branch of literature. Satire first signified a basket of first fruits offered to Ceres; then a hotchpot or olla podrida, then a medley; and so the name was given to poems written without any definite design. We might therefore conclude that they possessed no uniform character, but merely contained a mixture of miscellaneous matter. But we find in them no allusions to politics or war, and but few to the literature and philosophy of the day—their variety being due to their social complexion. One feeling and character pervades them all—they were called forth by a scornful indignation at the degeneracy of the age as represented by the rich and powerful, or even by certain leading individuals. The appearance of such a kind of literature denoted greater activity in society, an increase of profligacy among some, and of moral sensibility among others. Satire was a social scourge. It was not a philosophical investigation into the nature and origin of vice, but a denunciation of it as inimical to the interests of society. It was practical not theoretical—and sought to bring vice into contempt, by making it both odious and ridiculous. In the latter attempt, the satirists may have had more success than we credit them with, for in our day such virulent attacks would be distasteful, immorality being regarded as essentially a matter for grave and serious condemnation. Satire differs from abuse, not only in being declamatory, but in being deserved. The amusement in it mostly depends upon the deformity of the sensual, the failures of the wicked, and the exposure of guilt in a kind of moral pillory. It did not aim at mere accidental losses or imperfections, and made no fanciful accusations merely to amuse, but it was often lightened by metaphor, by coined words, and especially by exaggeration.

The satire of Rome, though in a certain sense new, seems to have been somewhat derived from Greece. Ennius, who commenced it, a man younger than Plautus and older than Terence, was himself half a Greek. He wrote epic poems and comedies, and also introduced this comic literature for private reading. Lucilius, who was the first eminent Roman satirist, is said to have imitated the old Greek comedies. His attacks are very severe and personal, reminding us a little of Archilochus, though apparently not written to gratify any private spleen. The tendency to personalities marked a time when the range of society and the tone of thought were equally narrow. Moral depravity was considered to be centred in a few individuals, and in the broken fragments of Lucilius' rage, which have descended to us, we find a man stigmatised as an "ulcer," "gangrene," a "poison," "jibber," "shuffler," "a hard-mouthed obstinate brute." Sometimes he ridicules the bodily infirmities of the depraved; but Lucilius' attacks seem less ill-natured and more justly humorous from being always directed against the vicious and demoralised. Occasionally he indulges in such uncomplimentary expressions as "There is no flummery-maker equal to you," while some are hailed with "Long life to you, glutton, gormandizer, and belly-god." He might truly say in his metaphorical language, "I seize his beak and smash his lips, Zopyrus' fashion, and knock out all his front teeth."

The satire of Horace was exceptionally mild; with him its social character was much more marked than its acerbity. In many places he shows Greek reflections, for he had received a liberal education, duly completed at Athens. But his philosophy did not consist of dreamy theories and arbitrary rules—it was directed to practical ends, to the harmonizing of the feelings, and the elevation of society. As a man of the world, he was not carried away by fancies, nor given to exaggerated views; and as a companion of the great, he was not inclined to inveigh bitterly against the degeneracy of the times. On the contrary, so kindly were his feelings, that he tells us that we should overlook the vices of our friends. His teaching, both in spirit and range, was broader than that of his predecessors; his shafts were directed against classes rather than individuals, and wherever he is more pointed, his object is not to gratify personal spite, but to make his warning more forcible by illustration. Moreover, his names are generally unreal. In this way he attacks Nasidienus on the excessive luxury of the table, and his advice was applicable not only to the rich and great, but to more ordinary men. Thus, he shows the bad tendencies of avarice and love-intrigues, and the meanness of sycophantism and legacy-hunting. Many of the faults he condemns are rather errors in taste than serious moral delinquencies. Sometimes he criticises merely trivial matters, such as a costume or a scent. "Rufillus smells all perfumes, Gorgonius like a goat," and the most humorous of his pieces is that in which he ridicules the ignorance and impudence of a manoeuvring chatterer. But in this line he is not very successful, and his contests of rival jesters are as much beneath the notice of any good writer of the present day, as his account is of Porcius, the jack-pudding "swallowing cakes whole."

Horace says that men are more impervious to slashing reproach than to fine ridicule, and he was unusually adroit in hitting foibles without inflicting pain. He was not a man who held strong opinions on subjects. This is especially evident where he speaks of his own fickleness; and while he reiterates his dislike of Rome, with its noise and bustle, he makes his slave say that this is but affectation, and when an invitation comes from Mecænas, "Mulvius and the 'scurræ' are turned out," from which we learn that parasites had their parasites, and that Horace in the country played the patron to the rustic wits.

Although the Romans generally have no claim to be called a humorous people, many of them became celebrated for their talent in repartee. Scipio Africanus Æmilianus above mentioned, was remarkable in this way, as was Crassus, Granius, Vargula, and others. There was a good old joke that Nasica having called at the house of the poet Ennius, and the maid-servant having told him that Ennius was not at home, he perceived she had said so by her master's order; and when, a few days afterwards, Ennius called at Nasica's house, and inquired for him, Nasica cried out that he was "not at home." "What!" says Ennius, "do I not know your voice?" "You are an impudent fellow," replied Nasica, "I believed your servant when she said you were not at home, and you will not believe me."

A vein of humour seems to have run through the Cæsar family. Caius Julius Cæsar Strabo Vopiscus was so noted for the gift that Cicero in his work on Oratory makes him deliver his observations on the subject. Julius Cæsar himself was as remarkable for pleasantry as for clemency. His "Veni, vidi, vici," in which his enemies saw so much arrogance, was no doubt intended and understood by his friends to be humorous. In his youth he was accused of effeminate habits, and when on his obtaining the entire command of Gaul, he said that he would now make his enemies his suppliants, and a senator replied sarcastically, "That will not be an easy task for a woman." He rejoined with gaiety, "Semiramis reigned in Assyria, and the Amazons possessed a great part of Asia." We have already seen him lamenting over the loss of comic force in Terence as compared with Menander, and in the triumphal games given in his honour in the year 45, he commanded Decimus Laberius, though a man of sixty, to appear on the stage in the contest of wit. This knight was a composer of mimes—a light kind of comedy, somewhat to be compared to the "entertainments" given by humorists at the present day. Julius Cæsar obliged him to perform in person—an act of degradation—but afterwards gave him 500,000 sesterces, and restored him to his rank. This act of Cæsar's has been regarded as having a political significance, but it may merely have shown his love of humour. He may have wished to bring out the talent of the new mime, Publius, a young Syrian, who had acquired great celebrity both for beauty and wit. It is said that when his master first took Publius to see his patron, the latter observed one of his slaves, who was dropsical, lying in the sunshine, and asking him angrily what he was doing there, Publius answered for him "Warming water." On the same visit, in jesting after supper, the question was asked, "What is a disagreeable repose?" When many had attempted answers, Publius replied, "That of gouty feet."

Some of the sayings of Publius, have been preserved.

"He receives a benefit who gives to a worthy person."

"He to whom more than is just is allowed, wishes for more than he gets."

"A man who talks well on the road is as good as a carriage."

"He unjustly accuses Neptune who is ship-wrecked twice."

"By overlooking an old injury you invite a new one."

These sayings are of a worldly-wise and proverbial character, and, therefore, as has been already observed, although not actually humorous, are easily capable of being so regarded.

Cæsar awarded the prize to Publius instead of Laberius, because, as it is supposed, of some reflections the latter made upon him. But it may have been that Cæsar was right, and Publius' wit was the most salient.

Scarcely any specimens remain of Laberius' talent. Aulus Gellius says that he coined many strange words, and he seems to have made considerable use of alliteration.

We may suppose that the humour of Cicero was somewhat hereditary, for he records a saying of his grandfather that "the men of our time are like Syrian slaves; the more Greek they know, the greater knaves they are!" It is fortunate the grandson inherited the old man's wit without his plebeian prejudices, and became as celebrated for his culture as for his readiness. In his work entitled "The Orator," he commends humour as a means of gaining influence, and a vehicle for moral instruction. "Orators," he says, "joke with an object, not to appear jesters, but to obtain some advantage." But we may feel sure he did not keep this dry and profitable end always in view, for he wrote a jest-book, and was nick-named by his enemies "Scurra Consularis,"[21] the consular buffoon.

A man can scarcely have a talent for humour without being conscious of its fascination, and being sometimes led away by it— as Cicero says, "it pleases the listeners"—but he need not therefore descend to buffoonery. We should not be inclined to accuse a man of that, who tells us that "a regard to proper times, moderation and forbearance in jesting, and a limitation in the number of jokes, will distinguish the orator from the buffoon;" who says that "indelicacy is a disgrace, not only to the forum, but to any company of well-bred people," and that neither great vice nor great misery is a subject for ridicule. From all this we may gather that Cicero was full of graceful and clever jocosity, but did not indulge in what was vapid and objectionable. Both by precept and practice he approved good verbal humour. The better class of puns was used in the literature of the time, as we find by St. Paul and others, not in levity, but merely as embellishments.[22]

Cicero replied to Vibius Curius, who was telling a falsehood about his age: "Then when we declaimed at the schools together, you were not born;" and to Fabia, Dolabella's wife, who said she was thirty, "No doubt, for I have heard you say so twenty years." When he saw Lentulus, his cousin—a little man girt with a big sword: "Who," he asked, "has fastened my cousin to that sword?" and on being shown a colossal bust of his brother, who was also small, he exclaimed, "The half of my brother is greater than the whole." One day Cicero had supped with Damasippus, and his host had said—putting some inferior wine before him—"Drink this Falernian, it is forty years old!" "It bears its age well," replied Cicero.

We have a most interesting collection of good sayings in "The Orator," which although not spoken by Cicero himself, were those which he had from time to time noticed, and probably jotted down. Here is one of Cæsar's (Strabo). A Sicilian, when a friend made lamentation to him that his wife had hanged herself upon a fig tree: "I beseech you," he said, "give me some shoots of that tree that I may plant them." Some one asked Crassus whether he should be troublesome if he came to him before it was light. Crassus said, "You will not." The other rejoined, "You will order yourself to be awakened then." To which Crassus replied, "Surely, I said that you would not be troublesome."

To return to the Cæsars. The humorous vein which we have traced in the family descended to Augustus—the great nephew of Julius. Some of his sayings, which have survived, show him to have been as pleasant in his wit as he was proverbially happy in his fortunes.

When the inhabitants of Tarraco made him a fulsome speech, telling him that they had raised an altar to him as their presiding deity, and that, marvellous to relate, a splendid palm tree had grown up on it: "That shows," replied the Emperor, "how often you kindle a fire there." To Galba, a hunchback orator, who was pleading before him, and frequently saying, "Set me right, if I am wrong," he replied, "I can easily correct you, but I cannot set you right."

The following will give a slight idea of the variety of his humour.

When he heard that, among the children under two years old whom Herod had ordered to be slain, his own son had been killed, he said, "It is better to be Herod's pig than his son." Being entertained on one occasion with a very poor dinner, and without any ceremony, as he was passing out he whispered in the ear of his host, "I did not know that I was such a friend of yours." A Roman knight having died enormously in debt, Augustus ordered them to buy him his bed-pillow at the auction, observing: "The pillow of a man who could sleep when he owed so much must be truly soporific." A man who had been removed from a cavalry command and asked for an allowance, "not from any mercenary motive, but that I may seem to have resigned upon obtaining the grant from you," he dismissed with the words: "Tell everybody you have received it. I will not deny it."

Augustus kept a jester, Gabba, and patronised mimes, and among other diversions with which he amused himself and his friends, was that of giving presents by lottery; each drew a ticket upon which something was named, but on applying for the article a totally different thing was received, answering to a second meaning of the name. This occasioned great merriment, a man who thought he was to get a grand present was given a little sponge, or rake, or a pair of pincers; another who seemed to have no claim whatever, obtained something very valuable. The humour was not great, but a little refreshing distraction was thus obtained from the cares of state. There is no loss in light literature so much to be deplored as that of the correspondence between Augustus and Mecænas. The latter prided himself upon his skill in poetry and humour, and we may be sure that he sent some of his choicest productions to Augustus, who in turn exerted himself to send something worthy of the eye of so celebrated a critic. It is not impossible that the Emperor showed himself equal, if not superior to the friend of Horace.

Those who succeeded to the imperial purple proved very different from their illustrious predecessor, and in Persius the severity of Roman satire re-appears. We could scarcely expect a man who lived under Nero, and after the reigns of Tiberius, Caligula, and Claudius to write with the mild placidity of the Augustan poet. Moreover, the satires of Persius were written at an early age—twenty-eight, and youth always feels acutely, and expresses strongly. Some of his attacks are evidently aimed at Nero, but his principal object is to denounce the vices of the times. Hence, indolence and prurient literature are stigmatised. He ridicules the extremes of extravagance, and of that parsimony by which it is usually accompanied. "Am I on a festive day to have a nettle dressed for me, and a smoked pig's cheek with a hole in its ear, in order that that grandson of yours may be surfeited with goose liver, and indulge in patrician amours. Am I to be a living anatomy that his pope's stomach may shake with fat."[23] Alluding to the absurdity of the prayers generally offered up, he uses language worthy of a Christian. "You ask for vigour, but rich dishes and fat sausages prevent the gods from granting your behest. You ask what your fleshly mind suggests. What avails gold in sacrifice? Offer justice to God and man—generous honour, and a soul free from pollution."

In Persius we miss the light geniality of Horace and the pure language of the Augustan age, but we mark the complexity and finesse of a later date, a form of thought bespeaking a comprehensive grasp, and suitable to subtle minds. But as regards his humour it depends much on exaggeration, and is proportionally weak, and beyond this we have little but the coining of some words,[24] the using others in unaccustomed senses, and a large seasoning of severity. He evidently aimed rather at being corrective than amusing, and his covert attacks upon Nero were, no doubt, well understood. Humour of a poor kind was evidently fashionable at the day—the Emperor himself wrote Satires and was so fond of comic performances that he first encouraged and rewarded a celebrated pantomimic actor named Paris, and then put him to death for being his rival in the mimetic art. Even Seneca could not resist the example of his contemporaries, and we find the sedate philosopher attacking his enemy with severe ridicule. Claudius had him sent into exile for eight years to the picturesque but lonely Island of Corsica; and Seneca who liked something more social and luxurious, held him up in a satire bordering upon lampoon. The fanciful production was called the Apolokokyntosis of Claudius; that is his apotheosis, except that, instead of the Emperor being deified, he is supposed to be "gourdified," changed not into a god, but into a pumpkin. Seneca, after deriding Claudius' bodily defects, accuses him of committing many atrocities, and finally sends him down from heaven to the nether world, where a new punishment is invented for him—he is to be always trying to throw dice out of an empty box.

One of the most remarkable characters in the reign of Nero was Titus Petronius Arbiter. He was a great favourite with the Emperor, and held some official appointment—the duties of which he is said to have discharged with ability. In his writings he is supposed to condemn immorality, but he enlarges so much upon what he disapproves that we doubt whether he does not promote the vice he pretends to condemn.[25] His "Satyricon" is not intended to be a satire, but an imitation of one of those old Greek comedies which treated of the doings of Satyrs and grotesque country deities. It is the first comic prose work, for in early times verse was thought as necessary to humour as to poetry. The whole work is enveloped in a voluptuous atmosphere; it is written in a gay roystering style, but although the indelicacy is great the humour is small. Occasionally it is interesting, as giving an insight into private life in the days of Nero. Here we find Trimalchio, a rich man, providing for the amusement of his guests, as well as for their sumptuous entertainment. One dish was a wild boar, which was placed on the table with a cap of liberty on its head. Petronius asked the meaning of this. "Why," said he, "your servant could explain that, it is no riddle. This boar escaped from yesterday's dinner where it was dismissed by the guests, and he now returns to table as a freedman." Afterwards a much larger hog was brought in. "What!" cried Trimalchio, looking closely at it, "is not his inside taken out? No! it is not; call the cook, call the cook." The cook being brought in, excused himself saying that he forgot. "Forgot!" cried Trimalchio, "why, he talks as if it were only a pinch of pepper omitted. Strip him." In a moment the cook was stripped to be flogged. All interceded for him, but Petronius felt somewhat indignant at such an oversight, and said he must be a careless rascal to forget to disembowel a hog. Trimalchio with a pleasant look said, "Come, you with the short memory, see if you can bowel him before us." The cook slashed with his knife, and out tumbled a load of puddings and sausages. All the servants raised a shout, and the cook was presented with a cup of wine, and a silver crown.

Petronius shared the fate of Seneca. He was suspected of conspiring against the Emperor, and his life being demanded, he preferred to suffer by his own hand rather than by that of the executioner. He caused his veins to be opened, but strangely whimsical to the last, and wishing to die slowly, he had them closed at intervals. In his dying state he was daily carried about the streets of Cumæ, and received his friends, made love verses and humorous epigrams, and endeavoured to withdraw his thoughts from the sad reality by indulging in all kinds of amusing caprices. At length he expired—another distinguished victim of Nero's cruelty.

Juvenal, who wrote under Domitian, a little later than Persius, equalled him in severity—due either to his natural disposition or to the spectacle presented by the ever increasing demoralization of Rome. Like Persius, he makes use of much metaphor and involution in his works—showing the literary taste and intellectual acumen of a settled state of society, but an early age is impressed upon his pages in the indelicacy with which he is frequently chargeable. His depiction of guilt was appreciated at that day, but under the Christian dispensation vice is thought too sinful, and in a highly civilised state too injurious to be laughable. The views then held were different, and Tacitus considered it a mark of great superiority in the Germans that they did not laugh at crimes. Juvenal tells us that the Romans jeered at poverty. There was much in the character of this satirist to raise him in the estimation of right-minded men. His tastes were simple, he loved the country and its homely fare, and although devoid of ambition, was highly cultivated. No doubt he was rather austere than genial: his aim was to instruct and warn rather than amuse; and where he approaches humour it is merely from complexity of style, in coining words and barbarisms, or in comparisons mostly dependent upon exaggeration. The following is one of his best specimens, though over-weighted with severity. It gives an idea of the state of Rome at the time. A drunken magnate and his retinue stop a citizen in the street, and insolently demand—

"With whose vinegar and beans are you blown out? What cobbler has been eating leeks and sheepshead with you? Answer, or be kicked." "This," says Juvenal "is a poor man's liberty. When pummelled, he begs that he may be allowed to escape with a few of his teeth remaining."

Juvenal longs for the sword of Lucilius, and the lamp of Horace, that he may attack the vices of Rome, but he himself is more severe than either. Forgers, gamblers and profligates are assailed, and names are frequently given, though we often cannot now decide whether they belonged to real persons. Laughing at those who desire length of years without remembering the concomitant infirmities of age, he says:

"All kinds of disease dance around the aged in a troop, of which if you were to ask the names I could sooner tell you how many lovers Hippia had, how many patients Themison killed in one autumn, or how many allies Basilus and Hirrus defrauded." He condemns the increased desire for luxury. "Do not," he warns, "long for a mullet, when you have only a gudgeon in your purse." The rule of the day was to purchase sensual indulgence at any cost, "Greediness is so great that they will not even invite a parasite." Excessive selfishness leads to every kind of dishonesty. "A man of probity is as rare as a mule's foal, or as a shower of stones from a cloud." "What day is so sacred that it fails to produce thieving, perfidy, fraud, gain sought through every crime, and money acquired by bowl and dagger. The good are so scarce that their number is barely as great as that of the gates of Thebes, or the mouths of the fertilizing Nile."

He attacks every kind of social abuse, and does not even spare the ladies—some are too fast, some are learned and pedantic, some cruel to their slaves—even scourging them with cowhides. "What fault," he asks, "has the girl committed, if your own nose has displeased you?" As to religion, that has disappeared altogether. "What a laugh your simplicity would raise in public, if you were to require of anyone that he should not perjure himself, but believe that there was some deity in the temple, or at the ensanguined altar! That the souls of the departed are anything, and the realms below, and the punt-pole and frogs of the Stygian pool, and that so many thousands pass over in one boat, not even the boys believe, except those who are too young to pay for their bath."

The language used in the last passage is no doubt an example of the profane manner in which some men spoke at that day, but in general, we must remember that these pictures are humorous and overdrawn. Still, some of the offences spoken of with horror by Juvenal were treated almost as lightly by contemporary poets as they had been by Aristophanes.

There is a slightly foreign complexion about the productions of Martial, which reminds us that he was a Spaniard. Even at this time there seems to have been a sparkle and richness in the thoughts that budded in that sunny clime. Martial was a contemporary of Juvenal, and addressed two or three of his epigrams to him. His works consisted of fourteen books, containing altogether more than fifteen hundred of these short poems.

The appearance of such works may be taken as indicative of the condition of Rome at the time. The calls of business had become more urgent from the increase of the population and development of commerce, while the unsatisfactory state of the Government and of foreign affairs kept men's minds in agitation and suspense. Martial himself observes that those were no times for poems of any length, and that some of his friends would not even read his longer pieces, though they never exceeded thirty lines. The period demanded something light and short—a book which could be taken up and laid down without any interruption of the narrative. But the swifter current of affairs had also produced a keener or more active turn of mind, so that it was necessary not only to be short, but also pithy. It was not necessary to be humorous, but it was essential to be concise and interesting, and thus Martial gave to the epigram that character for point which it has since maintained.

Nothing could be more attractive than allusions to contemporary men, passing scenes, or novelties of the day, and when we read his works we seem to be transported by magic into the streets and houses of ancient Rome. On one page we have the sanguinary scenes of the circus; in another we see the ladies waving their purple fans, and hear them toasted in as many glasses as they have letters to their names.

From this kind of gaiety Martial graduates into another—that of pleasantry. In an epitaph on his barber, he bids the earth lie light upon him, adding, "It could not be lighter than his artistic hand." From his censure of bad wit, it is evident that he drew great distinctions between broad and subtle humour. "Every man," he says, "has not a *nose*," *i.e.*, a keen perception—cannot smell a fault. He is very seldom guilty of a pun, and says in one place that he has not adopted verbal tricks, imitating echoes, or making lines which can be read backwards or forwards.[26] Nor has he any intention to indulge in bitter reflections; he says,—

"My page injures not those it hates, and no reputation obtained at the expense of another is pleasing to me. Some versifiers wish publications which are but darts dipped in the blood of Lycambus to be mine, and vomit forth the poison of vipers under my name. My sport is harmless."

But he well saw that some little severity was necessary for humour, for he chides a dull poet:

"Although the epigrams which you write are always sweetness itself, and more spotless than a white-leaded skin, and although there is in them neither an atom of salt, nor a drop of bitter gall, yet you expect, foolish man, that they will be read. Why, not even food is pleasant if wholly destitute of acid seasoning, nor is a face pleasing which shows no dimples. Give children your honey, apples, and luscious figs—the Chian fig, which has sharpness, pleases my taste."

Following this view we find him often sarcastic, but not personal, the names being fictitious, or if not, those of well known public men. In a few instances he is a little ill-natured, and writes, "Laugh, if thou art wise, girl, laugh, said Ovid, but he did not say this to all girls, not, for instance, to Maximina, who has only three teeth, and those the colour of pitch and boxwood. Avoid the pantomimes of Philistion and gay feasts. It befits you to sit beside an afflicted mother, and a wife lamenting her husband. Weep, if thou art wise, girl, weep."

Martial often uses the figure called by the Greek grammarians "contrary to expectation." The point of the whole epigram lies in the last word or line, which changes the drift of the whole.

> "His funeral pile was strewn with reed,
> His tearful wife brought fragrant myrrh,
> The bier, the grave, the ointment were prepared,
> He named me as his heir, and he—got well."

> "Sorry is Athenagoras not to send the gifts,
> Which in mid-winter he is wont to send;
> Whether he be sorry I shall shortly see,
> But sorry he has certainly made me."

> "You feast so often without me, Lupercus,
> I've found a way by which to pay you out,
> I am incensed, and if you should invite me,
> What would I do, you ask me? Why—I'd come."

The growing appreciation of this kind of writing had already led Meleager, a cynic philosopher of Gadara, to form the first collection of Greek epigrams, which he prettily termed the anthology or bouquet. Martial has been commended at the expense of the Greeks, but he borrowed considerably from them in form and matter. His epigrams were more uniformly suggestive and concentrated than those of any previous writer, and he largely contributed to raise such compositions from being merely inscriptive into a branch of literature. He opened a new field, and the larger portion of these productions in Greek were written about this time. They are not generally humorous, with the exception of a few from Philo and Leonidas of Alexandria who lived about 60 B.C., from Ammianus in 120 B.C., and from Lucilius, a great composer of this kind, of whose history nothing is known but that he lived in the reign of Nero. The following are from the last-mentioned.

"Some say, Nicylla, that thou dyest thy hair, which thou boughtest most black at the market."

"All the astrologers prophesied that my uncle would be long-lived except Hermocleides, who said he would not be so. This, however, was not until we were lamenting his death."

The following are free translations from the same writer.

> "Poor Cleon out of envy died,
> His brother thief to see
> Nailed near him to be crucified
> Upon a higher tree."

On a bad painter.

> "You paint Deucalion and Phaeton,
> And ask what price for each you should require;
> I'll tell you what they're worth before you've done,
> One deserves water, and the other fire."

The works of Lucian are generally regarded as forming a part of Roman literature, although they were written in Greek by a native of Samosata in Syria. In them we have an intermingling of the warm imagination of the East with the cold sceptical philosophy of the West. Lucian was originally brought up to be a stone-cutter, but he had an insatiable desire for learning, and in his "Dream" he tells us how he seemed to be carried aloft on the wings of Pegasus. He became a pleader at the bar, but soon found that "deceit, lies, impudence, and chicanery" were inseparable from that profession. In disgust he betook himself to philosophy, but could not restrain his indignation when he found so many base men throwing the blame of their conduct on Plato, Chrysippus, Pythagoras, and other great men. "A fellow who tells you that the wise man alone is rich, comes the next moment and asks you for money—just as if a person in regal array should go about begging." He says they pay no more attention to the doctrines they teach than if their words were tennis balls to play with in schools. "There is," he continues, "a story told of a certain king of Egypt, who took a fancy to have apes taught to dance. The apes, as they are apt to mimic human actions, came on in their lessons and improved very fast, and were soon fit to appear on the public stage, and display their skill, dressed in purple robes, with masks on their faces. The spectators were much pleased with them for a considerable time, when a wag who was present, having brought with him a quantity of nuts, threw a handful amongst them. The dance was immediately forgotten, and the performers from pyrrhic dancers, relapsed into apes, who went chattering and snapping at one another, and fighting for nuts; so that in a few moments the masks were crumpled, the clothes torn to rags, and the ape dance, which had been so much extolled, terminated amidst peals of laughter. Such is the history of mock philosophers."

The above story may serve to exhibit Lucian's views, and his love of humorous illustration. He indulges in many fancies, such as the complaint of the letter S against T, which had in Attic been substituted for it.

Another kind of pleasantry which he brings forward is interesting, inasmuch as after having been in fashion among the grammarians, and reviving among the monks in the middle ages it has now fallen entirely out of use. It may be regarded as being a kind of continuation of the philosophical "hard questions" of ancient times, originated with the Sophists, and was entirely confined to logical subtleties affording diversion, but not awakening any emotion sufficient to cause laughter. Lucian makes a parasite ask his host after dinner to solve such riddles as "The Sorites and the

Reaper," and the "Horned Syllogism." The latter proposition was, "What you have not lost that you still have. You have not lost horns, therefore you have horns." In "The Sale of the Philosophers," in which Jupiter puts them all up to auction to see what will be bid for them, Chrysippus gives some similar examples. "A stone is a substance, is it not?" "Certainly." "A living being is also a substance." "Yes." "And you are a living being—therefore you are a stone." Chrysippus then offers to turn him back into a man. "Is every substance a living being?" "No." "Is a stone a living being?" "No." "But you are a substance?" "Yes." "And a living being; then, although you are a substance you are not a stone, because you are a living being."

Lucian's crusade against vice is of so general a kind as to remind us more of some of the old philosophers than of the Roman satirists. At the same time he says he has only spoken against impostors, and is only the enemy of false pretence, quackery, lies, and puffing. But we may suppose that he would not be sparing of his lash in any direction, for in the "Resuscitated Philosophers," he observes, "Philosophy says that ridicule can never make anything worse than it is in itself, and whatever is beautiful and good comes out with more lustre from it, and, like gold, is rendered splendid by the strokes of the hammer."

Following this view, he makes pretty sport of the parasites, whom he represents as forming a large and educated class. Patroclus he counts as Achilles' parasite, and includes several philosophers, who, he says, sponged upon Dionysius of Syracuse, "but Plato failed in the art." He commends them in merry irony, and describes the parasite as stout and robust—bold, with an eye full of fire and spirit. Who could venture a bet against a parasite, whether in jesting or feasting? Who could contribute more to the diversion of the company? A parasite is obliged to be strict in his conduct. He has an annual salary, but is always beaten down in it. He does not receive the same food as the chief people, and in travelling he is put with the servants. Jokes are made at his expense by the company, and when he receives a present of his patron's old clothes, he has to fee the servants for them. Of philosophers, some are poisoned, some are burned alive. None ever tell of a parasite who came to such an end—he dies gently and sweetly, amidst loaded dishes and flowing bowls, and should one of them come to a violent death, it is merely from indigestion. The parasite does honour to the rich man—not the rich man to the parasite.

Lucian's "True History" deserves especial notice as having been the first extravagant story written under the form of a circumstantial narration of travels. It was the precursor of "The Voyage to the Moon," Baron Münchausen, and various Utopias. We must therefore allow it the merit of originality, and it evinces talent, for mere exaggeration would not be entertaining. The intention was to ridicule the marvellous travellers' stories then current. Much of this history is merely florid, and we may compare it to a waving line, in which the fable is constantly undulating between humour and poetry.

Lucian says he is going to write about what never can be. He sets sail on a voyage of discovery for the Western Ocean, and reaches a beautiful island. There they find a river of wine, navigable in many places. He could not trace the source of it, but near the place where it seemed to rise, were several vines full of grapes, and at the root of every one wine flowed out. They found fish in the stream, and after eating some, felt intoxicated; when they cut them up, they found grape-stones in them. Passing the river, they found a most wonderful species of vine; the lower parts, which touched the ground, were green and thick, the upper formed the most beautiful women, from the top of whose fingers branches sprang forth full of grapes; and on their heads, instead of hair, they had leaves and tendrils. Two of his companions, going up to embrace them, became so entangled that they could not again disengage themselves. After this, they left the island, and were caught in such a violent storm that the vessel was lifted out of the water, so high that it could not come down again. Then they came to another island, round and shining. Here they found Hippogypi, men riding upon vultures—birds so large that each of their feathers was like the mast of a ship. The voyagers join the Hippogypi in a battle against the inhabitants of the sun, and have various allies—some mounted on fleas about the size of twelve elephants, and spiders, each as big as one of the Cyclades islands. The travellers were taken prisoners, and conveyed to the Sun, but he returned to the Moon, of which he gives a description. The inhabitants there make use of their stomachs—which are empty and lined with hair—as bags or pockets to put away things. They take their eyes in and out, and borrow them. "Whoever does not believe me, had better go and see." Returning from the air to the earth and sea, they saw several enormous whales, one of whom swam up to them with its mouth wide open. Coming near he swallowed them up—ship and all. It was dark inside, until he opened his mouth again. There was a large extent of land inside, and hills and woods, in which birds were building nests.

From this last fancy, we might conclude that Lucian had read the Book of Jonah, and a description he afterwards gives of the Isles of the Blessed, seems to be written in imitation of the Revelation.

The age in which Lucian lived was marked by theological contests between Pagans, Jews, and Christians, and such times have generally caused an increase of scepticism and profanity. Lucian was a follower of Democritus, and his Confabulations consist of a succession of squibs and satires on the mythological legends of the gods and goddesses. He laughs at curing diseases by charms and incantations. People pretended to fly, walk on water and through fire—they are called Babylonians and Hyperboreans. A Syrian from Palestine professes to drive devils out of people (perhaps alluding to the exorcists of the early church.) He makes Eucrates speak of one Pancrates, who would take a broom or the pestle of a wooden mortar, and upon saying a couple of magical words, it appeared to become a man, drew water, and ordered food. When Pancrates had no further need of him, he spoke a couple of words, and the man was a pestle again. Eucrates tried this himself, but having made the pestle a man, and told him to bring water, he forgot how to change him back again. So he kept on bringing water. Eucrates then split the pestle in two, and both halves still continued to bring water.

Demonax, the friend of Lucian, was as remarkable for his wit and repartee as for his kindly nature. A man who over-rated his austerity, expressed one day his surprise at seeing him eat sweet-cakes. "Do you think," he replied, "that the bees make their honey only for fools?" He seems to have had as little respect as Lucian for the idolatry of his day, for on one of his companions saying to him "Let us go to the Temple of Æsculapius to pray for my son," he answered, "Is the god then so deaf that he cannot hear us where we are?"

He lived and died a bachelor, and we are told that on being blamed by Epictetus, with whom he studied, for not marrying and having a family as a philosopher should, he replied "Very well, give me one of your daughters." Epictetus was an old bachelor.

He counselled a bad orator to practise and exercise himself in the art of speaking, and on his replying, "I am always doing so—to myself," he added, "It is therefore not surprising you speak as you do—having a fool for your audience."

When the sophist Sidonius, delivering a long panegyric on himself, said that he was acquainted with all the tenets of the philosophers: "If Aristotle calls me to the Lyceum, I obey; if Plato to the Academy, I come; Zeno to the Stoa, I take up my abode there; if Pythagoras calls, I am silent:" Demonax jumped up in the middle of the Assembly and cried out, "Pythagoras calls you."

His humour was purely genial and jocose, as when, on the point of setting sail in winter, he replied to a friend who asked him whether he was not afraid he should be ship-wrecked and go to feed the fishes, "Should I not be ungrateful were I unwilling to be devoured by fishes, when I have feasted on so many myself?"

But there is one speech of his which must ever make his memory dear to all good men. When the Athenians wished to emulate the Corinthians by exhibiting a gladiatorial combat, he said, "Do not vote this, Athenians, before ye have taken down the Altar of Mercy."

Demonax lived to a ripe old age, and we are told that he was so much beloved in Athens that, as he passed the bread-shops, the bakers would run out to beg his acceptance of a loaf, and thought it a good omen if he complied; and that the little children called him father, and would bring him presents of fruit.

Apuleius wrote in Latin in the second century. He was a native of Carthage—not the celebrated Carthage of Terence, but that of Cyprian—a new city. He travelled like many of the learned men of his time to Athens and Alexandria, and thus, most probably, became acquainted with his contemporary Lucian. At any rate, his "Golden Ass" seems taken from the work by that author. Bishop Warburton has seen in his production a subtle attack upon Christianity, but we may take it as intended to ridicule magical arts, and those who believed in them. He was likely to feel keenly on this subject, for having married a rich widow, Pudentilla, her relatives accused him of having obtained her by witchcraft, and even dragged him into a court of justice.

Lucian ridiculed the religion of his day, Apuleius its superstitions. Apuleius speaks of his "book of jests," but it is lost—the few lines he gives out of it are a somewhat matter-of-fact recommendation of tooth-powder. His enemies thought that tooth-powder was something magical and unholy—at any rate, they made his mention of it a charge against him. In reply, he says that perhaps a man who only opens his mouth to revile ought not to have tooth-powder.

In the "Golden Ass," Apuleius gravely supposes that transformations take place between men and the lower animals. He makes Aristomenes tell a story in which a witch appears, "able to drag down the firmament, to support the world on her shoulders, crumble mountains, raise the dead, dethrone gods, extinguish the stars, and illuminate hell." She changed one of her lovers, of whom she was jealous, into a beaver, and persecuted him with hunters. She punished the wife of another of them, who was about to increase her family, by condemning her to remain in that condition. "It is now eight years since she has been growing larger and larger, and seems as though about to produce an elephant."

Lucius goes to Thessaly, celebrated for its witches, and a good story is told how returning late from supper he finds three men battering against his door. Taking them for robbers he draws his dagger, and stabs them, and the ground is covered with blood. Next day he is tried for murder, and about to be crucified, when the corpses are brought into court, and are found to be three wine-skins. He is told that this was a trick played on him upon the day when they usually celebrated the festival of the god of laughter, but it seems to have been really owing to an incantation. He sees Pamphile, his hostess, change herself into an owl, thinks he also will transform himself into a bird, and anoints himself with some of the witch's preparations. By mistake, taking the wrong ointment, he transforms himself into a donkey. He then goes to look for his horse, who, thinking he is coming to eat his food, kicks him out, and soon afterwards he is well thrashed by his servant boy. He is told that eating fresh roses will restore him to his former self, but for various reasons he cannot get any. Being hungry he goes into a kitchen garden, and makes a good meal of the vegetables, for which transgression he is nearly killed by the gardener. To prevent this he kicks the man over, whereupon a general outcry was raised, and great dogs rush upon him. After this persecution he is in danger of dying of starvation—"spiders began to spin their webs on his lips," but becoming instrumental in saving a young girl, he receives better treatment. He is then bought by vagrants, who go about playing cymbals, and carrying an image of the Syrian goddess. He is accompanied by a troop of fanatical priests, who dance and scourge themselves. While the priests are being royally entertained by one of their votaries, a dog runs off with a haunch of venison, and the cook, not knowing what to do, conceives the project of killing the ass, and dressing one of his haunches instead. To avoid this the donkey breaks loose, and gallops into the supper room. After the band of priests is dispersed, owing to their thieving propensities, the donkey is sold to a baker, and by him to a gardener, and nearly dies of cold and exposure. Then he becomes the property of the servants of a very rich man, and is found eating up the remains of their supper. This greatly amuses them all, and their lord orders him to be brought to his table. A buffoon, or parasite, who sat among the guests, exclaims "Give him a cup of wine," and he was taught various tricks. His fame increases so that his master only admits people to see him on payment. Finally being taken to the circus, and afraid that some of the wild beasts might eat him by mistake, he slips away and gallops to Cenchroea, where he prays to the goddess Iris, and is by her restored to his human form. The descriptions in this work are often very beautiful, and the humour in describing the misfortunes of the ass is excellent.

In contrast to the humour of Lucian and Apuleius, we may place that of the Emperor Julian, an ascetic and devotee, who was nephew of Constantine the Great, and brought up a Christian. Julian's early life was spent in terror, for Constantius, Constantine's son, imprisoned him at Milan, after having put his elder brother to death. Perhaps this treatment at the hands of a Christian may have prejudiced him against the new religion, or his mild disposition may have been scandalized at the fierceness of theological controversies, or at the lives of many of the converts. His early education and experiences of life were more inclined to imbue him with principles of toleration than to make him a zealous Christian, and, finally, when he arrived at the age of twenty, he determined to return back into Paganism. This retrograde movement, not altogether out of keeping with his quaint character and love of antiquity, has stamped him with the opprobrious title of the "Apostate," but in moral excellence he was superior to the age in which he lived. Many of his writings show a sense of humour, such as that he wrote in Lutetia (Paris) on "Barley wine" the drink of the Gauls.

> "Who and whence art thou, Dionyse? for, by true Bacchus
> I know thee not, but Jove's great son alone,
> He smells of nectar, thou of goats, truly the Celts
> For want of grapes made thee of ears of corn;
> Wherefore thou shouldst be Cereal called, not Bacchus,
> Pyrogenes and Bromos, not Bromion."[27]

Julian's principal work is on the Cæsars. He commences it by saying that he is not addicted to jesting, but he will relate a sort of fable in which all the gods and Cæsars are called to a great banquet. Accordingly, he introduces various characters. Julius Cæsar seems in his pride to wish to dispute the throne even with Jupiter. Augustus he compares to a chameleon, sometimes one colour, sometimes another; one moment a visage full of sorrow, another smiling.

Tiberius has a fierce countenance, and shows the marks of intemperance and debauchery. "Take care he does not pull your ear," says Bacchus, "for thus he treated a grammarian." "He had better," returned Silenus, "bemoan himself in his solitary island, and tear the face of some miserable fisherman."[28]

Constantine, not finding among the gods any type of his character, betook himself to the goddess of pleasure. She, receiving him softly and embracing him, trimmed him up and adorned him, dressed him in a shining and many-coloured woman's gown, and led him away to demoralization. With her he found one of his sons, who loudly proclaimed to all, "Whosoever is a seducer, a murderer, or shameless, let him advance boldly, for by washing him with water I will immediately make him pure; and if he should be again guilty of such things, I will grant him to be pure on striking his breast, or beating his head."[29] At the end of this "fable," the Emperors are called upon to speak in their defence. Constantine being asked what object he had in view, replied "to amass great riches and spend them on myself and friends." Silenus burst into a fit of laughter, and retorted "You now wish to pass for a banker, but how can you forget your living like a cook, or a hair-dresser?" alluding to his luxurious feastings, and his wearing gold-flowered stuffs, and a diadem of jewels.

Gibbon calls this work on the Cæsars one of the most agreeable and instructive productions of ancient wit.

Julian prided himself on his primitive and severe life, and made himself ridiculous by wearing a long unfashionable beard— either in imitation of the Gauls, or of the ancient philosophers. It is probable that he persisted in this habit to discountenance the effeminacy of the times. He says that soon after he entered Constantinople, he had occasion to send for a barber. An officer, magnificently dressed, presented himself. "It is a barber," said the prince, "that I want, and not a minister of finance." He questioned the man about his profits, and was informed that besides a large salary and some valuable perquisites, he enjoyed a daily allowance of twenty servants and as many horses! Not only was Julian strongly opposed to luxury, but he was, as far as his light went, a religious man, and was strict in observing the feasts and festivals of the heathen deities. All his antiquated peculiarities are brought strongly before us on the occasion of his visit to Antioch. Strabo tells us that this was one of the largest cities in the world—little inferior in extent to Alexandria and Seleucia. It was noted for its gaieties, and seems now to have been the centre of fashion. The new religion had been, at least nominally, adopted, and also the new costumes, as well as every kind of luxury and dissipation. Chrysostom bears witness to the same effect. The town was full of dancers, pipers, and players, camels "adorned like brides" stalked through the porticos, and fish and poultry had come to be considered as necessaries of life. There were here many people of leisure and cultivation, fond of light and fanciful pursuits, and among others of forming verbal conceits. Hence, we find that the disciples were first called *Christians* at Antioch, no doubt, derisively,[30] and in Julian's time they had a cant saying that they had suffered nothing from the X or the K (Christ or Constantius). A celebrated school of rhetoric was established here, and no doubt some of the effusions penned at this time, abounded with rich and epigrammatic humour.

It must have been a rare sight for these polished and satirical Christians of Antioch to behold Julian celebrating the festivals of the pagan gods. To view the procession of Venus—a long line of all the dissolute women in the town, singing loose songs—followed by the lean, uncouth Roman Emperor, with his shaggy beard, and terminated by a military train. No wonder they hooted him, and wrote lampoons upon him. But Julian thought he was performing a solemn duty; he by no means intended to countenance immorality. "Far from us," he says, "be all licentious jests and scurrilous discourse—let no priest read Archilochus or Hipponax." He gives an amusing account of his reception at the celebrated grove of Daphnæ, near Antioch, which he visited at the time of the annual festival. He expected to see a profusion of wealth and splendour. He pictured to himself the solemn pomp, the victims, the libations, the dancers, the incense, the children in white robes. When he entered the temple, full of such elevated thoughts, he found there neither incense, cake, nor victims. Much surprised, he could only suppose that the people were waiting at the gate, by way of respect, for a signal from the sovereign Pontiff. He therefore asked the priest what offering the city was about to make on this great anniversary; to which he replied, "The city has furnished nothing, but I have brought the god a goose from my own house."

Julian says the people of Antioch had transfixed him with sarcasms, as with arrows. In accordance, however, with his peaceful disposition, he only retaliated by writing the Misopogon or "Beard-hater." "No law," he says, "forbids me to satirise myself." He begins with his face and says,

"Although naturally good-looking, moroseness and bad manners have led me to wear a long beard for no apparent reason but that nature has not made it handsome. Therefore, I allow lice to run about in it like wild beasts in a wood, nor have I the power of eating or drinking much, for I must be cautious, lest I eat hairs along with bread. About being kissed, or kissing, I do not much care; still a beard has this inconvenience among others, that it does not allow us to join pure lips to those that are pure, and, therefore, the sweeter. You say that ropes should be twisted out of it, and I would willingly grant this, if only you were able to draw out the bristles, so that your soft and delicate hands should not suffer from their roughness."

He says that he never goes to the theatre, and hates horse-races. As to domestic matters, "I pass sleepless nights upon a bed of straw, and insufficient food makes my manners severe and offensive to a luxurious city. Do not think that I do this on your account—a great and senseless mistake has led me from my childhood to wage war with my stomach." He is not at all surprised that they should follow the dissolute habits of the founder of their city, Antiochus, and that they think of nothing but dressing, bathing, and love-making—charges which could not be brought against himself. He esteems dancers and players "no more than the frogs of the lakes," and tells a story, that when Cato came into the city of Antioch, seeing all the young men under arms, and the magistrates in their robes, he thought the parade was in his honour. He blamed his friends for having told them he was coming, and advanced with some hesitation, when the master of the ceremonies came up and asked, "Stranger, how far off is Demetrius?" a man who had been a slave of Pompey, but had become immensely rich. Cato made no reply, but exclaimed, "O, miserable city!" and departed.

The Misopogon is unique as a mock disparagement of self. Although written in condemnation of the Antiochians, a vein of pleasantry runs through it, which shows that Julian was not vindictive, and had a considerable gift of humour. Had he lived to mature age, he would probably have left some brilliant literary work. But shortly after his visit to Antioch, he led an expedition into Persia, and with his usual disregard of danger, entered the battle without his armour, and was mortally wounded.

We read that the Roman girls were very fond of amusing themselves in their leisure hours by making "scirpi" or riddles. They do not seem to have indulged much in puns, or to have attempted anything very intricate, but rather to have aimed at testing knowledge and memory. We have few specimens remaining of their art, but such as we have are of that early kind, which demand some special information for their solutions. Aulus Gellius has preserved one "old by Hercules," which turns on the legend that when Tarquinius Superbus was installing Jupiter at the Capitol, all the other gods were ready to leave except Terminus, who being by his character immovable, and having no legs, refused to depart.[31] Two other specimens are found in Virgil's bucolics:—

> "Say in what lands grow flowers inscribed with names
> Of kings—and Phyllis shall be yours alone,"

referring to the hyacinth, on whose petals the word Ajax was supposed to be found. The responding couplet runs:—

> "Say, and my great Apollo thou shalt be,
> Where heaven's span extends but three ells wide;"

the answer to which is not known.

Probably some riddles of an earlier date may be incorporated in the book of Symposius. Nothing is known of the life of this author, and it has been suggested that the word should be Symposium or the "Banquet"—these enigmas being supposed to be delivered after dinner. But most authorities consider Symposius to have lived in the fourth century, although an examination of his prosody might lead us to place him not earlier than the fifth. Very few of the riddles are really ingenious; among the best we may reckon:—

> "Letters sustain me—yet I know them not,
> I live on books, and yet I never read,
> The Muses I've devoured and gained no knowledge."

This is tolerably self-evident, but some require special information as:—

> "You can behold what you can scarce believe
> There is but one eye, yet a thousand heads,
> Who sells what he has, whence shall he get what he has not?"

Few would ever guess that this referred to a one-eyed man selling garlic. But the greater number of these conceits are merely emblematic descriptions of well-known things, and are more vague than epigrammatic, as,

> "I am the purple of the earth suffused with lovely tints and girt, lest I be wronged with pointed spears. Happy indeed! had I but length of life."
>
> "There's a new capture of some well-known game, that what you catch not, you bear off with you."

"Hoarsely amidst the waves I raise my voice
It sounds with praise with which it lauds itself,
And though I ever sing, no one applauds."

"Spontaneous coming, I show various forms,
I feign vain fears, when there is no true conflict,
But no one can see me till he shuts his eyes."

"By art four equal sisters run
As if in contest, though the labour's one,
And both are near, nor can each other touch."[32]

We know little of Macrobius except that he was a Greek, and lived in the fifth century. His principal work was his "Saturnalia," and he selected for it this title and plan, because, as he tells us, men were in his day so much occupied with business, that it was only in the annual festival of misrule that they had any time for reflection or social intercourse. The "Saturnalia," occupied the greater part of December, and Macrobius represents a company of magnates and wits agreeing to meet daily to discuss in the morning topics of importance, and to spend the evening in light and jocund conversation. His work treats of astronomy, mythology, poetry and rhetoric, but it is most interesting with regard to our present subject, where he brings before us one of those scenes of convivial merriment of which we have often heard. The party are to relate humorous anecdotes in turn. Avienus says that they should be intellectual not voluptuous, to which the president, Prætextatus, replies, that they will not banish pleasure as an enemy, nor consider it to be the greatest good. After these suggestions they commence:—

Prætextatus records a saying of Hannibal. Antiochus, to whom he had fled, showed him in a plain a vast army he had collected to make war with the Romans; the men were adorned with gold and silver, there were chariots with scythes, elephants with towers, cavalry shining with ornamental bits and housings. Then turning to Hannibal, he asked him if he thought they would be enough for the Romans. The Carthaginian, smiling at the weakness and cowardice of the gaudily accoutred host, replied, "Certainly, I think they will be enough for them, however greedy they may be."

Furius Albinus says that after the flight at Mutina, on some lady asking what Antony was doing, one of his friends replied, "What the dogs do in Egypt—drink and run!" "It is well known," he adds, "that there the dogs run while they drink, for fear of the crocodiles."

Avenienus says that the sister of Faustus, the son of Sylla, had two lovers—one of them, Fulvius, the son of a fuller; the other Pomponius, nick-named Spot. "I wonder," he said, "that my sister should have a spot, when she has a fuller."

The remaining guests speak more at length, and their discourses occupy a considerable portion of the book.

The example set by Martial gradually led to a considerable development of epigrammatic literature. A humorous epigram survives, written by Trajan on a man with a large nose:

> "By placing your nose and gaping mouth opposite the sun
> You will tell wayfarers the hour."

Justinian in the sixth century is supposed to have assisted Paul the Silentiary—a sort of master of the ceremonies—in his compositions; but it may be hoped that the Emperor was not an accomplice in producing the impurities with which they are disfigured. Here and there, however, a few sweet flowers are found in his poisonous garland. We may hope that he often received such a cool welcome as that he commemorates in his "Drenched Lover."

Hierocles and Philagrius are supposed to have lived in the fifth century, but the jests and stories which bear their names seem to be much later. They are based upon violations of the primary laws of nature and mind, but have not the subtlety of the syllogistic quibbles, which were the work of learned grammarians or the logicians of a better period. Being little more than Bulls, they excite scarcely any emotion and no laughter, although evincing a certain cleverness. The hero is generally a "Scholastic," who is represented as a sort of fool. A friend of Scholasticus going abroad asks him to buy him some books. Scholasticus forgets all about it, and when he meets his friend on his return, says, "By the way, I never received that letter you wrote about the books." A man meeting Scholasticus says, "The slave you sold me died." "Did he? By the gods," replied the other, "he never played me that trick." Scholasticus meeting a friend exclaims, "Why, I heard you were dead!" The other replies, "Well, I tell you that I'm alive." "Yes," persists Scholasticus, "but the man who told me so was more veracious than you!" A promising son apostrophizes his father, "Base varlet! don't you see how you have wronged me? If you had never been born and stood in the way I should have come into all my grandfather's money."

The humour which has come to us from classic times, brings the life of ancient Greece and Rome near to our own firesides. It is not that of a primitive or decaying civilization, but of one advanced and matured, resembling our own, in which density of population has brought a clashing of interests, and enlarged knowledge has produced a variety of thought upon a great multiplicity of home and foreign subjects. We can thus bridge over two thousand years, and obtain, as it were, a grasp of the Past, in which we find men so very like ourselves, not only in their strong emotions, but in their little conceits and vanities, and their opinions of each other.

ENGLISH HUMOUR.

CHAPTER I.

MIDDLE AGES.

Relapse of Civilization in the Middle Ages—Stagnation of Mind—Scarcity of Books—Character of reviving Literature—Religious Writings—Fantastic Legends—Influence of the Crusades—Romances—Sir Bevis of Hamptoun—Prominence of the Lower Animals—Allegories.

Those ancient philosophers who believed in a mundane year and a periodical repetition of the world's history, would have found a remarkable corroboration of their theory in the retrogression of learning during the middle ages, and its subsequent gradual revival. This re-birth contained all the leading characteristics of the original development of thought, although, amid the darkness, the torch handed down from the past afforded occasionally some flickering light. The great cause of the disappearance of literature and civilization was, of course, the sword of the Goths, which made the rich countries of Southern Europe, a wilderness and desolation. A lesser cause was the intolerance of the ecclesiastics, who, in their detestation of Pagan superstition and immorality endeavoured to destroy all classical writings which touched upon mythological subjects, or contained unseemly allusions. But, although we regret its action in this respect, and the intellectual stagnation thus generally produced, we must admit that we are indebted to the Church for the preservation of many valuable works. There were many men of learning in the monasteries, and some of sufficient enlightenment to be able to venerate the relics of Greek and Latin literature. We find that in the East the works of Aristophanes were so much admired by St. Chrysostom that he slept with them under his pillow. Perhaps the Saint enjoyed the reflections of the comedian upon the superstitions of his day, or he may have had a secret liking for the drama, and in one place he observes how much the world resembles a stage. There seems to have been a conflict in his breast, as no doubt there was in many at the time, between love of the classics and religious scruples; he tells us that he dreamed one night that he was being whipped by the devil for reading Cicero.

We may observe that the Eastern world was not at this time in such a benighted state. Theodosius the younger founded in A.D. 425, an academy and library at Constantinople, which, when it was destroyed by the Turks contained 120,000 volumes. Nothing brings before us more forcibly the state of ignorance in which the Western world was now sunk than the scarcity of books. The price of them in the middle ages was so great that a man who presented one to a monastery, thought he merited eternal salvation. Documents were drawn up and duly signed when a book passed from one person to another—and in the eighth century a library of 150 volumes was regarded as something magnificent.[33]

The state of ignorance among the Saxons may be imagined from the fact that Alfred was twelve years old before he could get a master capable of teaching him the alphabet, and even after the invention of paper in the eleventh century books were very scarce. The cause of the scanty supply of literature was not only the general destruction which had taken place, but also that there was no demand for it. Archbishop Lanfranc, with a view to improve education in England, directed in 1072 that a book should be given to each of the monks, who were to be allowed a year to read it, and what follows gives us some idea of the indolence of these representatives of learning, for it was ordered that if the monk has not then read it he is to prostrate himself, and ask pardon of the abbot. The monks of Winchester were probably not much troubled in this way, for some time afterwards the library of the bishop of that diocese only consisted of seven books. What must then have been the ignorance of the masses of the population! We should scarcely believe that such a relapse could have taken place had we not seen the centres of civilization in the world successively succumbing, and the greatest cities becoming desolate, and did we not reflect that, but for such vicissitudes, mankind must have attained a far greater degree of excellence than has been reached at the present day.

The first kind of composition attempted by the mind of man is that which expresses religious feelings, and the idea that there exists a being greater than himself. That dim searching after something beyond experience could seldom confine itself to its legitimate direction, but by dreams and hopes, and by the love of the marvellous—that early source of idealism—strayed into a variety of fabulous and legendary mazes. Hence arose all the strange and grotesque myths about heathen gods and Christian saints which occupy the shadowy borders between chaos and history. The stories which were current in this country in early times spoke of miracles worked by the Virgin, represented St. Christopher as a giant twenty-four feet high, and related how "Seynt Pateryk" banished the "wormes" from Ireland; or sometimes would draw from the rich mine of Rabbinical tradition such allegorical fictions as that, when Noah planted the vine, Satan was present and sacrificed a sheep, a lion, an ape, and a sow, representing the different stages of inebriety.[34]

But man's awakening thoughts turn not only to his Protector above, but also to his enemies below, and thus the exploits of warlike heroes, who generally combine the religious with the military character, easily became tempting themes for the exercise of fancy.

There is reason to believe that the earliest British legends recorded the glories of King Arthur—the defender of Christianity against the worshippers of Odin. The origin of these accounts have been traced by some to Scandinavian, by some to Arabian sources, but we may suppose them to have arisen among those ancient British people who inhabited Wales and Cornwall,[35] and passed over in the fifth and sixth centuries to Brittany (Armorica). It matters little for our present purpose whence they came, they were full of extravagant and supernatural occurrences. The names of two shadowy warriors, Sir Bevis and Sir Guy, seem to have been handed down from Saxon times, probably by oral tradition; the former is said to have performed prodigies of valour in the South, and the latter in the North of England. The literature which has come down to us from this date (with the exception of an ode of triumph) is purely of a religious character, and adorned with a variety of miraculous circumstances—a considerable part of it consists of the hymns of Cædmon, an ignorant cowherd, who was inspired to sing by an angel appearing to him in a vision.

Bede's Ecclesiastical History is full of strange stories, and although Acca, his contemporary, adorned his cathedral of Hexham in Northumberland with what was then considered to be a magnificent library, it was entirely composed of histories of the Apostles and martyrs to whose relics he had dedicated the altars of his church.[36] Meanwhile, the glorification of Charlemagne and his paladins, the great champions of Christendom, exercised the invention of the minstrels of France. But activity of mind increasing, additional subjects for entertainment were demanded, and the old pagan kings and heroes appeared in entirely new characters. The marvellous and magnificent career of Alexander the Great seemed to invite a little additional ornamentation, and the Roman Emperors were introduced in very fantastic habiliments.

It would seem that traditional accounts of Roman times had been preserved in some of the Western monasteries, as well as portions of the old Homeric and mythological history in Latin translations[37]—Greek had been fading out of Europe since the time of Theodosius. No doubt there were still here and there a few genuine classical books, and we hear of Aristotle being prized—the obscurity and subtlety of his works having led to his being now regarded as a magician.

The following will give some idea of the kind of stories then appreciated. A beautiful princess, nourished with poison, was sent as a present to Alexander. Aristotle discovered the danger, and a slave was ordered to kiss her, who immediately fell down dead.

The gigantic body of Pallas, the son of Evander, was found at Rome. It exceeded in height the walls of the city, and had remained uncorrupted, and accompanied with a burning lamp for two hundred and forty years. His wound was fresh, and we may suppose caused instant death, for it was four feet and a half long.

Magical rings are often mentioned. There is some pretty sentiment in the story of Vespasian and a wife whom he had married in a distant country. She refuses to return home with him, and yet declares that she will kill herself if he leaves her. The Emperor orders two rings to be made, one bearing the image of Oblivion, the other that of Memory. The former he gives to the Empress, the latter he wears himself.

Virgil, who is represented as an enchanter, places a magical image in the centre of Rome, which every day communicates to the Emperor Titus all the secret offences committed in the city.

From such fanciful sources, and with a discrimination such as they display, Geoffrey of Monmouth drew up in the eleventh century a fabulous history of England. His story of Gogmagog, the British giant, supposed to have been destroyed by Brutus, the great grandson of Æneas, on his landing in this country, is said to have been derived from that of two Arabian giants Gog and Magog. The stones which compose Stonehenge, each containing some medicinal virtue, are fabled to have been transported by giants from the deserts of Africa to Ireland, and to have been carried thence by Merlin's enchantment to form a monument over the British slain by Hengist. The state of criticism existing at this time may be imagined from the fact that even afterwards, in the reign of Edward I., the descent of the Britons from the Trojans through Brutus was solemnly alleged in a controversy of great importance concerning the subjection of the crown of England to that of Scotland, showing an amount of credulity which might almost have credited the legend that St. James, mounted on horseback, led the Christian armies in Spain in their battles against the Moors, or that there was in that country a golden image of Mahomet as high as a bird could fly, in which the false prophet had sealed up a legion of devils.

But the imaginative powers were soon to be developed upon more attractive themes. War and Religion were about to be blended in the grand drama of the Crusades, prompted alike by zeal for the faith, by hatred of the Moslem, and by thirst for military glory. The first nobles of the West arrayed themselves in their armour, collected their retainers, and set out for the lands of the rising sun. Here they came into contact with an Eastern civilization, ornate and dazzling, superior to their own, but still in a state of childhood, and revelling in the fanciful creations which please the infantine mind.[38] Foremost among the Christian knights went the Barons of Provence, accompanied by troops of minstrels—troubadours to sing their praises; and we might well suppose that some of the wonders of the dreaming East would now find their way into Europe, interwoven with the doughty deeds of the Christian heroes. This view is corroborated by the fact that almost all our early romances recount some great exploits performed against the Saracens; but the marvels they relate, from whatever source they come, were in accordance with the times in which they were written, for as alchemy preceded chemistry, so romance-writing was the commencement of literature. Some of the Arabian stories had considerable grace and beauty, and are even now attractive to the young. But whether our poets borrowed from this prolific source or not, it is certain that about this time they became more ambitious, and produced regular tales of considerable length, in which the northern gallantry towards the fair sex was combined with extravagances resembling those of Eastern invention.

Not until this time were the early heroic legends of this country developed, and committed to writing, and as they appeared first in French, some writers—among whom is Ritson—have concluded that they were merely the offspring of our neighbours' fertile imagination. But although the poets who recounted these stories wrote in French, they were in attendance at the English Court, in which, even before the Conquest, French was the language used, while Latin was that of the learned, and Saxon that of the country-people. Henry the First, the great patron of letters, sometimes held his Court at Caen, so that the Norman poets who were competing for his favour, were doubtless familiar with the legendary history of England. The first important works in the French language seem to have come from Normandy, and it is not improbable that some of them were written in England. They were called romances, because they were composed in one of the languages of Southern Europe, containing a large element of the Roman, which we find was still used among the soldiery as late as the seventh century. It has been supposed that all our early Anglo-Norman romances were translations from the French, except the "Squyr of Lowe Degre," and of some the originals are still extant.

These productions, from whatever source they came, were the kind of literature most acceptable at the time. There seemed then nothing harsh or contemptibly puerile in stories we should now relegate to the nursery, and no doubt people derived an amusement from them, for which that of humour was afterwards gradually substituted.

Examples of such stories are found in that of Robert, King of Sicily, who for his pride was changed, like Nebuchadnezzar, into one of the lower animals, and in that of Richard "Coeur de Lion," who rode a horse possessed by the devil, and whose wife flew away like a bird.

In the romance of Sir Bevis of Hamtoun, (Earl of Southampton,) he is represented as a kind of infant Hercules, who, when fifteen, killed sixty Saracen knights. He afterwards was imprisoned at Damascus in a den with two dragons, but destroyed them. He was kept in a dungeon, however, and

> "Rats and mice, and such small deer,
> Was his meat that seven year."

During this time he was cheered by an angel visiting him. An adversary shortly appears in Ascapard:

> "This geaunt was mighty and strong,
> And full thirty foot was long,
> He was bristled like a sow;
> A foot he had between each brow.
> His lips were great, and hung aside,
> His eyen were hollow, his mouth was wide,
> Lothy he was to look on than,
> And liker a devil than a man."

He was overcome, and became page to Sir Bevis. Ascapard is very useful, as he is able to take Bevis, Josyan, and even the horse Arundel under his arm. An attempt at humour is introduced here, which is said to have amused the people of Cologne. The bishop prepared to christen the giant,

> "For Ascapard was made a tun,
> And when he should therein be done,
> He lept out upon the brench (brink)
> And said, 'Churl! wilt thou me drench?
> The devil of hell mote fetche thee!
> I am too much (big) christened to be!'"

We will finish this sketch of the romancing tendencies of our early literature by a description of a dragon from "Sir Degoré:"

> "There was a dragon great and grymme,
> Full of fyre, and also venymme,
> Wyth a wyde throte, and tuskes grete,
> Uppon that knygte fast gan he bete,
> And as a lyon then was hys feete,
> Hys tayle was long, and full unmeete;
> Between hys head and hys tayle
> Was xxii fote withouten fayle;
> His body was lyke a wyne tonne,
> He shone ful bryght agaynst the sunne;
> Hys eyen were bryght as any glasse,
> Hys scales were hard as any brasse:
> And thereto he was necked lyke a horse,
> He bore hys hed up wyth grete force;
> The breth of hys mouth that did not blow
> As yt had been a fyre on lowe.
> He was to loke on, as I you telle
> As yt had been a fiende of helle."

These romances were often called "Gestes," from the great "Gesta" or exploits they recorded.

The author of "Cursor Mundi," a book of religious legends, says,

> "Men lykyn jestis for to here
> And romans rede in divers manere
> Of Alexandre the conquerour,
> Of Julius Cæsar the Emperour, &c."

It may be doubted whether such tales as the above were ever regarded as true, but it was not until thought became more active that the falsity of them was fully appreciated, and "jests" gradually acquired their present signification. The word romance has also come to be used not only for a pleasant poetical narrative, but especially for something utterly devoid of truth. "Story" is used in the same sense, but not "novel," for in our present works of fiction there is seldom so much improbability as to be offensive in our day, though it may be so to our successors.

In the above extracts it may have been observed that there is a prominence and importance given to the lower animals which we should not find in writings of the present day. As civilization fell back into barbarism, fables re-appeared, and some indifferent literature of this kind was produced in the fourth century by Aphthonius in Greek, and afterwards by Flavius Avianus in Latin. In the Saxon ode on the victory of Athelstan, a very particular account is given of the beasts of prey present at the carnage.

Theodosius, the blind Emperor, is said to have been restored to sight by a serpent, whom he had benefited, coming in while he was asleep, and placing a precious stone upon his eyes. In one of the early romances of Marie, a baron is transformed into a bisclaveret,[39] or wolf, for three days every week, much to his wife's discomfort; in another a falcon changes into a knight, who is finally caught in a bird-trap; in another a lady falls into a trance, and is supposed to be dead, until her rival, seeing a weasel restore another one by placing a vermilion flower in its mouth, she places it in the lady's mouth and thus awakens her. The same element is largely present in the other romances.

Alexander Neckam, who lived in the latter part of the twelfth century, shows how fond our forefathers were of animals, and how they kept them in their houses. The castles were often full of them, some roving about, others necessarily in confinement. Monkeys were in high favour. Some of them were taught to fight as in a tournament, which we are told caused great laughter. In mediæval times there was a love of all kinds of hybrid animals, and there was a certain amount of belief that all sorts of monsters came from the East or North. Giraldus Cambrensis tells us that there were in Ireland such mixtures as half ox and half man, half dog and half monkey.

All these stories remind us of the fabular period in old Greek history, and bespeak a time, when both taste and knowledge were in their infancy; but when, at the same time, the rays of the ideal were breaking upon the mind, and "men appeared as trees walking."

Allied to a love of fabling was that of allegory, which, as soon as literary activity began to appear in the early church, produced an abundant harvest. This tendency exhibited itself in the first progress of thought in England. Philippe de Than, one of the most ancient Anglo-Norman poets, wrote a work describing the character of each bird and beast, upon which he grounded moral reflections. Robert Grosseteste, Bishop of Lincoln, who died in 1253, was celebrated for a copious dissertation on mystical divinity, and a poem is extant ascribed to him, called the "Castle of Love" by Leland, in which the creation and redemption are represented as an allegory—our Lord being supposed to enter a magnificent castle, the body of the Virgin. The "Gesta Romanorum" strongly exhibits the want of discrimination at this time, for although the dramatis personæ are generally Roman Emperors, the deepest Christian mysteries are supposed to be shadowed forth by their actions. Some of the stories are evidently invented to enforce religious teaching. We read of an angel accompanying a hermit on his wanderings, the angel robs or murders all who receive him, but explains afterwards that it is for their good. He gives a golden goblet to a rich man who refuses to entertain them, to comfort him in this world, as he will go to hell in the next.

Vincent of Beauvais, a learned Dominican of France, who flourished in the thirteenth century, observes that it was a practice of preachers to rouse their congregation by relating a fable of Æsop. In the British Museum there is a collection of two hundred and fifteen stories, romantic, allegorical, and legendary, evidently compiled for the use of monastic preachers. Mystic similitudes were at this time greatly affected in all branches of learning. In the "Romaunt of the Rose," the difficulties of a lover are represented under the form of a man seeking a rose in an inaccessible garden. This flower, alchemists considered to be emblematic of the Philosopher's Stone, while theologians referred it to the white rose of Jericho—a state of grace into which the wicked could not enter.

CHAPTER II.

Anglo-Saxon Humour—Rhyme—Satires against the Church—The Brunellus—Walter Mapes—Goliardi—Piers the Ploughman—Letters of Obscure Men—Erasmus—The Praise of Folly—Skelton—The Ship of Fools—Doctour Doubble Ale—The Sak full of Nuez—Church Ornamentation—Representations of the Devil.

The rude character of the Anglo-Saxon humour may be gathered from our having derived from it the word *fun*. This term which we often apply to romping and boisterous games, refers principally to the sense of feeling, and always implies some low kind of amusement connected with the senses. We also discover among the Anglo-Saxons an unamiable tendency to give nicknames to people from their personal peculiarities. But if we look for anything better, we can find only a translation of the Latin riddles of Symposius by Aldhelm, Bishop of Shirburn. This prelate, who was a relation of Ina, King of the West Saxons, was in attainments far superior to his age. He was celebrated as a harper, poet, and theologian, and wrote several works, especially one in praise of Virginity. His translations from Symposius were probably intended for the post-prandial delectation of the monks.

Aristophanes seems to have made the first approach to rhyming, for he introduced some repetitions of the same word at the end of lines. He probably thought the device had an absurd effect and used it as a kind of humour. Aulus Gellius blames Isocrates, who lived about 400 B.C., for introducing jingles into his orations, and as he also refers to Lucilius' condemnation of them, he would probably have objected to them in poetry.

Classic Latin versification is supposed to have died out with Fortunatus, Bishop of Poitiers in the sixth century, but an advance was made towards playing with words by the introduction of rhymes in the church hymns. Some trace of them is found in the verses of Hilary in the fourth century, but we find them first regularly adopted in a Latin panegyric written for Clotaire II. in France at the commencement of the seventh. Some suppose that "Leonine verses" were invented shortly afterwards by Pope Leo II. As in the days of Greece and Rome, the development of poetry was accompanied by a considerable activity in the fabrication of metres. This did not limit itself to a distich or alternate rhyme called "tailed" or "interlaced," but included the "horned," "crested," and "squared" verses—the last forming double acrostics. Sometimes half a dozen lines were made to rhyme together. This movement, pedantic as it was, showed an advance in finding similarities in things dissimilar, a change in the appreciation of the harmony. Previously rhymes were considered ludicrous, as they seem to us now in prose, and even in the French drama. The old Welsh poetry depended merely upon alliteration—as in the words ascribed to the British Queen—

"Ruin seize thee, ruthless king."

And among our old proverbs we have "Many men of many minds." "Fools build houses, for wise men to live in." "First come, first served." The motto of the Duke of Athole runs "Furth fortune and fill the fetters."

The "Exeter Book," presented to his cathedral by Leofric, first Bishop of Exeter in 1046 deserves notice, as indicative of the course of early Anglo-Saxon literature. Here we have first religious meditations and legends of Saints, then proverbial, or as they are called "gnomic" verses, next allegorical descriptions by means of animals, and finally riddles. The last are very long, and generally consist of emblematic descriptions.

It is a part of the great system of compensation under which we live, that those who are most highly praised are most exposed to the attacks of the envious, and that those who stand on an eminence above others should have their bad as well as their good deeds recorded. And thus we find that the earliest shafts of censure were directed against princes and priests, and the first Norman satires of which we hear were some songs called Sirventois, against Arnould, who was chaplain to Robert Courthose in the time of William Rufus. He was apparently an excellent man, established schools at Caen, and was afterwards promoted to be patriarch of Jerusalem. The next attack of which we have any record was that made by Luc de la Barr against Henry I. The nature of the imputations it contained may be conjectured from the fact, that the king ordered the writer's eyes to be put out. Another satire was directed against Richard, "King of the Romans," who was taken prisoner at Lewes. It was written to triumph over him, and taunt him with his defeat, and the nearest approach to humour in it is where it speaks of his making a castle of a windmill, which is supposed to refer to his having been captured in such a building. The humour in the satires of this time was almost entirely of a hostile or optical character. We have two metrical ballads of the thirteenth century directed against the Scotch and French, but containing little but animosity. There is also one complaining of heavy taxation in the reign of Edward I., but generally the church was attacked, as the clergy formed a prominent mark in every parish in the country, and were safer game than the king or barons. Thus, in the Harleian MSS., there is an ancient French poem pretending to eulogise a new conventual order for both men and women, who are to live together in great luxury and be bound to perpetual idleness. Several monasteries in England are mentioned as affording instances of such a mode of living.

The earliest literary assault we have on the church in this country was written probably in the thirteenth century—Warton says, soon after the conquest—in a mixture of Saxon and Norman. A monastery, composed of various kinds of gems and delicacies, represents the luxury of the monks—

> "Fur in see, bi west Spayngne
> Is a lond ihote Cokaygne:
> Ther nis lond under heuen-riche
> Of wel of godness hit iliche.
>
> "Ther is a wel fair abbei,
> Of white monkes and of grei,
> Ther beth bowris and halles
> Al of pasteiis beth the walles

Of fleis, of fisse, and rich met,
The likfullist that man mai et.

Fluren cakes beth the schingles[40] alle
Of cherche, cloister, boure, and halle.
The pinnes[41] beth fat podinges
Rich met to princez and kinges.

"An other abbei is ther bi
For soth a gret fair nunnerie;
Vp a riuer of sweet milke,
Whar is gret plente of silk."

He goes on to speak of the monks and nuns as dancing together in a very indecorous manner.

The clergy were often humorous themselves—Nigellus Wireker, a monk of Canterbury, who is supposed to have lived in the time of Richard I., wrote a very amusing attack on his brethren. It is in Latin elegiac verse, and as being directed against ambition and discontent may be compared with the first satire of Horace. But he wrote in a less advanced state of civilisation to that in which the Roman poet lived, and he carries on his discourse by means of conversations of animals. The work is called the Brunellus—the name of an ass.

The poem is directed against passion and avarice—and especially against the monks, who, he says deserve to be called pastors, not *a pascendo* but *a poscendo*. But he takes so much interest in the animals he introduces, that he seems to lose sight of his moral object. He delights in the speeches of a cock and crow, but his main story is that the ass, Brunellus, is dissatisfied, because, having long ears he thinks he ought to have a long tail. He betakes himself to Galienus to consult him, who endeavours to dissuade him from adopting any surgical or medical means, and reminds him that if he has a short tail he has a very large head. He inculcates contentment by a story of two cows, one of which, through impatience when her tail has stuck in the mud, says it is not an *honour* but an *onus*, and so pulls it off, and becomes a laughing stock to the world. The other cow waits patiently, and makes a long speech containing references to Cato and the Trojan war.

Prescription given by Galienus to the ass Brunellus to make his tail grow:

> "Some marble's fat and seven fold furnace shade
> The offspring of a male and female mule,
> A little of the milk of goose and kite
> A punchbowl's racing, and a wolf's alarms;
> Of dogs and hares alliance take a drachm,
> And kisses which the lark gives to her hawk."

The ass begs Galienus to bestow upon him his blessing, which he does with mock gravity—

> "May Jove to thee a thousand omens give,
> And to thy tail ten thousand omens more;
> Mayst thou drink water, and on thistles feed,
> Be thy bed marble, and thy covering dew.
> May hail and snow and rain be ever near,
> Ice and hoar frost thy constant comfort be!"

The ass, whose extraordinary performances are narrated, is appointed the "nuntius" of a bishop.

The man who showed at this time the greatest judgment in humour and insight into its nature, was John of Salisbury. His Polycraticus is worthy of a religious character; but he speaks in it of "Court Trifles" under which he places dice, music and dreams. Many of his observations show a taste and knowledge in advance of his time. "Our age," he says, "has fallen back to fables," and he speaks as though the jesters of the day indulged in very questionable jokes and performances. He notices the force of a jest made by a man who would himself fall under it, as when a pauper laughs at poverty. Also he refers to the effect of accusing a man of the faults to which his virtues may lead, as of telling a liberal man he is a spendthrift. "So Diogenes told Antisthenes, his master, that he had made him a doctor instead of a rich man—a dweller in a tub, instead of in a mansion." Well-timed pleasantries, he says, are of use in oratory, but convivial jesting is dangerous, remarks or personal defects are objectionable, and as Lycurgus ordered, all jokes should be without bitterness.

But Walter Mapes seems to have been the first man of note, who reconciled "divinity and wit." He was born on the borders of Wales about the beginning of the twelvth century, and having studied at the University of Paris became a favourite of Henry II., and was made a Canon of St. Paul's, and Archdeacon of Oxford. It may be worth notice that his name was really a monosyllable, "Map," a man's appellation being not always without influence in determining his character and conduct. From being a man of humour he obtained the credit of being a man of pleasure, but as far as we can collect from the writings, which are with certainty attributed to him, he was strongly imbued with religious feelings. He delights to recount the miracles of saints. Peter of Tarentaise exorcised, he tells us, a devil from one possessed, and the man proved his cure by exclaiming, "Mother of God, have mercy upon me!" whereupon John the bishop said of Peter. "This is the only bishop—the rest of us are dogs unable to bark." Mapes also reflects the credulity of the age in which he lived, by narrating extraordinary stories of infidels walking about after death, and calling people by name, who always died shortly afterwards. He gives us a collection of Welsh "apparitions."

We must suppose that even at that day there was something peculiarly fanciful in the mind of the man who collected such tales. But, although he commends his favourite saints as being jocund and pleasant men, we are disappointed when we look for his own wit. It is either verbal or sententious, and does not rise higher than, "Few things are impossible to women." "May God omnipotent grant you not to be deceived by woman omnipotent." "The dog does not gnaw a dry bone, nor the leech stick to an empty vein." His "Mirror of the Church" is full of violent attacks upon the monastic orders, especially the Cistercian, evidently written in serious indignation, although he sometimes indulges in a play upon words. In this he was unlike many writers, who attacked the monks merely to amuse, for which there was a good opening, as the brethren, though in some cases weak, were generally viewed with respect, and tales about them were easily regarded as humorous. There is a story of Walter Mapes having been called to see a Cistercian Abbot, when dangerously ill, and the Archdeacon recommended him to quit his order, and give up avarice and rapacity. The Abbot refused, and even administered to the Archdeacon the rebuke, "Get thee behind me, Satan." Shortly afterwards Mapes was taken ill, and the Abbot going to visit him, strongly recommended him to renounce his light jesting habits, to give up his pluralities, and take refuge in the bosom of the Cistercian order—at the same time producing a gown and cowl, with which he proposed to invest him. Mapes, with characteristic humour called his servants, and told them that, if ever in a fit of sickness he expressed a desire of becoming a monk, they were to consider it a sign that he had lost his senses, and keep him in close confinement.

The character which Mapes obtained for himself, caused a large amount of poetry of a somewhat later date to be attributed to him. It is called "Goliardic," as it gives the views of a class of wild ecclesiastical or University men, who spent their time in composing lampoons, and were called Goliards, from their supposed gluttony. In an epigram, one of these men is represented coming to a bishop's palace, and stating that he is "all ready to dine," somewhat in the way of the old Greek parasites. The bishop tells him he does not want such disreputable company, but that as he has come, he may have his food. We may suppose, however, that he and his poorer brethren did not occupy any dignified position at the repast, as one of them complains

> "Abbas ire sede sursum,
> Et prioris juxta ipsum,
> Ego semper stavi dorsum
>   Inter rascalilia."

All these poems are in Latin rhyme. Two of them are especially attributed to Mapes. One is "on not marrying;" Golias here sets forth a very appalling catalogue of the miseries of matrimony. The husband is a donkey who is spurned by his wife. Her tongue is a sword. He thanks heaven he has escaped from the danger he was once in from the fascinations of a beautiful lady. The other piece is the "Confessions of Golias," which are very frank with regard to various unclerical weaknesses. Some of the stanzas may be translated as follows,

> "I purpose in a tavern to die,
> Place to my dying lips the flowing bowl,

May choirs of angels coming from on high
Sing, 'God be gracious to the toper's soul.'[42]

"The race of poets shun both drink and food,
Avoid disputes, withdraw from public strife,
And to make verses that shall long hold good
O'ercome with labour, sacrifice their life.

"Nature allots to each his proper course,
In hunger I could never use my ink,
The smallest boy then equals me in force,
I hate as death the want of food and drink."

In one of these poems, Golias calls down every kind of misery, spiritual and temporal, upon the man who has stolen his purse. He hopes he may die of fever and madness, and be joined to Judas in hell. One of the most amusing pieces is a consultation held among the priests, on account of the Pope having ordered them to dismiss their women-servants. They finally come to the conclusion that parish priests should be allowed two wives, monks and canons three, and deans and bishops four or five. We are not surprised to hear that such effusions as these called down the displeasure of the heads of the Church, and in 1289, a statute was published that no clerks should be "joculatores, goliardi seu bufones."

About the middle of the fourteenth century, a French monk, Robert Langlande, wrote the "Vision of Piers Plowman," an account of a dream he is supposed to have had when among the Malvern Hills. It is possible that the sight of the grand old abbey may have suggested his theme, for he inveighs not only against the laity, but especially against the ecclesiastics for their neglect of the poor. The poem is remarkable for being without rhythm, but alliterative, such as was common in the neighbouring district of Wales. It somewhat resembles one of the old "Mysteries," introducing a variety of allegorical characters. Some of the personifications are very strange. He says that,

"Dowel and Dobet and Dobest the thirde coth he
Arn thre fair vertues and ben not fer to fynde."

"Dobest is above bothe, and berith a bieschopis crois
And is hokid on that on ende to halie men fro helle
And a pike is in the poynt to putte adon the wyked."

In another place, the effects of starvation are described "both the man's eiyen wattred," and "he loked like a lanterne."

In another work by the same hand, "Piers, the Ploughman's crede," the author—a simple man—wishes to know how he is to follow Christ, and betakes himself to the friars for information. But he finds that each order thinks of little beyond railing against some other. The friars preachers are thus described,

"Than turned I ayen whan I hadde al ytoted
And fond in a freitoure a frere on a benche
A greet chorl and a grym, growen as a tonne,
With a face so fat, as a ful bleddere
Blowen bretful of breth, and as a bagge honged."

All the humour of Piers the Ploughman seems to be more or less of this personal kind.

We must here notice the humorous though scurrilous attack made upon the Roman clergy in the "Letters of Obscure Men," published in Germany at the commencement of the sixteenth century. There was something novel in the idea of a series of ironical letters, and from their appearance, the steady progress of the Reformation may be dated. The greater part of them seems to have been written by Ulrich von Hutten, and are addressed to Ortuin Gratius, a professor of the University of Cologne, who had attacked Reuchlin, a celebrated Hebraist. The original quarrel was only about some translations of Rabbinical works, but it extended into a contest between the Church party, represented by Gratius, and those desirous of reformation. Doctrine is scarcely touched upon in these letters, but accusations of immorality abound. There is great variety in the plan upon which the irony and satire are conducted. For instance, the writer says he has just heard from Gratius that he is sending flowers and gifts to another man's wife. "Reuchlin has written a defence of himself against Gratius, in which he calls him an ass. Reuchlin ought to be burnt with his book. Some people say the monks are grossly dishonest—it is a horrible lie. A preacher, after taking a little too much wine, has actually said that the principals of the University are given to drink and play. Some profane men say that the coat of our Lord at Treves is not genuine, but only an old rag; he does not believe there is now any hair of the Virgin in the world; and the preaching friars who sell indulgences are only a set of buffoons who deceive old apple-women. Another fool says that the preaching friars committed fearful abominations at Berne, and one day put poison into the consecrated elements. A great calamity has happened! A thief has stolen three hundred florins, which the preachers had gained by the sale of indulgences. The people who gave the money are in sad trouble to know whether they still have absolution—they need not be alarmed, they have as much as they had before they gave their money to the friars. Query. Is it a sin to play at dice in order to buy indulgences? Gratius, in a letter to another Father of the Church, expresses his astonishment at hearing that he thinks so much about the ladies. Such thoughts come from the devil; wherever they are suggested, he must make the sign of the cross on his back, and put a pinch of blessed salt on his tongue. Women make him ill by employing charms and sorceries against him; it is no wonder, for he has grey hair and eyes, a red face, a large nose, and a corporation. No man should ever make use of necromancy to obtain a woman's love, for a student of theology once fell in love with a baker's daughter at Leipzig, and threw an enchanted apple at her,[43] which caused her to fall violently in love with him, and finally led to a scandal in the church."

No one enjoyed these epistles more thoroughly than Erasmus,[44] who, perhaps, from being himself a monk, appreciated them the better. He is said to have laughed so immoderately over some parts of them, that he burst an abscess, which might have proved fatal to him. He was one of those few celebrated men who combine both humour and learning, and he seems to have imbibed somewhat of the spirit of Lucian, whose works he translated, and who also lived in an age of religious controversy and transition. There was such a love of amusement, and so little earnestness in Erasmus, that he could laugh on both sides of the question, with the Reformers and against them. When the monks told him that Luther had married a nun, and that the offspring of such an unholy alliance must needs be Antichrist, he merely replied: "Already are there many Antichrists!" Writing to a zealous Catholic in London, he says "that he grudges the heretics their due, because that, whereas winter is approaching, it will raise the price of fagots." In another place he attacks dignities: "No situation," he says, "could be more wretched than that of the vicegerents of Christ, if they endeavoured to follow Christ's life." There was scarcely anything sacred or profane which was safe from the lash of his ridicule, and if, as some say, he sowed the seeds of the Reformation, it was mostly because he could not resist the temptation to laugh at the clergy. He wrote a very characteristic Work entitled "The Praise of Folly," "Encomium Moriæ" (a play on the name of Sir Thomas More), in which he maintains a sort of paradox, setting forth the value and advantages of folly, *i.e.*, of indulging the light fancies and errors of imagination. With much humorous illustration he enumerates a great many conceits, and includes among them jests, but his main argument may be thus condensed.[45]

"Who knows not that man's childhood is by far the most delightful period of his existence? And why? Because he is then most a fool. And next to that his youth, in which folly still prevails; while in proportion as he retires from her dominion, and becomes possessed through discipline and experience of mature wisdom, his beauty loses its bloom, his strength declines, his wit becomes less pungent, until at last weary old age succeeds, which would be absolutely unbearable, unless folly, in pity for such grievous miseries, gave relief by bringing on a second childhood. Nature herself has kindly provided for an abundant supply of folly in the human race, for since, according to the Stoic definition, wisdom means only being guided by reason; whereas folly, on the other hand, consists in submitting to the government of the passions; Jupiter wishing to make life merry, gave men far more passion than reason, banishing the latter into one little corner of his person, and leaving all the rest of the body to the sway of the former. Man, however, being designed for the arrangement of affairs, could not do without a small quantity of reason, but in order to temper the evil thus occasioned, at the suggestion of folly woman was introduced into the world—"a foolish, silly creature, no doubt, but amusing, agreeable, and well adapted to mitigate the gloom of man's temper." Woman owes all her advantages to folly. The great end of her existence is to please man, and this she could not do without folly. If any man doubts it, he has only to consider how much nonsense he talks to a woman whenever he wishes to enjoy the pleasures of female society."

Erasmus wrote an ode in honour of Henry VII. and his children, and in it he recommends him to keep with him Skelton, "the one light and ornament of British literature." He says that no doubt the advice is unnecessary, as he hears the King is most anxious to retain his services. He was tutor to the young prince—afterwards Henry VIII. Skelton was born about 1460. Many of his humorous writings are lost, such as "The Balade of the Mustarde Tarte." He became a "poet laureate," at that time a degree in grammar, rhetoric and versification, on taking which, the graduate was presented with a laurel crown. Having taken orders in 1498, he was afterwards suspended for living with a lady whom he had secretly married. This suspension was much owing to his having incurred the anger of the Dominican Friars, whom he had attacked in his writings. We are told that he was esteemed more fit for the stage than the pulpit. The humour of Skelton consists principally of severe personal vituperation. In "Colyn Cloute" he assailed the clergy generally, but he wrote personal attacks on Garnesche (a courtier), and on Wolsey. The Cardinal had been his patron at one time, and Skelton had dedicated poems to him, among them "A Replycacion" against the followers of Wickliffe and Luther—of which pious effusion the following lines will give a specimen:—

> "To the honour of our blessed lady
> And her most blesed baby,
> I purpose for to reply
> Agaynst this horryble heresy
> Of these young heretics that
> > Stynke unbrent.

> "I say, thou madde marche hare,
> I wondre how ye dare
> Open your ianglyng iawes,
> To preche in any clawes
> Lyke pratynge poppyng dawes.

> "I say, ye braynless beestes,
> Why iangle you such iestes.

In your diuynite
Of Luther's affynite
To the people of lay fee
Raylying in your rages
To worshyppe none ymages
Nor do pylgrymages."

The cause of his quarrel with Wolsey is not known, but he afterwards wrote a severe personal attack upon him entitled, "Why come ye not to Courte?" The tone of this effusion may be gathered from such expressions as:—

"God save his noble grace
And grant him a place
Endlesse to dwell,
With the deuyll of hell,
For and he were there
We nede neuer feere,
Of the fendys blake;
For I vndertake
He wolde so brag and crake,
That he wolde then make
The deuyls to quake,
To shudder and to shake."

Owing to such attacks, he was obliged to flee and take sanctuary at Westminster, where he died. His most entertaining pieces are "Speke Parrot," "Phyllyt Sparrowe," and "Elynour Rummynge." In the first a fair lady laments the death of her bird, killed by "those vylanous false cattes." She sings a "requiescat" for the soul of her dear bird, and recounts all his pretty ways—

"Sometyme he wolde gaspe
When he sawe a waspe;
A fly or a gnat
He wolde flye at that;
And prytely he wold pant
When he saw an ant;
Lord, how he wolde pry
After the butterfly!

Lord, how he wolde hop
After the gressop,
And whan I said Phypp, Phypp,
Than he wolde lepe and skyp,
And take ane by the lyp.
Alas it will me slo
That Phillyp is gone we fro!"

She gives a long list of birds, who are to attend at his funeral, from which our nursery story of cock-robin may be taken. Skelton seems to have been fond and observant of birds. In Speke Parrot, he thus describes

"With my beeke bent, my lyttyl wanton eye,
My fedders freshe as is the emrawde grene,
About my neck a cyrculet lyke the ryche rubye
My lyttyl leggys, my feet both fete and clene,
I am a mynyon to wayt uppon a quene;
My proper parrot my lyttyl prety foole,
With ladyes I lerne and go with them to scole."

It will be observed that the humour in the above pieces is little separated from poetry. In Elynour Rummynge however, we have something undoubtedly jocose, and proportionally rustic and uncouth.

Skelton adopted, as we have seen, a quick, short metre, somewhat analogous to the "Swift Iambics," of the Greek humorists. Sometimes also he alternated Latin with English in a conceit not very uncommon towards the end of the fourteenth and in the fifteenth century as—

"Freeres, freeres, wo ye be!
Ministri malorum,
For many a mannes soul bringe ye,
Ad poenas infernorum."

No work became more popular than the Ship of Fools by Sebastian Brandt. It was published in Germany in 1494, and was speedily translated into Latin and French. Alexander Barclay altered it so considerably in the rendering as almost to make a new work, especially applicable to the state of things existing in this country. Ersch and Grüber speak of Brandt's fools as contemptible and loathsome, and say what he calls follies might be better described as sins and vices. But here and there we meet with touches of humour in the mishaps and absurd actions of those he censures. The whole work is rather of a moral and religious complexion, as the following heading of the poem will suggest—

"Of newe fassions and disgised garmentes. Of Avaryce and prodygalyte. Of vnprofytable stody. Of lepynges and dauncis and Folys that pas theyr tyme in suche vanyte. Of Pluralitees, of flatterers, and glosers. Of the vyce of slouth. Of Usurers and okerers. Of the extorcion of knyghtis. Of follisske, cokes, and buttelers."

Literature increased greatly in the fifteenth century, and began to take that general form it afterwards bore. One of the satires on the fashions of the period, which in every age seem to have afforded materials for mirth, begins as follows—

> "Ye prowd gallonttes hertlesse
> With your hyghe cappis witlesse,
> And youre schort gownys thriftlesse,
> Have brought this londe in gret hevynesse.
> With youre longe peked schone.
> Therfor your thrifte is almost don,
> And with youre long here into your eyen
> Have brought this londe to gret pyne."

There is a good satire written on a priest about the time of the Reformation, showing considerable humour both in matter, language and versification. It is called "Doctor Doubble Ale."

A little episode is given arising from the priest's ignorance—

> "His learning is exceeding
> Ye may know by his reading,
> Yet coulde a cobbler's boy him tell
> That he red a wrong gospell
> Wherfore in dede he served him well,
> He turned himselfe as round as a ball,
> And with loud voyce began to call,
> 'Is there no constable among you all

To take this knave that doth me troble?'
With that all was on a hubble shubble,
There was drawing and dragging,
There was lugging and lagging,
And snitching and snatching,
And ketching and catching,
And so the pore ladde,
To the counter they had,
Some wolde he should be hanged,
Or else he shulde be wranged;
Some sayd it were a good turne
Such an heretyke to burn."

A great many of the humorous poems written against the church were republished at the time of the Reformation to show that for centuries the misdoings of the clergy had been a source of comment. In "the Sak full of Nuez"—a rare book[46] referred to in 1575, containing a collection of humorous pieces of a rough and rude character—we find several hits at the expense of the church.

"A friar used to visit the house of an old woman, who, when he was coming, very prudently hid whatever she had to eat. One day coming with some friends, he asked her if she had not some meat. And she said, 'Nay.' 'Well,' quoth the friar, 'have you not a whetstone?' 'Yea,' quoth the woman, 'what will you do with it?' 'Marry,' quoth he, 'I would make meat thereof.' Then she brought a whetstone. He asked her likewise if she had not a frying-pan. 'Yea,' said she, 'but what the divil will ye do therewith?' 'Marry,' said the fryer, 'you shall see by and by what I will do with it;' and when he had the pan, he set it on the fire, and put the whetstone therein. 'Cocks-body,' said the woman, 'you will burn the pan.' 'No, no,' quoth the fryer, 'if you will give me some eggs, it will not burn at all.' But she would have had the pan from him, when that she saw the pan was in danger; but he would not let her, but still urged her to fetch him some eggs, which she did. 'Tush,' said the fryer, 'here are not enow, go fetch ten or twelve.' So the good wife was constrayned to fetch more, for feare that the pan should burn, and when he had them he put them in the pan. 'Now,' quoth he, 'if you have no butter, the pan will burn and the eggs too.' So the good-wife, being very loth to have her pan burnt, and her eggs lost, she fetcht him a dish of butter, the which he put into the pan and made good meat thereof, and brought it to the table, saying, 'Much good may it do you, my hostess, now may you say you have eaten of a buttered whetstone.'"

Another story runs as follows:—

"There was a priest in the country, which had christened a child; and when he had christened it, he and the clerk were bidden to the drinking that should be there, and being there, the priest drank and made so merry that he was quite foxed, and thought to go home before he laid him down to sleep; but, having gone a little way, he grew so drousie that he could go no further, but laid him down by a ditch-side, so that his feet did hang in the water, and lying on his back, the moon shined in his face; thus he lay till the rest of the company came from drinking, who, as they came home, found the priest lying as aforesaid, and they thought to get him away, but do what they could, he would not rise, but said, 'Do not meddle with me, for I lie very well, and will not stir hence before morning, but I pray lay some more cloathes on my feet, and blow out the candle.'"

At first it occasions us no little surprise to find the clergy of the early centuries so prone to attack and ridicule one another, but we must remember that there was then no reading public, and that the few copies of books in existence were mostly within the walls of the monasteries. Thus, the object of these writers would be like that of St. Jerome in his letters, not so much to disgrace the Church as to improve its discipline. We can also, perhaps, understand how the conflicts between the parish priests and monks led them sometimes to caricature each other in the grotesque heads of corbels and gargoyles; nor does it surprise us that Luther, indignant and rude, should portray the Pope to the public under the form of a jackass.

But how can we account for the strange and profane caricatures which are so numerous in the stone and wood carvings of our cathedrals? In the scriptural ornamentation of the thirteenth century in Strasburg Cathedral, there was the representation of a funeral performed by animals—a hare carried the taper, a wolf the cross, and a bear the holy water—while in another place a stag was celebrating mass, and an ass reading the gospel. We often find carvings in which foxes are habited as ecclesiastics, sometimes accompanied by geese, who represent their flock, and thus we can understand the significance of the design in Sherborne Minster and Wellingborough, where two geese are hanging a fox.

In St. Mary's, Beverley, are two foxes dressed as ecclesiastics, each holding a pastoral staff, while a goose's head is peeping out of his hood. At Boston Church we find a fox in a cope and episcopal vestments, seated on a throne, and holding a pastoral staff, while on the right is an ass holding a book for the bishop to read. The fact was that no means were left untried by the Church to make converts and to obtain a hold on the people. They wished to render religion as attractive as possible, and perhaps to direct and control tendencies which they could not destroy. It was then a favourite doctrine that the end justified the means—the Roman Church instituted persecutions, adopted heathen rites, and ordained fasts and festivals to impress the mind. It is recorded that Theophylact of Constantinople introduced into the Church, in the tenth century, the licentious "Feast of Fools," to wean the people from the revels of their old religion, and have we not until late years celebrated the Nativity of our Lord, not only by games and frolics, but gluttony and drunkenness, and riotous proceedings, under pagan misletoe! I believe that among the masses of the people the Roman saturnalia still survive. We need not then be surprised that the early Christians tried to recommend religion by unsuitable ornamentation. They adopted all kinds of floral designs, they represented fables and romances. In the old church of Budleigh, in Devonshire—which Sir Walter Raleigh attended, and where his head is buried—all kinds of devices are represented on the pews, from a pair of scissors to a man-of-war, including a cook holding a sheep by the tail. It was only a step from this to introduce humour, and as men's feelings had not then been chastened or brought into order by reflection, they probably overlooked the lowering tendencies of levity. Those who came to laugh, might remain to pray, and so a strange crop of incongruities germinated upon the sacred soil. Thus, in Beverley Minster, we have a monkey riding upon a hare—a bedridden goat, with a monkey acting as doctor; and at Winchester a boar is playing on the fiddle, while a young pig is dancing.[47] Even scenes of drunkenness and immorality are not always excluded. But the principal representations attributed human actions to birds and beasts—people who could laugh at stories of this kind, could also at depictions of them. It may be maintained that men were then highly emotional, and demanded but little complexity or truth in humour, so that they could see something amusing in a boar playing upon the bagpipes, or in such a device as a monster composed of two birds, with the head of a lion, or another with a human head on a lion's body! But there must have been something more than this—some peculiar estimation of animals to account for such numerous representations. They were common in the secular ornamentation of the day, for instance, in a MS. copy of Froissart of the fifteenth century, there is a drawing of a pig walking upon stilts, playing the harp, and wearing one of the tall head-dresses then in fashion.

This love of the comic seems to have been fostered by the leisure and the lively turn of some ecclesiastics. In the injunctions given to the British Church in the year 680, no bishop is to allow tricks or jocosities (ludos vel jocos) to be exhibited before him, and later we read of two monks, near Oxford, receiving a man hospitably, thinking he was a "jougleur," and could perform tricks, but kicking him out on finding themselves mistaken. We find some of the monks amusing themselves with "cloister humour," consisting principally of logical paradoxes; while others indulged in verbal curiosities, such as those of Tryphiodorus, the lipogrammatist, who wrote an Odyssey in twenty-four books without once using the letter A. Some were more fond of pictorial designs, and carved great figures on the chalk downs, such as the Giant of Cerne Abbas, in Dorsetshire, and the Long Man of Wilmington, in Sussex.

As we found reason to believe that the earliest kind of laughter was that of pleasure, so in this revival of civilization, we often see humour regarded as having no influence beyond that of ministering to amusement. The mind was scarcely equal to regarding things in more than one light. A jest was often viewed as entirely unimportant, its levity and depreciatory character being altogether overlooked. To this and to the hostile element then very prominent, we may attribute the caricatures of the devil, formerly so common. Before the tenth century, the devil was thought too dreadful to be portrayed, but afterwards, as the Church made a liberal exhibition of the torments of hell, the idea occurred of deterring offenders by representing evil spirits in as frightful a form as possible. Some think that such figures were suggested by the Roman satyrs, but they may have come from Jewish or Runic sources. There is a mediæval story of a monk having carved an image of the devil so much more repulsive than he really was, that the sable gentleman called upon him one night to expostulate. The monk, however, was inexorable. But the story says further that, although the holy man was proof against the entreaties of the devil, he was not so well armed against the fascinations of the fair, and owing to his suffering a defeat at the hands of the latter came afterwards to be shut up in prison. The original of his portrait again called upon him, and the monk agreed that, if he would obtain his release, he would represent him as a handsome fellow.

As times advanced, people began to fear the devil less, and to be amused at these strange carvings. From regarding them as ludicrous, it was only a step to make humorous caricatures—and there could be little harm in ridiculing the Devil. Thus we frequently find imps and demons brought in to perform the comic parts in the Church mysteries. It was a short advance from the ludicrous to the humorous, and thus we find the devil a merry fellow, playing all kinds of practical jokes on mankind. Such representations would now appear rather ludicrous than humorous, and are seldom seen, except to amuse children on Valentine's Day.

CHAPTER III.

As the early drama of Greece arose from the celebration of religious rites, so that of modern times originated in the church. This does not seem so strange when we remember that religion is in connection with abstract thought, and with an exercise of the representative powers of the mind. And if we ask how comedy could have been thus introduced, the reply must be that the ideal of former ages was very different from our own. In the days when the mind was dull and inactive, striking illustrations were very necessary to awaken interest in moral and spiritual teaching. They changed in accordance with the progress of the times and country—sometimes the medium was fables or other such impossible fictions, sometimes it was similitudes from nature, as parables, and sometimes dramatic performances. Whatever drama the Jews had was of a religious character. It is supposed by some that the words—"When your children shall say unto you, 'What mean ye by this service,'" refers to some commemorative representation. However this may be, we know that about the year 100 B.C., Ezekiel, an Alexandrian Jew, wrote a play in Greek on the Exodus, which somewhat resembled a "mystery." Luther thought that the books of Judith and Tobit were originally in a dramatic form; and, even among the Jews, a comic element was sometimes introduced—as in the ancient Ahasuerus' play at the feast of Purim—with a view of attracting attention at a time when people had little reflection, and were not very particular about the intermingling of utterly incongruous feelings, whether religion and cruelty, or religion and humour.

We have traced the gradual decline of the drama in Rome, until it consisted but of buffooneries and mimes; and so its revival in modern times commenced with performances in dumb show, the low intellectual character of the age being reflected in popular exhibitions. The mimi were people who performed barefooted, clothed in skins of animals, with shaven heads, and faces smeared with soot. The Italians gradually came to relish nothing but a sort of pantomime, and it seems to have occurred to the Roman Church, always enterprising and fond of adaptation, that they might turn this taste of the people to some account. Accordingly, we read of religious mummings in Spain as early as the sixth century, and in 1264 the Brotherhood of the Gonfalone was founded in Italy to represent the sufferings of Christ in dumb show and processions.[48] In France the performance of holy plays, termed Mysteries, dates from the conclusion of the fourteenth century, when a company of pilgrims from the Holy Land, with their gowns hung with scallop shells and images, assisted at the marriage of Charles VI. and Isabella of Bavaria. They were incorporated as a Society in Paris to give dramatic entertainments, and were known as the "Fraternity of the Passion." Originally the intention was to represent scenes in Scripture history, but gradually they introduced "Moralities"— fanciful pieces in which God, the Devil, the Virtues, &c., were the dramatis personæ. In one of these, for instance, the Devil invites the Follies to a banquet on their arrival in hell. When they sit down the table seems hospitably spread, but as soon as they begin to touch the food it all bursts into flame, and the piece concludes with fireworks. We can see that a comic element might easily be introduced into such performances. But Charles VI., who seems to have been fond of all mimetic exhibitions, formed another company named "L'Institution Joyeuse," composed of the sons of the best families in Paris, who, under the name of the "Enfans sans Souci," and presided over by the "Prince des Sots," made France laugh at the follies of the day, personal and political. The above mentioned religious fraternity joined these gay performers without apparently seeing anything objectionable in such a connection, and under the name of the "Clercs de la Bazoche," or clerks of the revels, acted with them alternately. Even in the Mysteries, an occasional element of humour was evidently introduced, although many things which would appear ludicrous to us did not so affect the people of that day. A tinge of buffoonery was thought desirable. Thus in the "Massacre of the Holy Innocents," a good deal of scuffling takes place on the stage, especially where the women attack with their distaffs a low fool, who has requested Herod to knight him that he may join in the gallant adventure. In France there was "The Feast of Asses," in which the priests were attired like the Ancient Prophets, and accompanied by Virgil! Balaam, armed with a tremendous pair of spurs, rode a wooden ass, in which a man was enclosed. Robert Grosseteste, Bishop of Lincoln, forbade the celebration in churches of the "Feast of Fools," in which the clergy danced and gesticulated in masks. The "Mysteries" seem sometimes to have been of extraordinary length, for there was a play called "The Creation," performed at Clerkenwell which lasted eight days.

Pageantry as well as humour—devices appealing to the senses—were largely employed to enliven the exhibitions of early times. In the Christmas games in the reign of Edward I., we find they made use of eighty tunics of buckram of various colours, forty-two vizors, fourteen faces of women, fourteen of men, and the same number of angels, as well as imitations of dragons, peacocks, and swans.

The taking of Constantinople in 1453 scattered the men of learning throughout the West, and led to a revival of literature. The drama recommenced with representations of the old plays of Plautus. They were performed at the Universities, and on state occasions, as in 1528, when Henry VIII. had a stage erected in his great hall at Greenwich.

But the first development seems to have been in Spain, where the old Romans had left their impress, and where the cruel games of the circus still survive in the form of bull-fights. Lopez de Reuda, of Seville, first brought comedy on the stage, but Cervantes tells us that then the whole wardrobe of an actor consisted of four sheep-skins, trimmed with gilt leather, four beards, four wigs, and four shepherds' crooks. Nevertheless, after the classical period, Spain became the repertory for the comedians of Europe.

So far we have traced the origin of comedy as to public performance. We now come to consider what tendencies of disposition opened the way for it, and led to its becoming a branch of literature. The love of amusement, which is so strong in man, induced the patronage, which in early times was extended to the various kinds of professors of light arts.

In the days of Greece, as in those of Rome, there were ball-players, and mountebanks, and we may remember an occasion on which Terence complained that a rope-dancer had enticed away his audience. In Sparta there were men who represented the tricks of thieves and impostors in dances, and whose entertainments, though poor, were superior to that of mere mountebanks. The mimes were a still greater improvement, in which a certain amount of amusing narrative was illustrated by dances, songs, contortions, and as the name implies by mimicry. We have seen Plato introducing mimi from Greece, and Julius Cæsar interesting himself in such performers. Our mediæval fool has been traced to the Roman mime, who continued to please the country-people with coarse and debased representations after Rome had fallen, and comedy had perished. Some have even given a classic origin to our pantomime, considering harlequin to be Mercury, the clown Momus, pantaloon Charon, and columbine Psyche. The Roman Sannio and Manducus certainly somewhat corresponded to our fool and clown, the latter especially in his gormandising propensities. But it is scarcely necessary to travel so far back, for the desire for amusement has in all countries produced an indigenous supply.

Court-jesters are heard of as early as the reign of Philip of Macedon, but they seem to have been at first little more than parasites of inferior rank and education. In Roman times they were little more than buffoons,[49] and not very different from the mediæval fools. They seem to have received nicknames, and Petronius describes a very low buffoon performing antics in a myrtle robe with a belt round his waist.

As in ancient times we find Achilles singing to his lyre, so the English musicians and story-tellers were originally amateurs of high rank. We read of King Alfred charming the Danes with his minstrelsy. So also in the Arthurian legends Sir Kaye is represented as amusing the company; but at the time of Hoel Dha's Welsh laws, the bard was paid, for we read that the king was to allow him a horse and a woollen garment, and the queen to give him a linen robe; the prefect of the palace is privileged to sit near him on festivals and to hand him his harp. Canute seems to have treated his scalds with less ceremony, for he threatened to put one of them to death because he recounted his exploits in too short a poem, but the man escaped by producing thirty strophes on the subject next day. The Saxon gleemen were generally of humble origin and not only performed music, but exhibited tricks. So also among the Normans we find the barons originally amusing one another with "gabs," *i.e.* boastful and exaggerated accounts of their achievements. But soon a greater amount of leisure and luxury led them to pay for amusement; professed musicians and story-tellers were introduced, and were classed with the *ministri* or servants, whence came the name minstrel, which was soon confined to them alone. We find Talliefer going before William the Conqueror at the battle of Hastings chanting the brave deeds of Charlemagne and making a display of skill in tossing and catching his sword and spear. This union of tricks and music became so common that the words minstrel and jougleur were soon synonymous, though there was originally a distinction between them. The word jougleur, sometimes by mistake written jonglleur, is derived from the latin *joculator*. This class of people were conjurers, as their name suggests, and often went about the country with performing animals, especially bears and monkeys. They gradually added songs to their accomplishments, which more assimilated them to the minstrels, and they became connected with, and were sometimes called "troubadours." In these minstrels or jougleurs, though sometimes strolling independently, being often attached to great households, we find an element of the domestic, or as he is called, court fool, and we find another in their performances being of that primitive character, which appeals chiefly to the perception of the senses. For although the "jocular" part, originally subordinate, had been increased, it took so rude a form that the ludicrous was not always easily distinguished from the humorous. The Fool was a strange mixture of both, varying from a mere idiot and butt to a man of genius, far superior to his masters. He made shrewd remarks, and performed senseless antics, the city fool, on Lord Mayor's day, was to jump clothes and all into a large bowl of custard. To a certain extent he generally corresponded with his name in having some mental weakness or eccentricity, and it was a recommendation if he were dwarfish or deformed. He wore a "motley" suit of discordant colours to make him ridiculous, and correspond with the incongruity of his mind and actions—a dress similar to the hundred patched *paniculus centunculus* of the Roman mimes. Sometimes he wore a petticoat or calf-skin to resemble an idiot. Finally, he had his head shaved and wore a cowl to make him like a monk, as his buffooneries would thus have a stranger character, and the nobles had no great affection for the church.[50] The domestic fool was common in the fourteenth and fifteenth centuries up to the time of Louis XIV.; but it is said that there were such men at the Court of Louis le Débonnaire. Giraldus Cambrenses writes that when he was preaching for the Crusades in South Wales, one John Spang "who by simulating fatuity, and having a quick tongue was wont to be a great comfort to the court," said to Resus, the king: "You should be greatly indebted to your relative the Archdeacon for sending a hundred of your men to day to follow Christ, and if he had spoken Welsh I do not believe that one of all your people would remain to you." This was towards the end of the twelfth century, but it does not seem clear that John Spang was a court jester. We may fairly consider that the institution of the domestic fools, the employment of men, who professed jocularity as a branch of art distinct from music and legerdemain increased mental activity, and a growing desire for humour. But the men who made jesting their profession were generally regarded with contempt, and an Act of Parliament in the reign of Edward III. ordered strollers of this kind to be whipped out of the town. An old satire written at the time of the Reformation brings together actors, dustmen, jugglers, conjurers, and sellers of indulgences.

But we want something more than wits and drolleries, and even public performances, to complete our idea of Comedy. We must have literary composition and artistic construction. From songs of warlike achievements such as were chanted by the old scalders to cheer their chiefs over the bowl, there arose by degrees fanciful tales with which the Saxons and their successors amused themselves after their dinner, and round the blazing hearth. In the tenth century the clergy found stories to amuse the post-prandial hour—extravagant, indelicate, or profane—such were the times, but marking improved activity of thought. Thus they enjoyed such a tale as that a "prophet" went to Heriger (Archbishop of Mayence about 920) and told him he had been to the nether world, a place, he said, surrounded by woods. The Archbishop replied that, if that was the case, he would send his lean swine there to eat acorns. The prophet added that afterwards he went to heaven, and saw

Christ and his saints sitting at table and eating; John the Baptist was the butler, and served the wine, and St. Peter was the cook. The Archbishop asked the stranger how he fared himself, and on his saying that he sat in the corner and stole a piece of liver—Heriger instead of praising his sanctity ordered him to be tied to a stake, and flogged for theft. The "Supper," as old as the tenth century, is another humorous description. A grave assembly of scriptural characters, from Adam and Eve downwards, are invited, Cain sits on a plough, Abel on a milk-pail &c.; two, Paul and Esau, are obliged to stand for want of room, and Job complains of having nothing to sit on but a dunghill. Jonah is here the butler. Samson brings honey to the dessert, and Adam apples—

> "Tunc Adam poma ministrat, Samson favi dulcia.
> David cytharum percussit, et Maria tympana,
> Judith choreas ducebat et Jubal psalteria
> Asael metra canebat, saltabat Herodias."[51]

Thus stories, by degrees, began to be not only composed, but written, and although not intended for acting, to be dignified with the old name of "Comedies." Such poems were written by Robert Baston, who accompanied Edward II. to Scotland.

The Tournament of Tottenham is a merry story of this kind, written in the reign of Henry VI. It is full of a rough kind of hostile humour, and shows the sort of things which amused at that time. Here we have a burlesque upon the deeds of chivalry. A mock tournament is held, the prize is to be the Reve of Tottenham's daughter, a brood hen, a dun cow, a grey mare, and a spotted sow. The combatants—clowns and rustics—provide themselves with flails, and poles, and sheep skins

> "They armed tham in mattes;
> They set on ther nollys (heads)
> For to kape ther pollys,
> Gode blake bollys (bowls)
> For t' batryng of battes (cudgels)."

The fierceness of the combat is described:

"And fewe wordys spoken,
There were flayles al to-slatered,
Ther were scheldys al to-flatred,
Bollys and dysches al to-schatred,
And many hedys brokyn."

We find some specimen of the kind of tales called Comedies, which preceded acted Comedy, in the works of Chaucer, who died in 1400. Scarcely any part of Chaucer's writings would raise a laugh at the present day, though they might a blush.[52] But he was by no means a man who revelled in indelicacy. We may suppose that he was moderate for the time in which he lived, and when he makes an offensive allusion, he usually adds some excuse for it. The antiquated language in which his works are written prevents our now appreciating much of the humour they contained; generally, there is more refinement and grace in his writings. No doubt at the time he was thought witty, and his tendency in this direction is shown by his praise of mirth in the "Romaunt of the Rose."

"Full faire was mirth, full long and high,
A fairer man I never sigh:
As round as apple was his face,
Full roddie and white in every place,
Fetis he was and well besey,
With meetly mouth and eyen gray,
His nose by measure wrought full right,
Crispe was his haire, and eke full bright,
His shoulderes of large trede
And smallish in the girdlestede:
He seemed like a purtreiture,
So noble was he of his stature,
So faire, so jolly, and so fetise
With limmes wrought at point devise,
Deliver smart, and of great might;
Ne saw thou never man so light
Of berd unneth had he nothing,
For it was in the firste spring,
Full young he was and merry of thought,
And in samette with birdes wrought
And with golde beaten full fetously

His bodie was clad full richely.
Wrought was his robe in straunge gise
And all slitttered for queintise
In many a place, low and hie,
And shode he was with great maistrie
With shoone decoped and with lace,
By drurie and by solace
His leefe a rosen chapelet
Had made, and on his head it set."

He speaks in equally high terms of "Dame Gladnesse."
We can appreciate Chaucer's address to his empty purse—

"To you my purse, and to none other wight
Complaine I, for ye be my lady dere,
I am sorry now that ye be light,
For certes ye now make me heauy chere
Me were as lefe laid vpon a bere,
For which vnto your mercy thus I crie
Be heauy againe or els mote I die.

"Now vouchsafe this day or it be night
That I of you the blissful sowne may here,
Or see your colour like the sunne bright
That of yelownesse had neuer pere;
Ye be my life, ye be my hertes stere
Queen of comfort, and good companie
Be heauy againe, or els mote I die.

"Now purse that art to me my liues delight
And sauiour, as downe in this world here,
Out of this towne helpe me by your might
Sith that you woll not be my treasure,
For I am shave as nere as any frere,
But I pray vnto your curtesie
Be heauy againe, or els mote I die."

Chaucer was very fond of allegory. This is especially visible
not only in the "Romaunt of the Rose," but in the "Court of Love,"
"Flower and Leaf," the "House of Fame," and the "Cuckoo and

Nightingale." In the "Assembly of Fowls" we have a fable. Chaucer was attached to the service of John of Gaunt, which may have led to his attacking the clergy, but in his youth he was fined two shillings for beating a Franciscan friar in Fleet Street. He favoured Wickliffe, and was for this reason eventually obliged to flee the country; but he returned and obtained remunerative appointments. It is said that on his death-bed he lamented the encouragement which vice might receive from his writings, but their indelicacy was not really great for the age in which he lived.

Henry Heywood has been called the "Father of English Comedy," and he was certainly one of the first that wrote original dramas, representing the ordinary social life of this country. His pieces, which all appeared before 1550, were short and simple, and seem to us very deficient in delicacy and humour. But in his day he was considered a great wit, and as a court-jester drew many a lusty laugh from old King Hal, and could even soothe the rugged brow of the fanatical Mary. One of his best sayings was addressed to her. When the Queen told Heywood that the priests must forego their wives, he answered. "Then your Grace must allow them *lemans*, for the clergy cannot live without sauce." He was called the epigrammatist, but the greater part of his jests seem to have little point. Some of them have been attributed to Sir Thomas More.

One of the earliest English comedies written by Nicholas Udall, and found entered in the books of the Stationers' Company in the year, 1566, is Royster Doister.

> "Which against the vayne glorious doth invey
> Whose humour the roysting sort continually doth feede."

The play turns on Ralph Royster Doister—a conceited fool—thinking every woman must fall in love with him. Much of the humour is acoustic, and depends on repetitions—

> "Then twang with our sonnets, and twang with our dumps,
> And hey hough for our heart, as heavie as lead lumps.
> Then to our recorder with toodle doodle poope,
> As the howlet out of an yvie bushe should hoope

Anon to our gitterne, thrumpledum, thrumpledrum thrum,

Thrumpledum,thrumpledum,thrumpledum,thrumpledum, thrum."

Royster is duped into sending Custance a love-letter, telling her that he seeks only her fortune, and that he will annoy her in every way after marriage. On discovering the deception, he determines to take vengeance on the scribbler who wrote the love-letter for him:—

"Yes, for although he had as many lives
As a thousande widowes and a thousande wives,
As a thousande lyons and a thousande rattes,
A thousande wolves and a thousande cattes,
A thousande bulles, and a thousande calves
And a thousande legions divided in halves,
He shall never 'scape death on my sworde's point
Though I shoulde be torne therefore joynt by joynt."

Where he prepares to punish Custance and her friends for refusing him, there is a play on the word "stomacke"—used for courage:

Ralph Royster. Yea, they shall know, and thou knowest I have a stomacke.

M.M. A stomacke (quod you) you, as good as ere man had.

R. Royster. I trowe they shall finde and feele that I am a lad.

M.M. By this crosse I have seene you eate your meat as well.

As any that ere I have seene of, or heard tell,

A stomacke quod you? he that will that denie,

I know was never at dynner in your companie.

R. Royster. Nay, the stomacke of a man it is that I meane.

M.M. Nay, the stomacke of a horse or a dogge I weene.

R. Royster. Nay, a man's stomacke with a weapon mean I.

M.M. Ten men can scarce match you with a spoon in a pie.

"Gammer Gurton's Needle" was acted in 1552. It bears marks of an early time in its words being coarsely indelicate, but not amatory. The humour is that of blows and insults and we may observe the great value then attached to needles. It is "a right pithy, pleasant and merry comedy"—a country story of an old dame who loses her needle when sewing a patch on the seat of her servant Hodge's breeches. The cat's misdoings interrupt her, and her needle is lost. The hunt for the needle is amusing, and Gammer Gurton and Dame Chat, whom she suspects of having stolen it, abuse and call each other witches. Hodge, the man with the patched breeches encourages Gammer Gurton, who seems little to require it.

> "Smite, I say Gammer,
> Bite, I say Gammer,
> Where be your nails? Claw her by the jawes
>   Pull me out both her eyen.
> Hoise her, souse her, bounce her, trounce her,
>   Pull out her thrott."

On some one giving Hodge a good slap, the needle runs into him, and is thus happily found.

At the opening of the second act of Gammer Gurton there is a drinking song, which deserves notice as it was the first written in English,—

> "I cannot eat but little meat
> My stomack is not good:
> But sure I think that I can drink
> With him that wears a hood.
> Though I go bare, take ye no care
> I nothing am a colde;
> I stuff my skin so full within
> Of ioly good ale and olde.
> Backe and side go bare, go bare,
> Booth foot and hand go colde;
> But belly, God send thee good ale inoughe,
> Whether it be new or olde;
>
> "I love no rost, but a nut browne toste
> And a crab laid in the fire;
> A little bread shall do me stead
> Moche bread I noght desire.

No frost, no snow, no wind I trowe
Can hurt me if I wolde.
I am so wrapt and throwly lapt
Of ioly good ale and olde.
      Backe and side, &c.

"And Tib my wife, that as her life
Loveth well good ale to seeke,
Full oft drinkes shee, till ye may see
The teares run downe her cheeke.
Then doth she trowle to me the bowle
Even as a mault-worm sholde,
And saith 'sweet heart I tooke my part
Of this ioly good ale and olde.'
      Backe and side, &c.

"Now let them drinke, till they nod and winke,
Even as good fellows should do;
They shall not misse to have the blisse
Good ale doth bring men to.
And al goode sowles that have scoured bowles,
Or have them lustely trolde,
God save the lives of them and their wives
Whether they be yong or olde.
      Backe and side, &c."

CHAPTER IV.

ROBERT GREENE.

Robert Greene—Friar Bacon's Demons—The "Looking Glasse"—Nash and Harvey.

One of the principal humorists at this time was Robert Greene, born at Norwich about 1560. He was educated at Cambridge, and was generally styled "Robert Greene, Maister of Artes." Early in life he became, as he tells us, "an author of playes and a penner of love pamphlets." From the titles of some of them, and from his motto, *"Omne tulit punctum qui miscuit utile dulci,"* it is evident that they were intended to be humorous. Thus, his "Euphues" professes to contain "Mirth to purge Melancholy;" his "Quips for an Vpstart Courtier" is "A Quaint Dispute between Velvet-breeches and Cloth-breeches," and his "Notable Discovery of Coosnage" has "a delightfull discourse of the coosnage of Colliers;" his "Second and last part of conny-catching" has "new additions containing many merry tales of all lawes worth the reading, because they are worthy to be remembered. Discoursing strange cunning coosnage, which if you reade without laughing, Ile give you my cap for a Noble." But in all these works there is but little humour, and what we learn in reading them is, that a very small amount of it was then thought considerable, and that stories, which we should think slightly entertaining, appeared in that simple age to be very ingenious and even comic. In the "Comicall Historie of Alphonsus, King of Arragon," we do not find anything that could have possibly been humorous, unless the speaking of a brazen head, and the letting Venus down from Heaven and drawing her up again, could have been so regarded. Greene is characteristic of his time in his love of introducing magic and enchanters, and of characters from classic and scripture history. In the "Looking-Glasse for London and England," in which our metropolis is compared to Nineveh, we have angels and magicians brought in. "A hand out of a cloud threateneth a burning sword," and "Jonas is cast out of the whale's belly upon the stage."

Greene is fond of introducing devils. In "The Honourable Historie of Frier Bacon and Frier Bongay," Ralph says, "Why, Sirrah Ned we'll ride to Oxford to Friar Bacon. O! he is a brave scholar, sirrah; they say he is a brave necromancer, that he can make women of devils, and he can juggle cats into coster-mongers." Further on in the same play a devil and Miles, Bacon's servant, enter.

> *Miles.* A scholar, quoth you; marry, Sir, I would I had been a bottle maker, when I was made a scholar, for I can get neither to be a deacon, reader, nor schoolmaster. No, not the clerk of the parish. Some call me dunce, another saith my head is full of Latin, as an egg's full of oatmeal: thus I am tormented that the devil and Friar Bacon haunt me. Good Lord, here's one of my master's devils! I'll go speak to him. What Master Plutus, how cheer you?
>
> *D.* Dost know me?
>
> *M.* Know you, Sir? Why are not you one of my master's devils, that were wont to come to my master, Doctor Bacon at Brazen-Nose?
>
> *D.* Yes, marry am I.
>
> *M.* Good Lord, Master Plutus, I have seen you a thousand times at my master's; and yet I had never the manners to make you drink. But, Sir, I am glad to see how comfortable you are to the statutes. I warrant you he's as yeomanly a man as you shall see; mark you, masters, here's a plain honest man without welt or guard. But I pray you Sir, do you come lately from hell?
>
> *D.* Ay, marry, how then?
>
> *M.* Faith, 'tis a place I have desired long to see: have you not good tippling houses there? May not a man have a lusty fire there, a good pot of ale, a pair of cards, a swinging piece of chalk, and a brown toast that will clap a white waistcoat on a cup of good drink.

D. All this you may have there.

M. You are for me, friend, and I am for you. But I pray you, may I not have an office there?

D. Yes, a thousand; what wouldst thou be?

M. By my troth, Sir, in a place where I may profit myself. I know hell is a hot place, and men are marvellous dry, and much drink is spent there. I would be a tapster.

In one play Greene introduces a court-fool, and he mixes with the stupidity and knavery of his clowns, a sort of artificial philosophy and argumentative ingenuity, which savours much of the old jesters. In "James the Fourth" Slipper says:—

O mistress, mistress, may I turn a word upon you?

Countess. Friend, what wilt thou?

Slipper. O! what a happy gentlewoman be you truly; the world

reports this of you, mistress, that a man can no sooner come to your house, but the butler comes with a black-jack, and says,

"Welcome, friend, here's a cup of the best for you," verily, mistress, you are said to have the best ale in all Scotland.

Countess. Sirrah, go fetch him drink *[an attendant brings drink.]* How likest thou this?

Slip. Like it mistress! why this is quincy quarie, pepper de watchet, single goby, of all that ever I tasted. I'll prove in this ale, and toast the compass of the whole world. First, this is the earth; it ties in the middle a fair brown toast, a goodly country for hungry teeth to dwell upon; next this is the sea, a fair pool for a dry tongue to fish in; now come I, and seeing the world is naught, I divide it thus: and because the sea cannot stand without the earth, as Aristotle saith, I put them both into their first chaos, which is my belly, and so, mistress, you may see your ale is become a miracle.

Further on Slipper again shows his readiness in dialogue—

Sir Bartram. Ho, fellow! stay and let me speak with thee.

Slip. Fellow! friend thou dost abuse me: I am a gentleman.

Sir B. A gentleman! how so?

Slip. Why, I rub horses, Sir.

Sir B. And what of that?

Slip. O simple-witted! mark my reason. They that do good service in the commonweal are gentlemen, but such as rub horses do good service in the commonweal, *ergo*, tarbox, master courtier, a horse-keeper is a gentleman.

Sir B. Here is over much wit in good earnest. But, sirrah, where is thy master?

Slip. Neither above ground nor under ground; drawing out red into white, swallowing that down without chawing, which was never made without treading.

Sir B. Why, where is he then?

Slip. Why in his cellar, drinking a cup of neat and brisk claret in a bowl of silver. Oh, Sir, the wine runs trillill down his throat, which cost the poor vintner many a stamp before it was made. But I must hence, Sir, I have haste.

Sir Bertram intimates that he wants his assistance, and will pay him.

Slip. A good word, thou hast won me; this word is like a warm caudle to a cold stomach.

Sir B. Sirrah, wilt thou for money and reward Convey me certain letters, out of hand, From out thy master's pocket?

Slip. Will I, Sir? Why were it to rob my father, hang my mother, or any such like trifles, I am at your commandment, Sir. What will you give me, Sir?

Sir B. A hundred pounds.

Slip. I am your man; give me earnest. I am dead at a pocket, Sir; why I am a lifter, master, by occupation.

Sir B. A lifter! what is that?

Slip. Why, Sir, I can lift a pot as well as any man, and pick a purse as soon as any thief in the country.

These humorous characters remind us a little of the slaves and parasites in Roman comedy, of whom, no doubt, Greene had read. His amusing fellows are free livers, and fond of wine like himself. In the "Looking-Glasse" above mentioned, Nineveh represents London, and a fast being proclaimed, we find Adam, a smith's journeyman, trying to evade it.

> *(Enter Adam solus, with a bottle of beer in one slop (trouser) and a great piece of beef in the other.)*
>
> *Adam.* Well, goodman Jonas, I would you had never come from Jewry to this country; you have made me look like a lean rib of roast beef, or like the picture of Lent, painted upon a red-herring's cob. Alas! masters, we are commanded by the proclamation to fast and pray! By my troth, I could prettily so, so away with praying, but for fasting, why 'tis so contrary to my nature, that I had rather suffer a short hanging than a long fasting. Mark me, the words be these: thou shalt take no manner of food for so many days. I had as lief he should have said, thou shalt hang thyself for so many days. And yet, in faith, I need not find fault with the proclamation, for I have a buttery and a pantry and a kitchen about me; for proof, *ecce signum*! This right slop is my pantry, behold a manchet; this place is my kitchen, for lo! a piece of beef. O! let me repeat that sweet word again!—for lo! a piece of beef. This is my buttery, for see, see, my friends, to my great joy a bottle of beer. Thus, alas! I make shift to wear out this fasting; I drive away the time. But there go searchers about to seek if any man breaks the king's command. O, here they be; in with your victuals, Adam.

> *(Enter two Searchers.)*

> *1st Searcher.* How duly the men of Nineveh keep the proclamation! how they are armed to repentance! We have searched through the whole city, and have not as yet found one that breaks the fast.
>
> *2nd Sear.* The sign of the more grace; but stay, there sits one, methinks at his prayers; let us see who it is. *1st Sear.* 'Tis Adam, the smith's man. How, now, Adam?
>
> *Adam.* Trouble me not; thou shalt take no manner of food, but fast and pray.

1st Sear. How devoutly he sits at his orisons! But stay, methinks I feel a smell of some meat or bread about him.

2nd Sear. So thinks me too. You, Sirrah, what victuals have you about you?

Adam. Victuals! O horrible blasphemy! Hinder me not of my prayer, nor drive me not into a choler. Victuals? why heardest thou not the sentence, thou shalt take no food, but fast and pray?

2nd Sear. Troth, so it should be; but, methinks, I smell meat about thee.

Adam. About me, my friends? these words are actions in the case. About me? no! no! hang those gluttons that cannot fast and pray.

1st Sear. Well, for all your words we must search you.

Adam. Search me? take heed what you do! my hose are my castles; 'tis burglary if you break ope a slop; no officer must lift up an iron hatch; take heed, my slops are iron.

2nd Sear. O, villain! See how he hath gotten victuals—bread, beef and beer, where the king commanded upon pain of death none should eat for so many days, not the sucking infant.

Adam. Alas! Sir, this is nothing but a *modicum non nocet ut medicus daret*; why, Sir, a bit to comfort my stomach.

1st Sear. Villain! thou shalt be hanged for it.

Adam. These are your words, I shall be hanged for it; but first answer me this question, how many days have we to fast still?

2nd Sear. Five days.

Adam. Five days! a long time; then I must be hanged.

1st Sear. Ay, marry must thou.

Adam. I am your man, I am for you, Sir, for I had rather be hanged than abide so long a fast. What! five days! Come, I'll untruss. Is your halter, and the gallows, the ladder, and all such furniture in readiness.

1st Sear. I warrant thee thou shalt want none of these.

Adam. But hear you, must I be hanged?

1st Sear. Ay, marry.

Adam. And for eating of meat. Then, friends, know ye by these presents, I will eat up all my meat, and drink up all my drink, for it shall never be said, I was hanged with an empty stomach.

It has been supposed that Greene was very indelicate in his language, as well as reckless in his life. But we cannot find in his plays anything very offensive, considering the date at which he wrote, and in the tract called "Greene's Funeralls," we read:—

> His gadding Muse, although it ran of love,
> Yet did he sweetly morralize his song;
> Ne ever gaue the looser cause to laugh
> Ne men of judgement for to be offended.

Greene died in "most woefull and rascall estate" at the house of a poor shoemaker near Dowgate. He had previously written his "Groat's-worth of Wit bought with a Million of Repentance;" in which he warns his former companions and "gentlemen who spend their wits in making playes," to take warning by his fate. He could get none of his friends to visit him at the last but Mistress Appleby, and the mother of "his base sonne Infortunatus Greene." He gave the following note for his wife—whom he had not seen for six years—to the shoemaker:

"Doll, I charge thee by the love of our youth, and by my soule's rest, that thow wilte see this man paide; for if hee and his wife had not succoured me, I had died in the streetes.

"ROBERT GREENE."

Gabriel Harvey writes, "My next businesse was to inquire after the famous author who was reported to lye dangerously sicke in a shop neere Dowgate, not of plague, but of a surfett of pickle herringe and rennish wine."

Thomas Nash was one of Greene's jolly companions at this fatal banquet. After Greene's death Harvey replied to some reflections made upon him by Greene, and called him in accordance with the amenities of the times, "a wilde head, ful of mad braine and a thousand crotchets; a scholler, a discourser, a courtier, a ruffian, a gamester, a lover, a souldier, a trauailer, a merchant, a broker, an artificer, a botcher, a pettifogger, a player, a coosener, a rayler, a beggar, an omnium-gatherum, a gay-nothing, a stoare-house of bald and baggage stuffe, unworth the answering or reading, a triuall and triobular autor for knaves and fooles," &c., &c.

Nash, although he seems to have forsaken Greene in his last distress, became the defender of his character after his death, and answered this vituperation by still coarser abuse and invective, saying, "Had hee lived, Gabriel, and thou shouldest vnartifically and odiously libel against him as thou hast done, he would have made thee an example of ignominy to all ages that are to come, and driven thee to eate thy owne booke buttered, as I saw him make an Appariter once in a tavern eate his Citation, waxe and all, very handsomely served 'twixt two dishes.'"

From this he proceeds to caricature Gabriel's person. "That word complexion is dropt forth in good time, for to describe to you his complexion and composition entred I with this tale by the way. It is of an adust swarth chollericke dye, like restie bacon, or a dried scate-fish; so leane and so meagre, that you wold thinke (with the Turks) he observed 4 Lents in a yere, or take him for a gentleman's man in the courtier, who was so thin-cheeked, and gaunt, and starv'd, that as he was blowing the fire with his mouth the smoke took him up like a light strawe, and carried him to the top or funnell of the chimney, wher he had flowne out God knowes whither if there had not been crosse barres overthwart that stayde him; his skin riddled and crumpled like a piece of burnt parchment; and more channels and creases he hath in his face than there be fairie circles on Salsburie Plaine, and wrinckles and frets of old age, than characters on Christ's sepulcher in Mount Calvarie, on which euerie one that comes scrapes his name, and sets his marke to shewe that hee hath been there; so that whosoever shall behold him

"Esse putet Boreæ triste furentis opus,"

will sweare on a book I have brought him lowe, and shrowdly broken him; which more to confirme, look on his head, and you shall find a gray haire for euery line I have writ against him; and you shall have all his beard white too, by that time he hath read over this booke. For his stature, he is such another pretie Jacke-a-

Lent as boyes throw at in the streete, and lookes in his blacke sute of veluet, like one of these jet-droppes which divers weare at their eares instead of a iewell. A smudge peice of a handsome fellow it hath been in his dayes, but now he is olde and past his best, and fit for nothing but to be a nobleman's porter, or a knight of Windsor."

Nash was so full of invective and personal abuse that he scarcely deserved the name of a satirist, and so great was the animosity with which the quarrel between him and Gabriel Harvey was conducted, that the Archbishop of Canterbury and Bishop of London issued an order in 1599 that all such books "be taken wheresoever they be found, and that none of the said books be ever printed hereafter."

His humour was remarkable, as it largely consisted of coining long and almost unintelligible words. This he laid great store by, and he speaks wrathfully of one who translated his "Piers Penniless," into what he calls "maccaronical language." In his "Lenten Stuffe or Praise of the Red Herring," *i.e.*, of Great Yarmouth, he calls those who despised Homer in his life-time "dull-pated pennifathers," and says that "those grey-beard huddle-duddles and crusty cum-twangs were strooke with stinging remorse of their miserable euchonisme and sundgery."

Peele was one of the gay play-writers to whom Greene addressed his warning. They seem at this time to have united the professions of dramatist and actor, and to have been infected with that dissipation which has since been attributed with more or less justice to the stage. Peele is as fond as Greene of surprises and miraculous interventions. In the "Arraignment of Paris" a golden tree grows up, and in the "Old Wives Tale," the most humorous of his works, the head of Huanebango rises from a well. He is fond of dealing in phonetic words Latinisms and barbarisms; in one place he makes Corebus say:

> "O *falsum Latinum*
> The fair maid is *minum*
> *Cum apurtinantibus gibletis* and all."

Peele was very popular in his day, and was often called upon to write pieces for the Lord Mayor and for royal receptions. He sometimes used Hexameter lines such as:

"Dub, dub-a-dub bounce, quoth the guns with a sulphurous
huff shuff."

Gabriel Harvey first introduced this metre into English, and he tried to induce Spenser to adopt it. Nash calls it "that drunken staggering kind of verse which is all vp hill and downe hill, like the way betwixt Stamford and Beechfeild, and goes like a horse plunging through the mire in the deep of winter, now soust vp to the saddle and straight aloft on his tip-toes."

CHAPTER V.

Donne—Hall—Fuller.

Already we have seen that some of our earliest humorists were ecclesiastics, and it would be unfitting that we should here overlook three eminent men, Donne, Hall, and Fuller. Pleasantry was with them little more than a vehicle of instruction; the object was not to entertain, but to enforce and illustrate their moral sentiments. Hence their sober quaintness never raises a laugh, much less does it border upon the profane or indelicate.

Donne was born in 1573, in London, and was educated, as was not then uncommon, first at Oxford, and then at Cambridge. His ability in church controversy attracted the attention of James, and he was made chaplain to the King. He became preacher at Lincoln's Inn, and afterwards was made Dean of St. Paul's. He lived to be fifty-eight.

His sermons are full of antitheses and epigrammatic diction. There is an airy lightness in his letters and poems, but he scarcely ever actually reaches humour. The following poem, an epistle to Sir Edmund Herbert at Juliers, will give an idea of his style.

> "Man is a lump, where all beasts kneaded be,
> Wisdom makes him an ark where all agree;
> The fool in whom these beasts do live at jar,
> Is sport to others, and a theatre.
> Nor scapes he so, but is himself their prey,
> All which was man in him is eat away,
> And now his beasts on one another feed,
> Yet couple in anger, and new monsters breed.
> How happy's he, which hath due place assigned
> To his beasts, and disaforested his mind!

Empaled himself to keep them out, not in,
Can sow, and dares trust corn where they've been;
Can use his horse, goat, wolf, and every beast,
And is not ass himself to all the rest."

Bishop Hall was born in 1574, and commenced his extensive literary labours by writing when twenty-three years of age, at Emmanuel College, Cambridge, three books of satires called Virgidemiæ. These books he calls *"Toothless* Satyres, *poetical, academical, and moral,"* and he attacks bad writers, astrologers, drunkards, gallants, and others. Alluding to the superabundance of indifferent poetry in his days, he says:—

"Let them, that mean by bookish business
To earn their bread, or holpen to profess
Their hard-got skill, let them alone for me
Busy their brains with deeper bookery.
Great gains shall bide you sure, when ye have spent
A thousand lamps, and thousand reams have rent
Of needless papers; and a thousand nights
Have burned out with costly candle-lights."

In the following year, he produced three books of "Byting Satyres." In these he laughs at the effeminacy of the times—the strange dresses and high heels.

"When comely striplings wish it were their chance
For Cænis' distaff to exchange their lance,
And wear curled periwigs, and chalk their face
And still are poring on their pocket-glass;
Tired with pinned ruffs and fans and partlet strips
And busks and verdingales about their hips;
And tread on corked stilts, a prisoner's pace,
And make their napkin for a spitting place,
And gripe their waist within a narrow span,
Fond Cænis that wouldst wish to be a man!"

The most severe is against the Pope:—

"To see an old shorn lozel perched high
Crossing beneath a golden canopy;
The whiles a thousand hairless crowns crouch low
To kiss the precious case of his proud toe;
And for the lordly fasces borne of old
To see two quiet crossed keys of gold;
But that he most would gaze and wonder at
To the horned mitre and the bloody hat,
The crooked staff, the cowl's strange form and store
Save that he saw the same in hell before;
To see the broken nuns, with new shorn heads
In a blind cloister toss their idle heads."

Although Bishop Hall wrote learnedly and voluminously on theological subjects, this light medley is now more esteemed than his graver works. He claimed upon the strength of it to be the earliest English satirist, and perhaps none of our writings of this kind had as yet been of equal importance. The work was one of those condemned to the flames by Whitgift and Bancroft.

Fuller was born in Northamptonshire, in 1608. He became a distinguished man at Cambridge, where he obtained a fellowship at Sidney Sussex College. He was also an eminent preacher in London, and a prebendary of Salisbury. In the Civil War, being a stanch Royalist, he was driven from place to place, and held at one time the interesting post of "Infant Lady's Chaplain" to the Princess Henrietta. In his "Worthies of England," Fuller not only enumerates the eminent men for which each country is distinguished, but gives an account of its products and proverbs. "A Proverb is much matter decocted into few words. Six essentials are wanting to it—that it be short, plain, common, figurative, ancient, true." The most ordinary subject is enlivened by his learned and humorous mind. Thus, in Bedfordshire, under the head of "Larks," he tells us, "The most and best of these are caught and well-dressed about Dunstable in this shire. A harmless bird while living, not trespassing on grain, and wholesome when dead, then filling the stomach with meat, as formerly the ear with music. In winter they fly in flocks, probably the reason why *Alauda* signifieth in Latin both a lark and a legion of soldiers; except any will say a legion is so called because helmeted on their heads and crested like a lark, therefore also called in Latin

Galerita. If men would imitate the early rising of this bird, it would conduce much unto their healthfulness."

Fuller abounds with figures and illustrations in which learning and humour are excellently intermingled. "They that marry where they do not love, will love where they do not marry." "He knows little, who will tell his wife all he knows." Speaking of children, he says that a man complained that never father had so undutiful a child as he. "Yes," said the son, "my grandfather had." Alluding to servants, and saying that the Emperor Charles the Fifth being caught in a tempest had many horses thrown overboard to save the lives of the slaves—which were not of so great market-value—he asks, "Are there not many that in such a case had rather save Jack the horse than Jockey the keeper?" Of widows' evil speaking he observes, "Foolish is their project who, by raking up bad savours against their former husbands, think thereby to perfume their bed for a second marriage." Of celibacy he says, "If Christians be forced to run races for their lives, the unmarried have the advantage of being lighter by many ounces!"

Speaking of the "Controversial Divine," he says, "What? make the Muses, yea the Graces scolds? Such purulent spittle argues exulcerated lungs. Why should there be so much railing about the body of Christ, when there was none about the body of Moses in the act kept betwixt the devil and Michael, the Archangel?" On schoolmasters he wrote, "That schoolmaster deserves to be beaten himself, who beats Nature in a boy for a fault. And I question whether all the whipping in the world can make their parts, that are naturally sluggish, rise one minute before the hour Nature hath appointed."

The following are some good sayings that have been selected from his works by an eminent humorist:—

> *Virtue in a short person.* "His soul had but a short diocese to visit, and therefore might the better attend the effectual informing thereof."
>
> *Intellect in a very tall one.* "Oft times such, who are built four storeys high, are observed to have little in their cock-loft."

> *Mr. Perkins, the Divine.* "He would pronounce the word Damn with such an emphasis, as left a doleful echo in his auditor's ears a good while after."
>
> *Memory.* "Philosophers place it in the rear of the head; and it seems the mine of memory lies there, because men there naturally dig for it, scratching it when they are at a loss."

To this we may add something from his "Holy State,"—a pleasant and profitable work, in which Fuller is happy in making his humour subserve the best ends:—Of "The Good Wife," he says, "She never crosseth her husband in the spring-tide of his anger, but stays till it be ebbing-water. And then mildly she argues the matter, not so much to condemn him as to acquit herself. Surely men, contrary to iron, are worst to be wrought upon when they are hot, and are far more tractable in cold blood. It is an observation of seamen, 'That if a single meteor or fire-ball falls on their mast, it portends ill-luck; but if two come together (which they count Castor and Pollux) they presage good success.' But sure in a family it bodeth most bad when two fire balls (husband's and wife's anger) both come together." In speaking of good parents, he says, "A father that whipt his son for swearing, and swore at him while he whipt him, did more harm by his example than good by his correction."

CHAPTER VI.

Shakespeare—Ben Jonson—Beaumont and Fletcher—The Wise Men of Gotham.

Greene, in his admonition to his brother sinners of the stage, tells them that "there is an vpstart crow beautified with our feathers an absolute Johannes factotum, in his own conceyt the onely Shakescene in a countrey," and in truth these olden writers are principally interesting as having laid the foundations upon which Shakespeare built some of his earliest plays. The genius of our great dramatist was essentially poetic, and some of his plays, which we now call comedies, were originally entitled "histories." How seldom do we hear any of his humorous passages quoted, or find them reckoned among our household words! From some of his observations we might think he was altogether averse from jocosity. Henry V. says

"How ill gray hairs become a fool—a jester!"

In "Much ado about Nothing," Beatrice speaks as follows—

"Why, he is the Prince's jester; a very dull fool, only his gift is in devising unprofitable slanders; none but libertines delight in him, and the commendation is not in his wit, but in his villany, for he both pleases men and angers them, and then they laugh at him and beat him."

But notwithstanding all this condemnation Beatrice is herself the liveliest character in Shakespeare, and her lady's wit is some of the best he shows—

Beatrice. For hear me, Hero; wooing, wedding, and repenting is as a Scotch jig, a measure and a cinque-pace; the first suit is hot and hasty, like a Scotch jig, and full as fantastical; the wedding mannerly-modest, as a measure full of state and ancientry; and then comes repentance, and with his bad legs, falls into the cinque-pace faster and faster, till he sinks into his grave.

Leonato. Cousin, you apprehend shrewdly.

Beat. I have a good eye, uncle; I can see a church, by daylight.

In the "Merchant of Venice" Lorenzo thus answers Launcelot—

"How every fool can play upon the word. I think the best grace of wit will shortly turn into silence, and discourse grow commendable in none but parrots."

Again Lorenzo—

"Oh, dear discretion, how his words are suited,
The fool hath planted in his memory
An army of good words: And I do know
A many fools that stand in better place
Garnished like him, that for a tricksie word
Defie the matter."

Comedians from Aristophanes downwards have been wont to complain in one place of that which they adopt in another—their object not being to adopt fixed principles so much as to show the varying shades of human thought. Shakespeare required something light to bring his deep reflections into bolder relief, and therefore frequently had recourse to humour. We are not surprised that he had no very high estimate of it, when we find him so much dependant upon "the alms-basket of words." There is so much of this in his plays, that it is almost superfluous to quote, but a few instances may be taken at random. Falstaff to Poins—

"You are straight enough in the shoulders; you care not who sees your back—call you that backing your friends? A plague upon such backing; give me a man who will face me."

Falstaff to Prince Henry. Act I. Scene II.

I prythee, sweet wag, when thou art king, as God save thy grace—majesty, I should say, for grace thou wilt have none—
P. Hen. What! none?
Fal. No, by my troth; not so much as will serve to be prologue to an egg and butter.

In Love's Labour Lost. Act I. Scene II.

Armado. Comfort me, boy. What great men have been in love?
Inoth. Hercules, master.
Arm. Most sweet Hercules! More authority, dear boy, name more; and, sweet my child, let them be men of good repute and carriage.
Inoth. Samson, master; he was a man of good carriage, for he raised the town gates on his back like a porter, and he was in love.

In the musicians scene, in Romeo and Juliet, Act IV. Scene V. we find—

Musician. Pray you put up your dagger, and put out your wit.
Peter. Then have at you with my wit. I will dry beat you with my iron wit, and put up my iron dagger. Answer me like:

When griping grief the heart doth wound,
And doleful dumps the mind oppress,
Then music with her silver sound—

Why *silver* sound? Why music with her silver sound? What say you, Simon Catling?
First Mus. Marry, Sir, because silver hath a sweet sound.

Peter. Pretty. What say you, Hugh Rebeck?

Sec. Mins. I say "silver sound," because musicians sound for silver.

Peter. Pretty, too! What say you, James Soundpost?

Third Mins. Faith! I know not what to say.

Peter. O! I cry for mercy; you are the singer; I will say for you. It is music with her silver sound, because musicians have no gold for sounding.

We may here observe that the puns of Shakespeare are never of the "atrocious" class; there is always something to back them up, and give them a shadow of probability. The tournaments of humour which he is fond of introducing, although good in effect upon the stage, are not favourable for any keen wit. Such conflicts must be kept up by artifice, cannot flow from natural suggestion, and degenerate into a mere splintering of words. One cause of the absence of "salt" in his writings is that he was not of a censorious or cynical spirit; another was that his turn of mind was rather sentimental than gay. Shakespeare evidently knew there might be humour among men of attainments, for he writes,—

> "None are so surely caught, when they are catched,
> As wit turned fool; folly is wisdom hatched,
> Hath wisdom's warrant and the help of school
> And wits' own grace to grace a learned fool."

But with him, those who indulge in it are clowns, simpletons, and profligates. Few of his grand characters are witty. Perhaps he was conscious of the great difficulty there would be in finding suitable sayings for them. Indelicacy and hostility would have to be alike avoided, and thus when the sage Gonzalo is to be amusing, he sketches a Utopian state of things, which he would introduce were he King of the island on which they are cast. He would surpass the golden age. Sebastian and Antonio laugh at him, and cry "God save the King," Alonzo replies "Prythee, no more, thou dost talk nothing *(i.e.* nonsense) to me." Gonzalo replies that he did so purposely "to minister occasion to those gentlemen, who are of such sensible and nimble lungs that they always use to laugh at nothing." They retort that they were not laughing at his humour, but at himself. "Who," he replies, "in this merry fooling am nothing to you" meaning, apparently, that he is acting the fool intentionally and out of his real character.

Hamlet, when his mind is distraught, "like sweet bells jangled," is allowed to indulge in a little punning, and Biron is humorous, for which he is reproached by Rosalind, who tells him that he is one

> "Whose influence is begot of that loose grace
> Which shallow laughing hearers give to fools;"

that only silly thoughtless people admire wit, and that

> "A jest's prosperity lies in the ear
> Of him that hears it—never in the tongue
> Of him that makes it."

Here the variable character of humour is recognised, but it is not to be supposed that Rosalind's arguments were intended to be strictly correct. Very much must depend upon the form in which a jest is produced, and without the tongue of the utterer, it cannot exist though the sympathy of the listener is required for its appreciation.

In Shakespeare's plays, and in most comedies we find humour in the representation of ludicrous characters. Words, which would be dull enough in ordinary cases, become highly amusing when coming from men of peculiar views. Sometimes people are represented as perpetually riding their hobby, or harping on one favourite subject. We have an instance of this in Holophernes and his pedantry; and the conversation between the two gravediggers in Hamlet, is largely indebted for its relish to the contrast between the language of the men and their occupation. In the same way, the ignorance and misrepresentations of rustics in play acting, which Shakespeare had probably often observed in the provinces—gives zest to the exaggerated caricature in "Midsummer Night's Dream."—

Bottom. There are things in this comedy of Pyramus and Thisbe that will never please. First, Pyramus must draw a sword to kill himself, which ladies cannot abide. How answer you that?

Snout. By'r lakin a parlous fear.

Starveling. I believe we must leave the killing out, when all is done.

Bottom. Not a whit. I have a device to make all well. Write me a prologue, and let the prologue seem to say, we will not do harm with our swords, and that Pyramus is not killed indeed; and for the more better assurance, tell them that I, Pyramus, am not Pyramus, but Bottom the weaver; this will put them out of fear.

* * * * *

Snout. Will not the ladies be afeard of the lion?

Sta. I fear it, I promise you.

Bottom. Masters, you ought to consider with yourselves to bring in—God shield us! a lion among ladies is a most dreadful thing; for there is not a more fearful wildfowl than your lion living, and we ought to look to it.

Snout. Therefore another prologue must tell, he is not a lion.

Bottom. Nay, you must name his name, and half his face must be seen through the lion's neck; and he must himself speak through, saying thus, or to the same effect—"Ladies," or "Fair ladies, I would wish you," or "I would request you," or "I would entreat you not to fear, nor to tremble: my life for yours. If you think I come hither as a lion, it were pity of my life: no, I am no such thing. I am a man as other men are," and there then let him name his name and tell them plainly he is Snug the joiner.

When the play comes on for performance and Snug the joiner roars "like any sucking dove," the Duke Theseus remarks—

A very gentle beast, and of a good conscience.

Demetrius. The very best as a beast, my lord, that e'er I saw.

Lysander. This lion is a very fox for his valour.

Theseus. True, and a goose for his discretion.

Demetrius. Not so, my lord, for his valour cannot carry his discretion, and the fox carries the goose.

Theseus. His discretion, I am sure, cannot carry his valour,
for the goose carries not the fox.

The enigmas and logical quibbles, which he occasionally intermingles with his verbal conceits, remind us of the old philosophic paradoxes. Sometimes a riddle is attempted; thus, he asks—"What was a month old at Cain's birth, that's not five weeks old now?" Answer—"The Moon."

Taken generally, there is such a remarkable uniformity in Shakespeare's humour as must acquit him of all charge of plagiarism in this respect, and may go some way towards proving the general originality of his plays. Certainly, verbal conceits were then in high favour, and the character of Shakespeare's humour is only one of many proofs that pleasantry had not at this time reached its highest excellence.

To Shakespeare's kindness and discretion Ben Jonson owed his first introduction to dramatic fame. The young poet had presented "Every Man in his Humour," to one of the leading players of the company to which Shakespeare belonged, and the comedian upon reading it, determined to refuse it. Jonson's fate was trembling in the balance; he was a struggling man, and, had he been unsuccessful, might have eventually, returned to his bricklayer's work, but he was destined to be raised up for his own benefit and that of others. Shakespeare was present when his play was about to be rejected, asked to be allowed to look over it, and, at once recognising the poet's talent, recommended it to his companions. From that moment Jonson's career was secured. But he was never destined to acquire the lasting fame of Shakespeare. With him the stream of Comedy was losing its deep and strong reflections, and beginning to flow in a swifter and shallower current, meandering through labyrinths of court and city life. Perhaps, also, his large amount of humorous illustration, which must have been mostly ephemeral, tended to cut short his fame. The best of it is interwoven with his several designs and plots, as where, in "The Alchemist," a gentleman leaves his house in town, and his housekeeper fills it with fortune-tellers vagabonds, who carry on their trade there; and in "The Fox" a rich and childless man is courted by his friends, from whom he obtains presents under the pretence that he will leave them his property. In this last play a parasite is introduced, and in general these plays abound with classical allusions, sometimes very incongruously intermixed with modern concerns. An indiscriminating admiration of ancient literature and art was as much one of the features of the day, as was its crude humour—a cleverness joined to folly and attributed to boobies and simpletons. Much of this jocosity scarcely deserves the name of humour, and we may remark that in Jonson's time it did not receive it. With him humour is thus defined—

> "To be a quality of air or water,
> And in itself holds these two properties,
> Moisture and fluxure . . . Now thus far
> It may by metaphor apply itself
> Unto the general disposition:
> As when some one peculiar quality
> Doth so possess a man, that it doth draw
> All his affects, his spirits, and his power."

The social peculiarities of the day are frequently alluded to by Jonson. In "Every Man out of his own Humour," we have complete directions for the conduct of a gentleman of the time. Smoking, then lately introduced, is especially mentioned as one of the necessities of foppery. Cob, a water-bearer says, "Ods me, I marle what pleasure or felicity they have in taking this roguish tobacco. It's good for nothing but to choke a man, and fill him full of smoke and embers: there were four died out of one house last week with taking of it, and two more the bell went for yesternight; one of them they say will never 'scape it: he cast up a bushel of soot yesterday."

In Cynthia's Revels a courtier is thus described—

"He walks most commonly with a clove or toothpick in his mouth: he is the very mint of compliment, all his behaviours are pointed: his face is another volume of essays, and his beard is Aristarchus. He speaks all cream skimmed, and more affected than a dozen waiting women. The other gallant is his zany, and doth most of these tricks after him, sweats to imitate him in everything to a hair, except his beard, which is not yet extant."

But the stamp of the age is especially prominent in the constant recurrence of verbal conceits. Jonson was fond of coining words, and of using such as are long and little known. He evidently found this a successful kind of humour, and may have partly imitated Plautus—

Lady Politick Would-be, to Volpone, supposed sick—

> Seed pearl were good now, boiled with syrup of apples,
> Tincture of gold, and coral, citron pills,
> Your elicampane root, myrobalanes—
> *Volpone (tired with her talk)* Ah me! I have ta'en a grasshopper
> by the wing.

In "The Alchemist" Subtle says to Face,

> Sirrah my varlet, stand you forth and speak to him
> Like a philosopher: answer in the language,
> Name the vexations and the martyrizations
> Of metals in the work.
>
> Face. Sir, putrefaction,
> Solution, ablution, sublimation,
> Cohabation, calcination, ceration and
> Fixation.

From "Every Man out of his Humour."

Macilente. Pork! heart! what dost thou with such a greasy
dish? I think thou dost varnish thy face with the fat
on't, it looks so like a glue-pot.

Carlo. True, my raw-boned rogue, and if thou wouldst farce
thy lean ribs with it too, they would not like rugged
laths, rub out so many doublets as they do; but thou
knowest not a good dish thou. No marvel though, that
saucy stubborn generation, the Jews, were forbidden
it, for what would they have done, well pampered with
fat pork, that durst murmur at their Maker out of
garlick and onions? 'Slight! fed with it—the strummel-
patched, goggle-eyed, grumbledones would have
gigantomachized.—

The following extracts will give a slight idea of Ben Jonson's
varied talent. At the conclusion of a play directed against plagiarists
and libellers, he sums up—

"Blush, folly, blush! here's none that fears
The wagging of an ass's ears,
Although a wolfish case he wears.
Detraction is but baseness varlet
And apes are apes, though clothed in scarlet."

From "The Alchemist."

Tribulation. What makes the devil so devilish, I would ask
 you.
Sathan our common enemy, but his being
Perpetually about the fire, and boiling
Brimstone and arsenic? . . .

Fastidious. How like you her wit.
Macilente. Her ingenuity is excellent, Sir.
Fast. You see the subject of her sweet fingers there *(the
 viol)* oh, she tickles it so that—she makes it laugh
 most divinely—I'll tell you a good jest just now, and
 yourself shall say it's a good one. I have wished myself
 to be that instrument, I think a thousand times, and
 not so few by heaven.

The two following are from "Bartholomew Fair."

Littlewit. I envy no man my delicates, Sir.
Winwife. Alas, you have the garden where they grow still. A
 wife here with a strawberry breath, cherry lips, apricot
 cheeks, and a soft velvet head like a melicotton.
Lit. Good i' faith! now dulness upon us, that I had not that
 before him, that I should not light on't as well as he!
 Velvet head! . . .
Knockem. Sir, I will take your counsel, and cut my hair, and
 leave vapours. I see that tobacco and bottle ale, and
 pig and whit, and very Ursula herself is all vanity.
Busy. Only pig was not comprehended in my admonition—
 the rest were: for long hair, it is an ensign of pride,
 a banner: and the world is full of those banners—
 very full of banners. And bottle ale is a drink of
 Satan's, a diet-drink of Satan's devised to puff us up,

and make us swell in this latter age of vanity; as the smoke of tobacco to keep us in mist and error: but the fleshly woman, which you call Ursula, is above all to be avoided, having the marks upon her of the three enemies of man—the world, as being in the Fair, the Devil, as being in the fire;[53] and the flesh as being herself.

Ben Jonson has a strange, and I believe original conceit of introducing persons to explain their plays, and make remarks on the characters. Sometimes many interruptions of this kind occur in the course of a drama, affording variety and amusement to the audience, or the reader. In "Midsummer's Night's Dream" we have the insertion of a play within a play. The following taken from Jonson's epigrams have fine complexity, and show a certain tinge of humour.

THE HOUR GLASS.

"Consider this small dust here in the glass,
  By atoms moved:
Could you believe that this the body was
  Of one that loved;
And in his mistress' flame, playing like a fly,
Was turned to cinders by her eye:
Yes; and in death as like unblest,
  To have't exprest,
Ev'n ashes of lovers find no rest."

MY PICTURE.—LEFT IN SCOTLAND.

I now think Love is rather deaf than blind,
For else it could not be
  That she,
Whom I adore so much, should so slight me,
And cast my suit behind;
I'm sure my language to her was as sweet,
And every close did meet
In sentence of as subtle feet,
As hath the youngest, he,

That sits in shadow of Apollo's tree.
Oh! but my conscious fears
That fly my thoughts between
Tell me that she hath seen
My hundreds of gray hairs,
Told seven and forty years,
Read so much waste, as she cannot embrace
My mountain belly, and my rocky face,
And all these through her eyes have stopt her ears.

Although fond of indulging in strong language, Jonson is scarcely ever guilty of any really coarse allusion—he expresses his aversion from anything of the kind, and this in the age in which he lived, argued great refinement of feeling.

In Fletcher we mark a progress in humour. Ben Jonson was so personal that he made enemies, and was suspected of attacking Inigo Jones and others, but Fletcher was general in his references, and merely ridiculed the manners of the age. The classic element disappears, and quibbling and playing with words—so fashionable in Shakespeare's time—is not found in this author, whose humour has more point, and generally more sarcasm, but of a refined character.

The name of Fletcher is invariably connected with Beaumont. The two young men lived together in the same house, and it is even said wore each other's clothes. But Beaumont only lived to be twenty-nine, and has left little in comparison with the voluminous works of Fletcher. They were both born in a good position, and, mingling in the fashionable society of their day, filled their pages with love intrigues, in colours not then offensive. Fletcher never married, and those who look for contrasts between fathers and children may learn that his father, who was Bishop of London, was suspended by Elizabeth for taking a second wife. Our author is said to have been himself a comedy, and his death, if we can believe the story, was consistent with his gay life, for we are told that, through waiting in London for a new suit of clothes, he died of cholera, which was raging there at the time.

Here is a specimen of his sketches—the character of a rich usurer—

Sanchio. Thou'art very brave.

Cacafogo. I've reason; I have money.

San. Is money reason?

Cac. Yes, and rhyme too, captain.
If you've no money you're an ass.

San. I thank you.

Cac. You've manners! ever thank him that has money.

San. Wilt thou lend me any?

Cac. Not a farthing, captain; captains are casual things.

San. Why, so are all men:
Thou shalt have my bond.

Cac. Nor bonds, nor fetters, captain:
My money is my own; I make no doubt on't.

Juan. What dost thou do with it?

Cac. Put it to pious uses—
Buy wine—

Juan. Are you for the wars, Sir?

Cac. I am not poor enough to be a soldier,
Nor have I faith enough to ward a bullet;
This is no living for a trench, I take it.

Juan. You have said wisely.

Cac. Had you but money

You'd swear it, colonel. I'd rather drill at home
A hundred thousand crowns, and with more honour,
Than exercise ten thousand fools with nothing;
A wise man safely feeds, fools cut their fingers.

The prurient coarseness of Fletcher is due to the peculiar licentiousness of the period. In his plays, although kissing is sometimes provocative of jealousy, it is generally regarded, even by persons of rank, as of less importance than it is now by boys and girls, who play "Kiss in the ring." In "Rule a wife and have a wife" Margarita says to the Duke

> "I may kiss a stranger,
> For you must be so now."

This lady is desirous of obtaining a very easy husband, who will let her do whatever she likes. A friend says she has found one for her in Leon, who is forthwith introduced. Margarita puts some questions to him to ascertain his docility, and then says—

> "Let me try your kisses—
> How the fool shakes!—I will not eat you, Sir.
> Beshrew my heart, he kisses wondrous manly!
> You must not look to be my master, Sir,
> Nor talk i' th' house as though you wore the breeches,
> No, nor command in anything . . . You must not be saucy,
> No, nor at any time familiar with me;
> Scarce know me when I call not."

After trying and approving his kisses again, she tells him that he is not to start or be offended if he sees her kissing anyone else. He is to keep in the cellar, when not wanted. The proposed husband promises to be most obedient and accommodating in everything, but as soon as he is accepted and the ceremony performed, he appears in a totally different character. He informs his wife, in whose magnificent house he goes to live—

> You've nothing to do here, Madam,
> But as a servant to sweep clean the lodgings,
> And at my farther will to do me service.
> *Margarita (to her servants.)* Get me my coach!
> *Leon.* Let me see who dare get it
> Till I command; I'll make him draw your coach
> And eat your couch, (which will be hard duty).

On Cacafogo making some slighting remark, this gentle individual exclaims—

> "Peace! dirt and dunghill!
> I will not lose mine anger on a rascal;
> Provoke me more,—I will beat thy blown body
> Till thou rebound'st again like a tennis-ball."

In "Monsieur Thomas" we have the following jovial passage—

Francisco. What hast thou there? a julep?

Hylas. He must not touch it;
'Tis present death.

Thomas. You are an ass, a twirepipe,
A Jeffery John Bo-peep! Thou minister?
Thou mend a left-handed pack-saddle? Out! puppy!
My Friend, Frank, but a very foolish fellow.
Dost thou see that bottle? view it well.

Fran. I do, Tom.

Tho. There be as many lives in it as a cat carries;
'Tis everlasting liquor.

Fran. What?

Tho. Old sack, boy.
Old reverend sack; which for ought that I can read yet
Was the philosopher's stone the wise King Ptolomus
Did all his wonders by.

Fran. I see no harm, Tom.
Drink with a moderation.

Tho. Drink with sugar,
Which I have ready here, and here a glass, boy.

* * * * *

> Hang up your juleps, and your Portugal possets,
> Your barley broths and sorrel soups; they are mangy
> And breed the scratches only: Give me sack!

The devil now becomes a constant resource for humour. In "The Chances" Antonio has lost his jewels. His servant suggests that the thieves have "taken towards the ports."

> *Ant.* Get me a conjurer,
> One that can raise a water-devil. I'll port 'em.
> Play at duck and drake with my money? Take heed,
> fiddler,
> I'll dance ye by this hand: your fiddlestick
> I'll grease of a new fashion, for presuming
> To meddle with my de-gambos! get me a conjurer,
> Inquire me out a man that lets out devils.

Beaumont and Fletcher were great conversationalists, their racy raillery is said to have been as good as their plays. They were members of the celebrated Mermaid Club in Fleet Street, a centre where the wits of the day sharpened their humour in friendly conflict. In his epistle to Ben Jonson, Beaumont writes—

> "What things have we seen
> Done at the 'Mermaid!' heard words that have been
> So nimble and so full of subtle flame,
> As if that every one from whom they came
> Had meant to put his whole wit in a jest,
> And had resolved to live a fool the rest
> Of his dull life."

Here it was that Shakespeare and Jonson often contended, the former like "a light English man-of-war" the latter like "a high-built Spanish galleon."

To some portion of the seventeenth century, we must attribute those curious stories called "The Merry tales of the Wise Men of Gotham" although by some they have been attributed to Andrew Gotham, a physician of Henry VIII. They are said to have been suggested by a circumstance which occurred in the time of King John. He intended to pass through Gotham, a village in

Northamptonshire, but the inhabitants placed some difficulties in his way. On his expressing his determination to carry out his project, and sending officers to make inquiries about the opposition offered, the inhabitants were seized with a panic and pretended to have lost their senses. This was the tradition upon which, in after-times, these tales were founded, and being unobjectionable they are well adapted for the nursery, but being mere exercises of ingenuity they afford but very slight pleasure to older minds. Although aimless, there is something clever in them. The Wise Men determine to hedge round a cuckoo to keep it in so that it should sing all the year. The bird seeing the hedge flies away. "A vengeance on her," say the Wise Men, "we made not the hedge high enough." There is the story of the young man, whose mother told him to throw sheep's eyes at his sweetheart, and who, literally, performed her bidding. One Good Friday the Men of Gotham consulted what to do with their red herrings, and other salt fish, and agreed to cart them into a pond that the number might increase next year. At the beginning of the next summer they drag the pond, and only find a great eel. "A mischief on him," they say, "he hath eaten up our fish." Some propose to chop him in pieces, but the rest think it would be best to drown him, so they throw him into another pond. Twelve men of Gotham go to fish, and some stand on dry land, and some in the water. And one says "We have ventured wonderfully in wading; I pray that none of us come home drowned." So they begin to count, and as each omits himself he can only count eleven, and so they go back to the water, and make great lamentation. A courtier, who meets them, convinces them of their mistake by laying his whip on each of them, who calls out in turn "Here's one," until twelve are counted. The minister of Gotham preaches that men should not drink in Lent. A man, who comes for absolution, and confesses to having been drunk in Lent, replies that fish should swim. "Yes," returns the priest, "but in water." "I cannot enjoin your prayer," he adds, "for you cannot say your Paternoster. It is folly to make you fast because you never get meat. Labour hard, and get a dinner on Sunday, and I will come and dine with you."

CHAPTER VII.

Jesters—Court of Queen Elizabeth—James I.—The "Counterblasts to Tobacco"—Puritans—Charles II.—Rochester—Buckingham—Dryden—Butler.

Professed fools seem to have been highly appreciated in the time of Shakespeare. They do not correspond to our modern idea of a fool, because there was intention in their actions, and yet we could not have considered them to be really sensible men. Nor had they great talent, their gifts being generally lower than those of our professed wits.

Addison observes that, "when a man of wit makes us laugh, it is by betraying some oddness or infirmity in his own character," and at the present day, not only do those who indulge much in humour often say things approaching nonsense, and make themselves in other ways ridiculous, but their object, being entirely idle diversion and pleasantry, appears foolish and puerile. Those who cultivate humour are not generally to be complimented on their success, and a popular writer has thus classified fools—"First, the ordinary fool; secondly the fool who is one, and does not know it; thirdly, the fool who is not satisfied with being one in reality, but undertakes in addition to play the fool." Thus, to a certain extent we may always regard a professed wit as a silly fellow, but still at the present day the acts or sayings of an absolute idiot or lunatic, would be depressing and offensive, and could afford little amusement in any way except accidentally.[54] They would resemble the incongruities in dreams which although strange are not generally laughable. And if we are not amused with a fool, neither are we with a man who imitates him, although Cicero says that humour consists in a man who is not a fool, speaking as though he were one. Some mistake supposed to be made by an ordinary man is what amuses us, and although humorous sayings originated in an imitation of ludicrous things, and Quintilian's observation sometimes holds good that the same things, which if they drop from us unintentionally are foolish, if we imitate them are humorous; still humour is not confined to this; there is generally no such imitation, and the witty sayings of the present day are seldom representations of such things as anyone would utter in earnest, whether he were a fool or not.

We must not confuse folly and wit, though they may exist in the same person and in close relationship. The latter requires intelligence and intention. If a humorous man ever purposely enacts the dullard, the impersonation is always modified—he is like Snug, the joiner, who does not "fright the ladies." There is always some peculiar point in his blunders; if he acted the fool to the life we should not laugh with him. We always see something clever and admirable in him, and to be successful in this way, a man should possess considerable mental gifts, and be able to gauge the feelings of others. Still we can hardly assent to the proposition that "it takes a wise man to make a fool." A man may be witty without having any constructive power of mind. It is easier to find fault than to be faultless, to see a blemish than to produce what is perfect—a pilot may point out rocks, but not be able to steer a safe course.

At the time of which we are now speaking, the double character of the court fool corresponded with that early and inferior humour which was always on the verge of the ludicrous. The connection thus established, long remained and led to witty observations being often spoken of as "foolerie." Upon this conceit or confusion Shakespeare founded the speech of Jaques in "As you like it."

Act II. Scene IV.

Jaques. A fool! a fool!—I met a fool i' the forest,
A motley fool:—a miserable fool!—
As I do live by food, I met a fool:
Who laid him down, and basked him in the sun,
And railed on Lady Fortune in good terms.
In good set terms—and yet a motley fool.

"Good morrow, fool," quoth I. "No, Sir," quoth he,
"Call me not fool till heaven hath sent me fortune."
And then he drew a dial from his poke,
And looking on it with lack lustre eye,
Says very wisely, "It is ten o'clock;"
"Thus we may see," quoth he, "how the world wags;
'Tis but an hour ago since it was nine,
And after one hour more t'will be eleven,
And so from hour to hour we ripe and ripe,
And then from hour to hour we rot and rot,
And thereby hangs a tale."

There is nothing very laughable in the above reflections, but they contain a deep satire, and afford a beautiful example of Shakespearian complexity. From the mixture of wisdom and folly compounded in the "fool" of the day—who was then, it must be remembered, the monitor of the great—it is here implied that in his awkward way he sometimes arrived at truth better than the sage. As supremely wise men are often regarded as fools, so what seems folly may be the highest wisdom—"motley's your only wear."

The fool is generally represented in Shakespeare as saying things which have a certain wit and shrewdness.

> *Clown.* God bless thee, lady.
> *Olivia.* Take the fool away.
> *Clo.* Do you not hear, fellows? Take away the lady.

* * * * *

Good Madonna, why mournest thou?
Oli. Good fool, for my brother's death.
Clo. I think his soul is in hell, Madonna.
Oli. I know his soul is in heaven, fool.
Clo. The more fool, Madonna, to mourn for your brother's
soul being in heaven. Take away the fool, gentlemen.

In King Lear.

Fool. Dost thou know the difference, my boy, between a
bitter fool and a sweet one?
Lear. No, lad, teach me.

Fool. That lord that counselled thee
To give away thy land,
Come place him here by me—
Do thou for him stand:
The sweet and bitter fool
Will presently appear,
The one in motley here,
The other found out there.
Lear. Dost thou call me fool, boy?
Fool. All thy other titles thou hast given away that thou wast
born with.
Kent. This is not altogether a fool, my lord.

The fact was that wit was now gradually improving, and was being wielded by so called fools in such a way that it could not be confounded with fatuity. The time was approaching when the humour manufactured by professed jesters would not be appreciated. Something higher and keener, such as Shakespeare has here shadowed forth would be required. This was not reached in Ben Jonson's time, but fools and their artifices are by him discarded for something more natural, for country bumpkins and servants, ludicrous in their stupidity, knavery and drunkenness. As civilization advanced, jugglers and clowns were relegated to country fairs.

Henry the Eighth, at the commencement of his reign was a great patron of men of wit and learning, and probably the humour of More, as well as his virtue, recommended him to the King. We read that at Cardinal Morton's entertainments of his Christmas company, the future Chancellor, then a boy, would often mount the stage and extemporize with so much wit and talent as to surpass all the professional players. During his university course, and shortly afterwards, he wrote many neat Latin epigrams of which the two following rough translations will give some idea—

> "A thief about to be accused, implored
> Advice, and sent his counsel many a pound,
> The counsel, when o'er mighty tomes he'd pored,
> Replied, 'If you'd escape, you must abscond.'

> "Once in the loving cup, a guest saw flies,
> Removed them, drank, and then put back a few.
> And, being questioned, sagely thus replies,
> 'I like them not—but cannot speak for you.'"

He was to the last fond of pleasantry and kept a jester.

The daughter of Henry the Eighth and Anne Boleyn[55] could scarcely have been deficient in mirthfulness, and we find that the dangers through which she passed in her youth were not able to extinguish Elizabeth's love of humour. According to the custom of the day she exhibited this not only in her sayings, but, as comedians were then often received in great houses, she ordered in 1583 that twelve of them should be made grooms of the chamber, be sworn the Queen's servants, and be arrayed in her livery. The most remarkable of these was Tarlton. He came of humble origin. Fuller says that, while tending his father's swine, a servant of Robert, Earl of Leicester, passing by was so pleased with his *happy unhappy* answers that he took him to court. But Tarlton's humour was often that of the common fool, and depended generally upon action, look, and voice. His face was in this respect his fortune, for he had a flat nose and squinting eyes. Nash mentions that on one occasion he "peept out his head," probably with a grimace, at the audience, which caused a burst of laughter, and led one of the justices, who did not understand the fun, to beat the people on the bare pates, inasmuch as they, "being farmers and hinds, had dared to laugh at the Queen's men." He was celebrated for his jigs, *i.e.* extempore songs accompanied with tabor and pipe, and sometimes with dancing.

Fuller says he had great influence with Elizabeth, and could "undumpish" her at pleasure. Her favourites were wont to go to him to prepare their access to her, and "he told the Queen more of her faults than most of her chaplains, and cured her melancholy better than all her physicians."

Bohun says that, "at supper she would divert herself with her friends and attendants, and if they made no answer she would put them upon mirth and pleasant discourse with great civility. She would then also admit Tarlton, a famous comedian and pleasant talker, and other men to divert her with stories of the town, and the common jests or accidents, but so that they kept within the bounds of modesty." Tarlton, on one occasion, cast reflections upon Leicester; and said of Raleigh, "the knave commands the Queen," at which she was so much offended that she forbade any of her jesters to approach her table.

The jests of Scogan, or rather those attributed to him, were very popular in Elizabeth's time. This man was court-fool to Henry VII., and is said to have been "of pleasant wit and bent to merrie devices." He was fond of practical jokes, and often attacked the clergy. Elizabeth seems to have had a natural gift of humour, and we read of many of her witty sayings. On one occasion, upon an archbishop finding fault with some of her actions, and quoting Scripture to prove she had acted more as a politician than a Christian. "I see, my lord," she replied, "that you have read the scriptures, but not the book of Kings." She was so well acquainted with proverbs, that on being presented with a collection of English aphorisms, and told by the author that it contained them all, she answered, "Nay, where is 'Bate me an ace, quoth Bolton.'"

Among the sayings, good for the period, which have been attributed to her, we read that when the Archduke raised the siege of Grave, the Queen who heard of it before her secretary, said to him, "Wot you that the Archduke is risen from the Grave." When at Lord Burleigh's she promised to make seven knights, and the gentlemen to be so honoured were placed in a line as the Queen was going out. The least worthy of them, however, were through interest with Lord Burleigh placed first, so that they might have precedence of creation. But the Queen passed down the row and took no notice of them; but when she had reached the screen, turned, and observing, "I had almost forgotten my promise," proceeded to knight from the lower end. On one of her Privy Council saying "Your Majesty was too politic for my Lord Burleigh," she replied, "I have but followed the scripture—'the first shall be last and the last first.'"

The cares of sovereignty, and the opposition of her Roman Catholic subjects led Elizabeth's humour to assume a somewhat severe complexion. Her thoughts gradually became more earnest, and her jests cynical. Moreover, as seen in Shakespeare, the age in which she lived was reflective, and the budding activity of mind was directed towards great interests. There was not that impression of the vanity of all things, which grows up with the extension and maturity of society, and attracts the mind to more fanciful and less grave considerations. A good contrast between Elizabeth's position, and that of James I. may be seen in the following occurrences. When Henry IV. had given the order of St. Michael to Nicolas Clifford and Anthony Shirley, she commanded them to return it. "I will not," she said, "have my sheep follow the pipe of a strange shepherd;"[56] but when James I. was told that several noblemen of his court and council, received pensions from Spain, the King replied that he knew it well, and only wished the King of Spain would give them ten times as much, as it would render him less able to make war upon him.

James was a man of a very eccentric and grotesque fancy, combined with a considerable amount of intelligence and learning. He was particularly fond of religious controversy, and wrote what he considered to be an important work on "Demonologie." From one passage we might suppose that he thought it sinful to laugh, as he says that man can only laugh, because he can only sin. But he kept two clowns for his amusement, and also appreciated Ben Jonson, to whom he gave the direction of the Court Masques. He occasionally made some caustic remarks, which have come down to us, such as, "Who denys a thing he even now spake, is like him that looks in my face and picks my pocket." "A travelling preacher and a travelling woman never come to any good at all."

Sir Henry Wooton told him how the Prince of Condé sued for the title of Altesse from the Synod of Venice. The King replied, "The Prince had good reason to sue for it, and that the Seigniory had done ill to deny it him, considering that the world knew how well he deserved it; it being his custom to raise himself upon every man's back, and to make himself the higher by every man's tail he could get upon. And for that cause he hoped to see him elevated by the just Justice of God to as high a dignity as the gallows at last."

James the First's writings were mostly of a religious character, and some of them were sufficiently ludicrous. But in his "Counterblaste to Tobacco," his indignation is often mixed with humour. He observes that smoking came from the Indians, and continues—

"And now, good countreymen let vs (I pray you) consider what honour or policy can move vs to imitate the barbarous and beastly maneres of the wilde, Godlesse and slavish Indians, especially in so vile and stinking a custome? Shall wee that disdaine to imitate the manners of our neighbour France . . . Shall wee, I say without blushing abase ourselves so farre as to imitate these beastly Indians, slaves to the Spaniards, refuse to the world, and as yet aliens from the Holy Covenant of God? Why doe wee not as well imitate them in walking naked as they doe? in preferring glasses, feathers, and such toyes to gold and precious stones, as they doe? Yea, why do wee not deny God, and adore the divel as they doe?"

He proceeds to combat the theory, "That the braines of all men beeing naturally cold and wet, all drie and hote things should be good for them." "It is," he says, "as if a man, because the liver is hote, and as it were an oven to the stomache, would therefore apply and weare close upon his liver and stomache a cake of lead; he might within a short time (I hope) bee susteined very cheape at an Ordinarie, besides the clearing of his conscience from that dreadful sinne of gluttonie."

Towards the end he gives some medical testimony—

"Surely smoke becomes a kitchin farre better than a dining chamber, and yet it makes a kitchin also oftentimes in the inward parts of men, soyling and infecting them with an vnctuous and oily kind of soote, as hath been found in some great tobacco takers, that after their death, were opened."

Addison, speaking of James' love of jesting, observes:—"The age in which the pun chiefly flourished was in the reign of King James the First. That learned monarch was himself a tolerable punster, and made very few bishops or privy-councillors that had not sometime or other signalized themselves by a clinch or a conundrum. It was therefore in this age that the pun appeared with pomp and dignity. It had been before admitted into merry speeches and ludicrous compositions, but was now delivered with great gravity from the pulpit, or pronounced in the most solemn manner at the council-table." Verbal humour continued to be admired for its ingenuity in the reign of Charles I. The childish taste of the time in this respect is prominently exhibited in the "Fames Roule," written by a Mrs. Mary Fage, in honour of the royal family and principal peers of the realm. It consists of short poems, and each one forms an acrostic, and commences with an anagram of the name.

The following will give specimens of this ridiculous composition:—

"To the high and mighty. Princesse Mary,
Eldest Daughter of our Soveraigne Lord King Charles.

MARY STVARTE.
Anagramma.
A MERRY STATV.

"M irth may with Princes very well agree,
A Merry Statv then faire Madam be;
R ightly 'twill fit your age, your vertues grace;
Y eelding A Merry Statv in your face.

"S mile then, high Lady, while of mirth write I,
T hat so my Muse may with alacrity,
U nto your Highness sing without all feare,
A nd a true Statv of your vertues reare:
R eaching whereto, that she may higher flee,
T hus humbly beg I on my bended knee,
E ver A Merry Statv be to me."

GEORGE MANNERS.
Anagramma.
NOR AS GREEN GEM.

"G reat honoured Peere, and *Rutland's* Noble Earle,
E ven in vertue shining like a Pearle
O ver all *Europe*, adding to your birth,
R adiant bright beames of your true honoured worth:
G em great and precious, see you are remaining
E ver the rayes of vertue's beames retaining.

"M aking all *Europe* stand amazed quite,
A nd wonder much at *Rutland's* glorious light,
N or *as a green gem* let your lustre be,
N o, *greenness* here betokens *levity*,
E ver more as a precious gem remain you,

R ed or some orient colour still retaine you;

S o *nor as green gem*, will the world proclaime you."

The jester still remained in office in Charles the First's reign and Archee assumed the old prerogative of the motley in telling home truths to his master. On one occasion he was ordered by the King to say grace, as the chaplain was away, upon which the jester pronounced it, "All glory be to God on high, and little Laud to the devil." At which all the courtiers smiled, because it reflected upon the Archbishop of Canterbury, who was a little man. The King said he would tell Laud, and what would he do then? "Oh!" said Archee, "I will hide me where he will never find me." "Where is that?" asked the King. "In his pulpit," answered Archee, "for I am sure he never goes there."

The rebellion against Charles the First and the success of the Puritans led to a remarkable development of religious feeling. Men seemed for the moment to think more of the next world than of the present, seasoned their language with texts, and from Scripture adopted new names suitable to a new life. Their usual tone of conversation is thus humorously described by Harrison Ainsworth.

Captain Stelfax pays Colonel Maunsel a domiciliary visit, and an old Royalist retainer tells the redoubtable Roundhead that he looks more like a roystering Cavalier than a Puritan, to which the latter replies—

"Go to, knave, and liken me not to a profane follower of Jehoram. Take heed that thou answerest me truthfully. Thou art newly returned from the battle-field whereat the young man Charles Stuart was utterly routed, and where our general, like Pekah the son of Remaliah slew many thousands of men in one day, because they had forsaken the Lord God of their fathers. Didst thou bear arms in the service of Ahaz?"

One Increase Micklegift soon afterwards fell into the captain's bad graces—

"I begin to suspect it was by thy instrumentality that he hath escaped."

"How could that be seeing I was with thee in the closet." Micklegift rejoined.

"It might easily be, since it was by thy devise that I was led into the snare. Bitterly shalt thou rue it, if I find thee leagued with the Amalekites."

All this affords a good idea of the phraseology of these men, some of whom indulged in such names as "Nehemiah, Lift-up-Hand" and "Better-Late-than-Never," and it must be remembered, to their credit, that there never was a more orderly army than that of Cromwell. In accordance with the sentiments then entertained all theatrical exhibitions were prohibited. Such austerity and self-denial could not be of long continuance—it was kept up by an effort, and led to an inevitable reaction, and so we find that the court of the "Merry Monarch" became notorious in history for its dissipation. Humour proportionally changed from what it had been under Charles I., and we read that that the old Earl of Norwich, who had been esteemed the greatest wit, was now quite out of fashion.

Barbarous nations have little idea of delicacy of any kind; and civilisation finds it hard entirely to change nature, so that where-ever the ground is allowed to lie fallow, the old weeds appear in their noisesome rankness. Hence from time to time we find indelicacy springing up, and made to serve the purposes of those who know that the evil plant is not radically extirpated. One of the most offensive men in this respect was Peter Aretinus, an Italian adventurer, who became a great favourite with the Emperor Charles V. He is said to have died from falling back over his chair in a fit of laughter, on hearing some indelicate joke. But modes of death have often been invented to accord with the lives of those who suffered them, just as dithyrambic Anacreon is said to have been choked by a grape stone.

Louis XI. was also addicted to this jesting which is not convenient. We read that he told Edward IV. in a jocose way that he was right glad to see him at Paris, and that if he would come and divert himself with the gay ladies there, he would assign for his confessor, the Cardinal of Bourbon, who, he knew, would grant him easy absolution for peccadilloes of love and gallantry. Edward was much pleased with this raillery, for he knew the Cardinal was a gay man. Louis was afterwards in great alarm upon Edward's acceptance of his invitation.

The humour of Charles II. and his court consisted more of jollity than wit. The king was always ready to laugh outright, even in church at the sermon. He encouraged and led the way in an indelicate kind of jesting, which he seems to have learned during his travels in France. On his telling Lord Shaftesbury, "I believe Shaftesbury, that thou art the wickedest dog in England," the statesman humbly replied, "May it please your Majesty, of a subject, I believe I am." We should not expect too much from the son of Henrietta Maria. It is related that one morning when at Exeter, pressing her hand to her head she said to her physician, "Mayerne, I am afraid I shall go mad some day." "Nay," he replied, "your Majesty need not fear *going* mad; you have been so some time."

But Charles owed much to his gay and easy manner. Notwithstanding his faults "he was so pleasant a man that no one could be sorrowful under his government." He sometimes dined at the annual civic banquet, and one of the company present on the occasion when Sir Robert Viner was Lord Mayor, refers to it as follows. "Sir Robert was a very loyal man, and if you will allow the expression, very fond of his sovereign, but what with the joy he felt at heart for the honour done him by his prince and through the warmth he was in with continual toasting healths of the royal family, his lordship grew a little fond of His Majesty, and entered into a familiarity not altogether so graceful in so public a place. The king understood very well how to extricate himself in all kinds of difficulties, and with a hint to the company to avoid ceremony, stole off and made towards his coach which stood ready for him in Guildhall yard. But the Mayor liked his company so well, and was grown so intimate, that he pursued him hastily and catching him fast by the hand, cried out with a vehement oath and accent, 'Sir, you shall stay and take t'other bottle.' The airy monarch looked kindly at him over his shoulder, and with a smile and graceful air (for I saw him at the time and do now) repeated this line of the old song 'He that's drunk is as great as a King,' and immediately turned back and complied with his request."

Tom Killegrew was the last of his cloth; forced and constant jesting becoming less and less appreciated. As the jesters approached their end, they had more of the moralist and politician in them than of the mountebank. We may judge of Killegrew's wit, when we read that one day on his appearance Charles said to his gay companions, "Now we shall hear our faults." "No," replied the jester, "I don't care to trouble my head with that which all the town talks of."[57] Killegrew must have had fine scope for his sarcasm. In these times the character of the monarch gave the tone to society, and was reflected in the dramatists. Thus we find the earnestness of Elizabeth in Shakespeare, the whimsicality of James in Jonson, and the licentiousness of Charles II. in the poets of the Restoration. The deterioration of men and of humour in the last reign is marked by the fact that ridicule was mostly directed not against vice as in Roman satire, but against undeserved misfortunes. Even virtue and learning did not afford immunity; Bishop Warburton writes: "This weapon (in the dissolute times of Charles II.) completed the ruin of the best minister of that age. The historians tell us that Chancellor Hyde was brought into his Majesty's contempt by this court argument. They mimicked his walk and gesture with a fire-shovel and bellows for the mace and purse."

The indelicacy of which Charles and his companions was guilty, was not of a primitive and ignorant kind, but always of an amatory character, and at the expense of the fair sex; jests formerly so common as to obtain the name of "japes." The writers of that day are objectionable not merely for coarseness of this kind, but for the large amount of it, as one artiste in complimentary attire might be tolerated where a crowd of seminude performers could not. The poems of Sedley and Rochester are as abundant in indelicacy as they are deficient in humour. The epigram of Sedley to "Julius" gives a more correct idea of his character than of his usual dullness.

"Thou swearest thou'll drink no more; kind Heaven
send Me such a cook or coachman, but no friend."

Rochester might have produced something good. His verses have more traces of poetry and humour than we should expect from a man who out of the thirty-four years of his life, was for five of them continually drunk. He nearly always attunes his harp to the old subject, so as to become hopelessly monotonous. Inconstancy has great charms for him, and he consequently imputes it also to the ladies—

> "Womankind more joy discovers
> Making fools, than keeping lovers."

Again:

> "Love like other little boys,
> Cries for hearts as they for toys,
> Which when gained, in childish play,
> Wantonly are thrown away."

He seems to have been oppressed by a disbelief in any kind of good in the world. His philosophy, whenever he ventured upon any, was sceptical and irreverent. His best attempt in this direction was a poem "Upon Nothing," which commences:

> "Nothing! thou elder brother ev'n to shade,
> That had'st a being 'ere the world was made,
> And (well fixt) art alone of ending not afraid.
> Ere Time and Place were, Time and Place were not,
> When primitive Nothing, Something straight begot,
> Then all proceeded from the great united—What?"

Sometimes he amused himself writing libels on the king, and some of his satires contain more or less truth, as—

> "His father's foes he does reward,
> Preserving those that cut off's head,
> Old Cavaliers, the crown's best guard,
> He lets them starve for want of bread.
> Never was a King endued
> With so much grace and gratitude."

Buckingham does not appear to have agreed with Rochester about Charles, for he writes, "He was an illustrious exception to all the common rules of physiognomy, for with a most saturnine and harsh sort of countenance, he was both of a merry and merciful disposition." Buckingham's humour was of a very poor description, but he wrote a Comedy "The Rehearsal," which was highly approved, mostly, however, because aimed at Dryden, and the heroic drama. From one passage in it, we observe that he noticed the difference between the effect of humour in the plot, and in the dialogue of the play—

> *Prettyman.* Well, Tom, I hope shortly we shall have another coin for thee; for now the wars are coming on, I shall grow to be a man of metal.
>
> *Bayes.* O, you did not do that half enough.
>
> *Johnson.* Methinks he does it admirably.
>
> *Bayes.* I, pretty well, but he does not hit me in't, he does not top his part.
>
> *Thimble.* That's the way to be stamped yourself, Sir, I shall see you come home like an angel for the king's evil, with a hole bored through you.
>
> *Bayes.* There he has hit it up to the hilt. How do you like it now, gentlemen? is not this pure wit?
>
> *Smith.* 'Tis snip snap, Sir, as you say, but methinks not pleasant nor to the purpose, for the play does not go on. The plot stands still.
>
> *Bayes.* Why, what the devil is the plot good for but to bring in fine things.

Dryden could scarcely be expected to remain silent under the blow here aimed at his plays. An opportunity for revenge soon presented itself, when he undertook to compose a political satire upon Monmouth and his intrigues. Some say that this remarkable poem was written at the command of Charles. It had a great success, five editions being sold within the year—one cause of its popularity being its novel character. The idea of introducing Scriptural impersonations into a poem was new or nearly so, and very successful. Monmouth had already been called Absalom, and as the King (David) was very fond of him, it was desirable to place his shortcomings to the account of his advisers, represented by Achitophel. The way in which Dryden handled his adversaries may be understood from such passages as:—

> "Levi, thou art a load: I'll lay thee down
> And show rebellion bare, without a gown;
> Poor slaves in metre, dull and addle-pated
> Who rhime below e'en David's psalms translated."

Doeg is another enemy:—

> "'Twere pity treason at his door to lay
> Who makes heaven's gate a lock to its own key.
> Let him rail on, let his invective muse
> Have four and twenty letters to abuse,
> Which, if he jumbles to one line of sense
> Indict him of a capital offence."

This satire led to some replies, which Dryden crushed in his "Mac Flecnoe," a poem named after an Irish priest—an inferior poet—who, but for this notice, would never have been known to posterity. Shadwell was the man really aimed at; Mac Flecnoe exclaims:—

> "Shadwell alone, of all my sons, is he
> Who stands confirmed in full stupidity,
> The rest to some faint meaning make pretence
> But Shadwell never deviates into sense."[58]

After much in the same strain, he finishes with:—

> "Thy genius calls thee not to purchase fame
> In keen iambics, but mild anagram.
> Leave writing plays, and choose for thy command
> Some peaceful province in acrostic land,
> There thou mayest wings display and altars raise,
> And torture one poor world ten thousand ways."

Dryden calls this kind of satire Varronian, as he weaves a sort of imaginary story into which he introduces the object of his attack. He was under the impression that this was the first piece of ridicule written in heroics, and his claim seemed correct as far as England was concerned, but Boileau and Tassoni had preceded him. Willmot says, "Dryden is wanting in the graceful humour of Tassoni, and exquisite power of Boileau. His wit has more weight than edge—it beat in armour, but could not cut gause." The greater part of Dryden's satire could not cut anything, nor be distinguished from elaborate vituperation. He wrote an essay on Satire, in which

189

he shows a much better knowledge of history than of humour. His best passages are in the "Spanish Friars," but they are weak and mainly directed against the profligacy of the Church. The servant says of the friar, "There's a huge, fat religious gentleman coming up, Sir. He says he's but a friar, but he's big enough to be a Pope; his gills are as rosy as a turkey-cock's; his great belly walks in state before him like an harbinger, and his gouty legs come limping after it. Never was such a ton of devotion seen."

Samuel Butler affords one of the many examples of highly gifted literary men who have died in great poverty. His works, recommended by Lord Dorset, were read largely, and even by the King himself; but there was then no great demand for books, and authors had to look to patrons, and eat the uncertain bread of dependence. We may suppose, however, that he was an improvident man, for during his life he held several offices, and was at one time steward of Ludlow Castle.

Butler possessed a real gift of humour, and an astonishing fertility of invention. To us there seems to be still too much indelicacy in his writings, though less than heretofore, and there is a considerable amount of bear-fighting, both in the literal and metaphorical sense. This rough and cruel pastime was very common in that day. We read of bear-baiting at Kenilworth to amuse Queen Elizabeth, and Alleyn, the munificent founder of Dulwich College, was not only a dramatic author and manager, but "Master of the bears and dogs," which seems to have been a post of honour. To the present day, a ring for such sports is to be seen outside the principal gate of Battle Abbey.

We have already observed that the drama of Spain became the model for that of modern Europe, and we are not therefore surprised to find that the main design in Sir Hudibras is to produce an English Don Quixote. All the accessories of the work point to this imitation; there is a long account of his arms, his Squire, and horse. But beyond this, he aimed at several well-known rogues of his day, especially those pretending to necromancy and prophetic powers, who seem to have been numerous.[59] This gave the poem an interest at that day which it cannot have now, and it was increased by the amusing hits he makes at the Puritans, who had lately convulsed the State, and whom he had been able to gauge when he was employed by Sir Samuel Luke.[60] The lines are well known in which he speaks of the time:—

> "When pulpit, drum, ecclesiastic,
> Was beat with fist, instead of a stick;"

and the general outcry against dignitaries is thus represented:—

> "The oyster women locked their fish up
> And trudged away to cry 'No Bishop';
> Botchers left old clothes in the lurch,
> And fell to turn and patch the church;
> Some cry'd the Covenant, instead
> Of pudding, pies, and gingerbread!"

Sir Hudibras is a Presbyterian "true blue."

> "Such as do build their faith upon
> The holy test of pike and gun;
> Decide all controversies by
> Infallible artillery:
> And prove their doctrine orthodox
> By apostolic blows and knocks.

> "Rather than fail, they will defy
> That which they love most tenderly;
> Quarrel with minced pies, and disparage.
> Their best and dearest friend, plum porridge;
> Fat pig and goose itself oppose,
> And blaspheme custard through the nose."

Sir Hudibras was learned in controversy:—

> "For he a rope of sand could twist
> As tough as learned Sorbonist
> And weave fine cobwebs fit for skull
> That's empty when the moon is full,
> Such as take lodgings in a head
> That's to be let unfurnished."

He had been at the siege of "Bullen," by Henry VIII., and his breeches were lined

> "With many a piece
> Of ammunition, bread and cheese,
> And fat black puddings, proper food
> For warriors that delight in blood.
> For as he said he always chose
> To carry victual in his hose,
> That often tempted rats and mice
> The ammunition to surprise."

Hudibras speaking of men fighting with an unworthy enemy, says:—

> "So th' Emperor Caligula
> That triumphed o'er the British sea,
> Took crabs and oysters prisoners,
> And lobsters 'stead of cuirassiers;
> Engaged his legions in fierce bustles
> With periwinkles, prawns, and mussels,
> And led his troops with furious gallops
> To charge whole regiments of scallops;
> Not like their ancient way of war,
> To wait on his triumphal car;
> But, when he went to dine or sup,
> More bravely ate his captives up."

Butler begins one canto with

> "Ah me! what perils do environ
> The man that meddles with cold iron."

His political views are seen in the following:

> "For as a fly that goes to bed
> Rests with its tail above its head,
> So in this mongrel state of ours
> The rabble are the supreme powers.
> That horsed us on their backs to show us
> A jadish trick at last, and throw us."

Several minor poems have been attributed to Butler, but most of them have been considered spurious. Some, however, are admitted—one of which is a humorous skit against the Royal Society, who were supposed at that day to be too minutely subtle. It is called "An Elephant in the Moon." "Some learned astronomers think they have made a great discovery, but it is really owing to a mouse and some gnats having got into their telescope."

The light, short metre in which Butler composed his comic narrative was well suited to the subject, and corresponded to the "swift iambics" of Archilochus. Dryden says that double rhymes are necessary companions of burlesque writing. Addison, however, is of opinion that Hudibras "would have made a much more agreeable figure in heroics," to which Cowden Clarke replies, "Why, bless his head! the whole and sole intention of the poem is *mock* heroic, and the structure of the verse is burlesque," and he also tells us that Butler's rhymes constitute one feature of his wit. Certainly he had some strange terminations to his lines. Hudibras speaking of hanging Sidrophel and Whackum says:—

> "I'll make them serve for perpendiclars
> As true as e'er were used by bricklayers."

One of the bear-baiting mob annoys Rapho's steed, who

> "Began to kick, and fling, and wince,
> As if he'd been beside his sense,
> Striving to disengage from thistle
> That gall'd him sorely under his tail."

Again we have:—

> "An ancient castle that commands
> Th' adjacent parts, in all the fabric
> You shall not see one stone, nor a brick."

The astrologers made an instrument to examine the moon to

> "Tell what her diameter per inch is;
> And prove that she's not made of green cheese."

By the interchange which often takes place between the poetical and ludicrous, this roughness of versification, then allowable, appears now so childish, that Lamb and Cowden Clark mistook it for humour. But we might extract from the writers of that day many ridiculous rhymes, evidently intended to be serious.

The humour of Butler was in his time more popular than the sentiment of Milton, but he obtained no commensurate remuneration. Wycherley kindly endeavoured to interest Buckingham on his behalf, and had almost succeeded, when two handsome women passed by, and the Duke left him in pursuit of them. John Wesley's father has written Butler's epitaph in imperishable sarcasm:—

"See him when starved to death and turned to dust,
Presented with a monumental bust;
The poet's fate is here in emblem shown,
He asked for bread, and he received—a stone."

CHAPTER VIII.

Comic Drama of the Restoration—Etherege—Wycherley.

The example set by Beaumont and Fletcher seems to have been much followed by their immediate successors. Decker wrote conjointly with Webster and Middleton, and it is sometimes difficult to distinguish his work. His power of invective was well known; and in his humour there is such straining after strong words and effective phrases, as to seem quite unnatural. His "Gull's Hornbook" is written against coxcombs, and he says their "vinegar railings shall not quench his Alpine resolutions."

Etherege and Wycherley ushered in the comic drama of the Restoration. They were both courtiers, and the successful writers of this period took their tone from that of "the quality."

George, (afterwards Sir George) Etherege was born in 1636. He was known as "Gentle George" or "Easy Etherege," and it is said that he was himself a fop, and painted the character of Dorimant in Sir Fopling Flutter from himself. In his principal plays there is very little humour, though he gives some amusing sketches of the affectations of the metropolis.

> *Mistress Loveit.* You are grown an early riser, I hear.
> *Belinda.* Do you not wonder, my dear, what made me abroad so soon?
> *Lov.* You do not use to do so.
> *Bel.* The country gentlewomen I told you of (Lord! they have the oddest diversions) would never let me rest till I promised to go with them to the markets this morning, to eat fruit and buy nosegays.
> *Lov.* Are they so fond of a filthy nosegay?

Bel. They complain of the stinks of the town, and are never well but when they have their noses in one.

Lov. There are essences and sweet waters.

Bel. O, they cry out upon perfumes they are unwholesome, one of 'em was falling into a fit with the smell of these Narolii.

Lov. Methinks, in complaisance, you should have had a nosegay too.

Bel. Do you think, my dear, I could be so loathsome to trick myself up with carnations and stock-gilly flowers? I begged their pardon, and told them I never wore anything but Orange-flowers and Tuberose. That which made me willing to go was a strange desire I had to eat some fresh nectarines.

Wycherley was the son of a Shropshire gentleman who being a Royalist, and not willing to trust him to the Puritans, sent him to be educated in France. He became a Roman Catholic, but afterwards recanted.

Wycherley was remarkable for his beauty, and stalwart proportions, he was called "manly" or "brawny" Wycherley; and the notorious Duchess of Cleveland was so captivated by his appearance, that she made his acquaintance when passing in her carriage by jocosely calling out at him some abusive epithets. Afterwards, we are told that she often visited Wycherley at the Temple, disguised as a country girl in a straw hat, with pattens on her feet, and a basket on her arm. Later, he had the misfortune to make the acquaintance of the Countess of Drogheda on the Pantiles at Tunbridge Wells, and by secretly marrying her incurred the King's displeasure. He was finally reduced to great distress, but James II., recognising his talent, gave him a pension, and saved him from destitution in his old age.

Wycherley wrote his first play in 1667. In comparing him with Shakespeare we find the same difference as existed between the old and new comedy in Greece. Political characters have disappeared together with hostility and combats on the stage, while amorous intrigue is largely developed. There is at the same time considerable sprightliness in the dialogue, and the tricks, deceptions and misadventures of lovers fill the pages with much that is ingenious and amusing. In the "Gentleman Dancing Master," a young spark pretends to a rich father that he is only visiting his daughter to teach her to dance. A rival lover—a Frenchified puppy—is made unconsciously to co-operate in his own discomfiture, while the duped father jokes with the supposed "dancing master," and asks him whether he is not engaged to one of his rich pupils, laughing heartily at the picture he draws to himself of her father's indignation. Again, in "A Country Wife," a jealous husband obliges his spouse to write a disdainful letter to a gallant, but the lady slyly substitutes one of quite a different character, which the husband duly and pompously delivers to him. The humour of Wycherley is almost entirely of this kind. Here are no verbal quips, no sallies of professed fools, no stupidities of country boobies. These have passed away from good comedy. Speaking of the change, he says that formerly they were contented to make serving-men fools on the stage, "but now you shall scarcely see a fool on the stage who is not a knight." The fact was that a higher kind of humour was required, and accordingly we now, for the first time, hear of "wits"—men of good birth and position, who prided themselves on their talent. They were generally remarkable for their manners and address, and affected a superiority in acuteness, but not always in humour. Wycherley speaks of wits not exactly in the sense of humorists, but rather as coxcombs, endued with a certain cunning: "Your court wit is a fashionable, insinuating, flattering, cringing, grimacing fellow, and has wit enough to solicit a suit of love; and if he fail he has malice enough to ruin the woman with a dull lampoon; but he rails still at the man that is absent, for all wits rail; and his wit properly lies in combing perukes, matching ribbons, and being severe, as they call it, upon other peoples' clothes."

> *Lydia.* Now, what is your coffee wit?
>
> *Dapperwit.* He is a lying, censorious, gossiping, quibbling wretch, and sets people together by the ears over that sober drink—coffee; he is a wit as he is a commentator upon the Gazette; and he rails at the pirates of Algiers, the Grand Signior of Constantinople, and the Christian Grand Signior.
>
> *Lydia.* What kind of wit is your pollwit?

Dap. He is a fidgetting, busy, dogmatical, hot-headed fop, that speaks always in sentences and proverbs, and he rails perpetually against the present Government. His wit lies in projects and monopolies, and penning speeches for Parliament men—

He goes on to speak of the scribble wit, and judge wit or critic, but in general wits were regarded as rakes and not long afterwards we find it debated whether a woman can be witty and virtuous.

Wycherley did not aim much at facetiousness, nor introduce many humorous episodes, but passages incidentally occur which show he had considerable talent in that direction. The first from "Love in a Wood," is an ironical conflict between one Gripe, a rich but parsimous Alderman, and a Mrs. Joyner, a sly, designing old woman.

Gripe. I am full of your praise, and it will run over.

Joyner. Nay, sweet Sir, you are—

Gripe. Nay, sweet Mrs. Joyner, you are—

Joy. Nay, good your worship, you are—

(Stops her mouth with his handkerchief)

Gripe. I say you are—

Joy. I must not be rude with your worship.

Gripe. You are a nursing mother to the saints; through you they gather together, through you they fructify and increase, and through you the child cries out of the hand-basket.

Joy. Through you virgins are married, or provided for as well; through you the reprobate's wife is made a saint; and through you the widow is not disconsolate, nor misses her husband.

Gripe. Through you—

Joy. Indeed you will put me to the blush.

Gripe. Blushes are badges of imperfection—Saints have no shame.

You are the flower of matrons, Mrs. Joyner.

Joy. You are the pink of courteous Aldermen.

Gripe. You are the muffler of secrecy.

Joy. You are the head-band of Justice.

Gripe. Thank you, sweet Mrs. Joyner; do you think so indeed? You are—you are the bonfire of devotion.

Joy. You are the bellows of zeal.

Gripe. You are the cupboard of charity.

Joy. You are the fob of liberality.

Gripe. You are the rivet of sanctified love or wedlock.

Joy. You are the pick-lock and dark-lantern of policy; and in a word a conventicle of virtues.

Gripe. Your servant, your servant, sweet Mrs. Joyner! You have stopped my mouth.

Joy. Your servant, your servant, sweet Alderman! I have nothing to say.

Indelicacy in words has by this time become very much reduced, although here and there we find some cant expressions of the day which shock our sensibilities. Much refinement in this respect could not be expected at a period where a young lady of fortune could be represented as calling her maid, and afterwards herself, a "damned jade," and a lady from the country as saying she had not yet had "her bellyful of sights" in London.

"The Plain Dealer" is a naval captain in the time of the Dutch war. Olivia says,

"If he be returned, then shall I be pestered again with his boisterous sea-love; have my alcove smell like a cabin, my chamber perfumed with his tarpaulin Brandenburgh, and hear volleys of brandy-sighs, enough to make a fog in one's room. Foh! I hate a lover that smells like Thames Street."

The Plain Dealer, *i.e.*, the sea-captain Manly, meets with a lawyer, and they converse in this way,

Manly. Here's a lawyer I know threatening us with another greeting.

Lawyer. Sir! Sir! your very servant; I was afraid you had forgotten me.

Man. I was not afraid you had forgotten me.

Law. No, Sir; we lawyers have pretty good memories.

Man. You ought to have by your wits.

Law. O, you are a merry gentleman, Sir; I remember you were merry when I was last in your company.

Man. I was never merry in your company, Mr. Lawyer, sure.

Law. Why I am sure you joked upon me, and shammed me all night long.

Man. Shammed! prithee what barbarous law-term is that?

Law. Shamming! why, don't you know that? 'tis all our way of wit, Sir.

Man. I am glad I don't know it, then. Shamming! what does he mean by it, Freeman?

Free. Shamming is telling an insipid dull lie with a dull face, which the sly wag, the author, only laughs at himself; and making himself believe 'tis a good jest, puts the sham only upon himself.

Manly meets an Alderman.

Man. Here's a city-rogue will stick as hard upon us as if I owed him money.

Ald. Captain, noble Sir, I am yours heartily, d'ye see; why should you avoid your old friends?

Man. And why should you follow me? I owe you nothing.

Ald. Out of my hearty respects to you; for there is not a man in England—

Man. Thou wouldst save from hanging at the expense of a shilling only.

Ald. Nay, nay, but Captain, you are like enough to tell me—

Man. Truth, which you wont care to hear; therefore you had better go talk with somebody else.

Ald. No, I know nobody can inform me better of some young wit or spendthrift, who has a good dipped seat and estate in Middlesex, Hertfordshire, Essex, or Kent; any of these would serve my turn; now if you know of such an one, and would but help—

Man. You to finish his ruin.

Ald. I' faith you should have a snip—

Man. Of your nose, you thirty in the hundred rascal; would you make me your squire-setter?

(Takes him by the nose.)

Two lovers, Lord Plausible and Novel, have the following dialogue about their chances of success with a certain lady who is wooed by both.

> *Novel.* Prithee, prithee, be not impertinent, my lord; some of
> you lords are such conceited, well assured impertinent
> rogues.
> *Plausible.* And you noble wits are so full of shamming and
> drollery, one knows not where to have you seriously.
> *Nov.* Prithee, my lord, be not an ass. Dost thou think to get
> her from me? I have had such encouragements—
> *Plau.* I have not been thought unworthy of 'em.
> *Nov.* What? not like mine! Come to an éclaircissement, as
> I said.
> *Plau.* Why, seriously then; she told me Viscountess sounded
> prettily.
> *Nov.* And me, that Novel was a name she would sooner
> change hers for, than any title in England.
> *Plau.* She has commended the softness and respectfulness
> of my behaviour.
> *Nov.* She has praised the briskness of my raillery in all
> things, man.
> *Plau.* The sleepiness of my eyes she liked.
> *Nov.* Sleepiness! dulness, dulness. But the fierceness of
> mine she adored.
> *Plau.* The brightness of my hair she liked.
> *Nov.* Brightness! no the greasiness, I warrant! But the
> blackness and lustre of mine she admires.
> *Plau.* The gentleness of my smile.
> *Nov.* The subtilty of my leer.
> *Plau.* The clearness of my complexion.
> *Nov.* The redness of my lips.
> *Plau.* The whiteness of my teeth.
> *Nov.* My jaunty way of picking them.
> *Plau.* The sweetness of my breath.
> *Nov.* Ha! ha! nay there she abused you, 'tis plain; for you
> know what Manly said: the sweetness of your pulvillio
> she might mean; but for your breath! ha! ha! ha! Your

breath is such, man, that nothing but tobacco can perfume; and your complexion nothing could mend but the small-pox.

CHAPTER IX.

Tom Brown—His Prose Works—Poetry—Sir Richard Blackmore—D'Urfey—Female Humorists—Carey.

Whether it was owing to the commotions of the Civil War in which "fears and jealousies had soured the people's blood, and politics and polemics had almost driven mirth and good humour out of the nation," or whether it was from a dearth of eminent talent, humour seems to have made little progress under the Restoration. The gaiety of the Merry Monarch and his companions had nothing intellectual in it, and although "Tom" Brown[61] tells us that "it was during the reign of Charles II. that learning in general flourished, and the Muses, like other ladies, met with the civilest sort of entertainment," his own works show that the best wits of the day could not soar much above the attempts of Sedley and Rochester. Had Brown not acquired in his day the character of a humorist, we should think that he equally well deserved that of a man of learning, for whereas he shows an acquaintance with the classics and modern languages, his writings, which are of considerable length, contain little Attic salt. He was born in 1663, the son of a substantial Shropshire farmer, and was sent to Christ Church, Oxford, where he became as remarkable for his quickness and proficiency, as for the irregularity of his conduct. On one occasion, owing to his having been guilty of some objectionable frolic, he was about to be expelled, when, upon his writing a penitential letter, the Dean, who seems to have known his talent, promised to forgive him on his translating extempore the epigram of Martial.

> "Non amo te, Zabidi, nec possum dicere quare;
> Hoc tantum possum dicere non amo te."

The young delinquent replied in words now better known than the original,

> "I do not love you, Dr. Fell,
> But why I cannot tell,
> But this I know full well,
> I do not love you, Dr. Fell."

At this period he occasionally indulged in such silly effusions as the "Adverbial Declaration," which he first wrote in Latin, on "Mother Warner's bellows at Oxford."

Brown was finally obliged to leave the University, and went up to London to seek his fortune. The unpromising and reckless spirit in which he set out, is probably reflected in one of his pieces entitled "A Dialogue between two Oxford scholars."

A. Well, I see thou art resolved to leave us. I will not say, "Go, and be hanged," but go and turn country parson.

B. That's almost as bad, as the world goes now. But thanks to my stars, I know a better trick than that.

A. It may be thou art fallen out with mankind, and intendest to turn quack; or as they call it in the country, doctor.

B. No such matter; the *French* can kill men fast enough, and for women thou knowest my kindness.

A. But some of them have lived too long; and there are others so miserable, that even compassion will incline thee to help them out of the world. I can assure thee 'tis a profitable calling; for whether thou dost kill or cure, thy fees will be put in thy hand.

B. Yes, when they are found. But, prithee, speak no more of it, for I am resolved against it.

A. What, then, art thou resolv'd for the law? Methinks thou should'st have too much University learning and wit for that profession—

B. And too much honesty. But I'll spare thee the pains of guessing, and tell thee in short what my condition is, and what I design. My portion is all spent—save fifty pounds; and with that I am resolved for London or some other wealthy place, where conventicles abound:

and as a man of tender conscience and infinitely dissatisfied with several things in the Church of England, I will endeavour by some means or other to force myself into an acquaintance with some of their leading men, and more especially with some of the most zealous and wonderful women among them; and this point once gained, I doubt not, but before my stock is half spent, I shall receive a call to be pastor or holder-forth in some congregation or other—why dost smile?

A. At my friend's design. And I cannot but admire how it came into thy head. Thy ability to manage such a design I know very well; but how thou wilt dispense with the knavery of it, I am yet to learn.

B. That's a small matter. As the world goes one must practise a little knavery, or resolve to leave the world. Dost thou know that religious cheats are licensed by a law? and shall I live and die without taking advantage of it? Believe me, friend, Nature has fitted me pretty well to be one of these godly mountebanks, and a little art, together with a few months' conversation with that sort of people will supply all natural defects. Cannot I put on, when I please, a grave and serious countenance, and with head depending on one shoulder a little more than on the other, sigh for the iniquities of the time and corruptions of the Church? Cannot I wipe mine eyes with the fair pocket-cloth, as if I wept for all your abominations? Cannot I grieve in spirit as if ready to burst with grief and compassion. And cannot I likewise, when time serves, and company is disposed to be kindly affected with it, smile and fleer as takingly? And what hurt is there in this? Sure I may use my own face as I please.

We need scarcely say that Brown failed in his shrewd scheming; and he was soon fain to take the humble position of a schoolmaster at Kingston upon Thames, for which his acquirements qualified him. But his literary ambition would not allow him to remain long at this drudgery, and we soon find him wandering up again to town, where he was again unfortunate. At this time, men of letters expected little from the sale of books; but often obtained patrons who conferred valuable appointments upon them. Brown's temper and position rendered him ineligible for this sort of promotion. Not being a gentleman by birth, he had no good introductions, nor would he have been very acceptable in the houses of the great. His coarseness in writing—excessive even in that day—was probably reflected in his manners and language, and he had so little prudence that he ridiculed not only the clergy, but was always ready to lose a friend rather than a joke. Mere literary talent will not procure success in society.

Brown wrote a variety of essays, generally rather admonitory than humorous. His "Pocket-book of Common Places" resembles a collection of Proverbs or good sayings. It commences,

"To see the number of churches and conventicles open every Sunday, a stranger would fancy London all religion. But to see the number of taverns, ale-houses, &c., he would imagine Bacchus was the only God that is worshipped there. If no *trades* were permitted but those which were useful and necessary, Lombard Street, Cheapside, and the Exchange might go a-begging. For more are fed by our *vanities* and *vices* than by our virtues, and the necessities of Nature."

But his favourite and characteristic mode of writing was under the form of letters. We have "Letters Serious and Comical," "Diverting Letters to Gentlemen." One letter is to four ladies with whom the author was in love at the same time.

He probably took his idea of "Letters from the Dead to the Living," from Lucian. He never spares Dissenters, and comically makes a Quaker relate his warm reception in the lower world:—

"A parcel of black spiritual Janissaries saluted me as intimately as if I had been resident in these parts during the term of an apprenticeship; at last, up comes a swinging, lusty, overgrown, austere devil, armed with an ugly weapon like a country dung-fork, looking as sharp about the eyes as a Wood Street officer, and seemed to deport himself after such a manner that discovered he had ascendancy over the rest of the immortal negroes, and as I imagined, so 'twas quickly evident; for as soon as he espied me leering between the diminutive slabbering-bib and the extensive rims of my coney-wood umbrella, he chucks me under the chin with his ugly toad-coloured paw, that stunk as bad of brimstone as a card-match new-lighted, saying, 'How now, Honest Jones, I am glad to see thee on this side the river Styx, prithee, hold up thy head, and don't be ashamed, thou art not the first Quaker by many thousands that has sworn allegiance to my government; besides, thou hast been one of my best benefactors on earth, and now thou shalt see, like a grateful devil, I'll reward thee accordingly.' 'I thank your excellence kindly,' said I, 'pray, what is it your infernal protectorship will be pleased to confer upon me?' To which his mighty ugliness replied, 'Friend Naylor, I know thou hast been very industrious to make many people fools in the upper world, which has highly conduced to my interest.' Then turning to a pigmy aërial, who attended his commands as a running footman, 'Haste, *Numps*,' says he, 'and fetch me the painted coat,' which was no sooner brought, but by Lucifer's command I was shoved into it, neck and shoulders, by half a dozen swarthy *valets de chambre*, and in a minute's time found myself tricked up in a rainbow-coloured coat, like a merry-Andrew. 'Now, friend,' says the ill-favoured prince of all the hell-born scoundrels, 'for the many fools you have made above, I now ordain you mine below;' so all the reward truly of my great services was to be made Lucifer's jester, or fool in ordinary to the devil; a pretty post, thought I, for a man of my principles, that from a Quaker in the outer world I should be metamorphosed into a jack-adam in the lower one."

The occupation of people in the Nether world is described after Rabelais, thus:—"Cardinal Mazarin keeps a nine-holes; Mary of Medicis foots stockings; and Katharine of Sweden cries 'Two bunches a penny card-matches—two bunches a penny!' Henry the Fourth of France carries a raree-show, and Mahomet sells mussels. Seneca keeps a fencing-school, and Julius Cæsar a two-penny ordinary."

At the present day it is rather amusing to read, "A Comical View of London and Westminster"—a weekly prophecy intended to ridicule the increasing use of barometers and other scientific instruments for predicting changes of weather.

"Wednesday October 16th. Cloudy, foggy weather at Garraway's and Jonathan's, and at most coffee-houses at about twelve. Crowds of people gather at the Exchange by one; disperse by three. Afternoon, noisy and bloody at her Majesty's bear-garden at *Hockly-in-the-Hole*. Night—sober with broken chaplains and others that have neither credit nor money. This week's transactions censured by the virtuosos at *Child's* from morning till night.

"Thursday 17th. Coffee and water-gruel to be had at the Rainbow and Nando's at four. Hot furmity at Bride-bridge at seven. Justice to be had at *Doctor's Commons*, when people can get it. A lecture at Pinner's hall at ten. Excellent pease-pottage and tripe in Baldwin's Gardens at twelve. A constable and two watchmen killed, or near being so in *Westminster*, whether by a lord or lord's footman, planets don't determine.

"Friday. Damsels whipped for their good nature at *Bridewell* about ten. Several people put in fear of their lives by their god-fathers at the *Old Bailey* at eleven. Great destruction of Herrings at one. Much swearing at three among the horse-coursers at Smithfield; if the oaths were registered as well as the horses, good Lord, what a volume 'twould make! Several tails turned up at St. Paul's School, Merchant Taylors, &c. for their repetitioning. Night very drunk, as the two former.

"Saturday 19th. Twenty butchers' wives in Leadenhall and Newgate markets overtaken with sherry and sugar by eight in the morning. Shop-keepers walk out at nine to count the trees in Moorfields, and avoid duns. People's houses cleansed in the afternoon, but their consciences we don't know when. Evening pretty sober.

"Sunday. Beggars take up their posts in Lincoln's Inn Fields and other places by seven, that they may be able to praise God in capon and March beer at night. Great jingling of bells all over the city from eight to nine. Parish clerks liquor their throats plentifully at eight, and chaunt out Hopkins most melodiously about ten. Sextons, men of great authority most part of the day, whip dogs out of the church for being obstreperous. Great thumping and dusting of the cushion at Salter's Hall about eleven; one would almost think the man was in earnest he lays so furiously about him. A most refreshing smell of garlic in Spittlefield's and Soho at twelve. Country fellows staring at the two wooden men at St. Dunstan's from one to two, to see how notably they strike the quarters. The great point of Predestination settled in Russell-court about three; and the people go home as wise as they came. Afternoon sleepy in most churches. Store of handkerchiefs stolen at St. Paul's. Night, not so sober as might be wished . . ."

The following are some of the best specimens of Brown's poems—squibs on the fashions and occurrences of the day—

> "The *emblem of the nation*, so grave and precise,
> On the *emblem of wisdom* has laid an excise;
> Pray tell me, grave sparks, and your answer don't smother,
> Why one representative taxes another?
> The *Commons* on *salt* a new impost have laid
> To tax *wisdom* too, they most humbly are pray'd;
> For tell me ye patrons of woollen and crape,
> Why the *type* should be fined and the substance escape?"

A song in ridicule of a famous musician, who was caught serenading his mistress with his bass-viol on a very frosty night:—

> Look down, fair garreteer bestow
>   One glance upon your swain,
> Who stands below in frost and snow.
>   And shaking sings in pain.
>
> Thaw with your eyes the frozen street,
>   Or cool my hot desire,
> I burn within, altho' my feet
>   Are numbed for want of fire.
>
> *Chorus.*
>
> Thrum, thrum, thrum, thrum,
> Come, come, come, come,
>   My dearest be not coy,
> For if you are (zit, zan, zounds) I
>   Must without your favour die.

The sentiment in the following is easily appreciated, but is there not also some slight essence of humour?

ON FLOWERS IN A LADY'S BOSOM.

Behold the promised land, where pleasures flow!
See how the milk-white hills do gently rise,
    And beat the silken skies!
Behold the valley spread with flowers below!
The happy flowers, how they allure my sense!
The fairer soil gives them the nobler hue
    Her breath perfumes them too:
Rooted i' th' heart they seem to spring from thence,
Tell, tell me why, thou fruitful virgin breast,
Why should so good a soil lie unpossest?

Brown's humour partook of the coarseness of most of the writers of his times, and scandalized the more religious and decent muse of Sir Richard Blackmore, who endeavoured to correct this general failing in his "Satire upon Wit." This called forth many sarcastic replies, and critiques on Blackmore's works; such as Brown's "Epigram occasioned by the news that Sir R—d B—e's paraphrase upon Job was in the Press—"

"When Job contending with the devil I saw
It did my wonder, not my pity draw;
For I concluded that without some trick,
A saint at any time could match old Nick.
Next came a fiercer fiend upon his back,
I mean his spouse, stunning him with her clack,
But still I could not pity him, as knowing
A crab tree cudgel soon would send her going.
But when the quack engaged with Job I spy'd,
The Lord have mercy on poor Job I cry'd.
What spouse and Satan did attempt in vain
The quack will compass with his murdering pen,
And on a dunghill leave poor Job again,
With impious doggrel he'll pollute his theme,
And make the saint against his will blaspheme."

Upon the knighting of Sir R—d B—e.

"Be not puffed up with knighthood, friend of mine,
A merry prince once knighted a Sir-loin,
And if to make comparisons were safe
An ox deserves it better then a calf.
Thy pride and state I value not a rush
Thou that art now Knight Phyz, wast once King Ush."

Blackmore, who was successively physician to William III. and Queen Anne, had been once a schoolmaster.

Tom Brown died at the early age of forty. His life was full of misfortunes, but we can scarcely say that he was unhappy, for nothing could conquer his buoyant spirit. At one time he was actually in prison, for what was deemed a libellous attack, but we are told that he obtained his "enlargement" from it, upon his writing the following Pindaric Petition to the Lords in Council.

"Should you order Tho' Brown
To be whipped thro' the town
For scurvy lampoon,
Grave *Southern* and *Crown*
Their pens wou'd lay down;
Even D'Urfey himself, and such merry fellows
That put their whole trust in tunes and trangdillioes
May hang up their harps and themselves on the willows;
For if poets are punished for libelling trash
John Dryden, tho' sixty, may yet fear the lash.
No pension, no praise,
Much birch without bays,
These are not right ways
Our fancy to raise,
To the writing of plays
And prologues so witty
That jirk at the city,
And now and then hit
Some spark in the pit,
So hard and so pat
Till he hides with his hat
His monstrous cravat.
The pulpit alone
Can never preach down

The fops of the town
    Then pardon Tho' Brown
And let him write on;
But if you had rather convert the poor sinner
His foul writing mouth may be stopped with a dinner.
Give him clothes to his back, some meat and some drink
Then clap him close prisoner without pen and ink
And your petitioner shall neither pray, write, or think."

Unfortunately his pecuniary difficulties were not removed, but accompanied him through life. What a strange mixture of gaiety, learning and destitution is brought before us, when on a clamorons dun vowing she would not leave him until she had her money, he exclaimed in an extempore version of two lines of Martial—

"Sextus, thou nothing ow'st, nothing I say!
He something owes, that something has to pay."

In an imitation of another epigram of Martial he gives an account of the unpromising position of his affairs:—

"Without formal petition
Thus stands my condition,
I am closely blocked up in a garret,
Where I scribble and smoke,
And sadly invoke
The powerful assistance of claret.
Four children and a wife
'Tis hard on my life,
Besides myself and a Muse
To be all clothed and fed,
Now the times are so dead,
By my scribbling of doggrel and news;
And what I shall do,
I'm a wretch if I know
So hard is the fate of a poet,
I must either turn rogue,
Or what's as bad—pedagogue,
And so drudge like a thing that has no wit."

How much are we indebted to the pecuniary embarrassments of poets for the interest we take in them. Who could read sentiment written by a man faring sumptuously every day? Towards the end of his life, Brown became acquainted with Lord Dorset, and we read of his once dining with that nobleman and finding a note for fifty pounds under his plate. Tom Brown seems to have regarded with great contempt his contemporary Tom D'Urfey—best known as a composer of sonnets—words and music. He addresses to him "upon his incomparable ballads, called by him Pindaric Odes," the following acrimonious lines—

> "Thou cur, half French half English breed,
> Thou mongrel of Parnassus,
> To think tall lines, run up to seed,
> Should ever tamely pass us.

> "Thou write Pindaricks and be damned
> Write epigrams for cutlers,
> None with thy lyricks can be shammed
> But chambermaids and butlers.

> "In t'other world expect dry blows;
> No tears can wash thy stains out,
> Horace will pluck thee by the nose
> And Pindar beat thy brains out."

Such unworthy attacks are not unfrequently made by ill-natured literary men. Brown was no doubt jealous of his rival, but Addison's generous heart formed a very different estimate of D'Urfey's talent. He says that after having "made the world merry he hopes they will make him easy" in his pecuniary affairs, for that although "Tom" had written more Odes than Horace, and four times as many Comedies as Terence, he was reduced to great difficulties by a set of men who had furnished him with the accommodations of life, and would not, as we say, "be paid with a song." "As my friend," he continues, "after the manner of all the old lyrics, accompanies his works with his own voice, he has been the delight of the most polite companies and conversations from the beginning of King Charles II.'s reign to our present times.

Many an honest gentleman has got a reputation in his country by pretending to have been in company with Tom D'Urfey." "I myself remember King Charles II. leaning on Tom D'Urfey's shoulder more than once, and humming over a song with him. It is certain that monarch was not a little supported by 'Joy to great Cæsar,' which gave the Whigs such a blow as they were not able to recover that whole reign. My friend afterwards attacked Popery with the same success—he has made use of Italian tunes and Sonatas for promoting the Protestant interest, and turned a considerable part of the Pope's music against himself."

Little need be added to this eloquent commendation, except that it was written to obtain patronage for a benefit in behalf of an aged poet and friend. D'Urfey wrote through the reigns of Charles II., James II., William and Anne, into that of George I. His plays, which were thought attractive at the time, contained much that was gross, and were deficient in humour and power. Thus, they were soon forgotten, and neither he nor his rival Brown were able to reach a point, which would give them a permanent position in literature.

The following description would have led us to expect something better of him, at least in farcical talent[62]—

"Mr. D'Urfey generally writes state-plays, and is wonderfully useful to the world in such representations. This method is the same that was used by the old Athenians, to laugh out of countenance or promote opinions among the people. My friend has therefore against this play is acted for his own benefit, made two dances which may be also of an universal benefit. In the first he has represented absolute power in the person of a tall man with a hat and feathers, who gives his first minister who stands just before him a huge kick; the minister gives the kick to the next before; and so to the end of the stage. In this moral and practical jest you are made to understand that there is in an absolute government no gratification, but giving the kick you receive from one above you to one below you. This is performed to a grave and melancholy air; but on a sudden the tune moves quicker, and the whole company fall into a circle and take hands; and then, at a certain sharp note, they move round and kick as kick can. This latter performance he makes to be the representation of a free state; where, if you all mind your steps, you may go round and round very jollily, with a motion pleasant to yourselves and them you dance with: nay, if you put yourselves out, at the worst you only kick and are kicked by friends and equals."

But D'Urfey's short songs and poems were his most successful productions—sometimes he breathed martial strains in honour of Marlborough's victories, sometimes formed adulatory addresses to members of the Royal Family. His "Pills to purge Melancholy," at times approached humour. The following is taken from the "Banquet of the Gods," and refers to Hermes visiting the Infernal regions—

> "Fierce Cerberus, who the gate did keep,
> First with a sop he lays asleep,
> Then forward goes to th' room of State,
> Where on a lofty throne of jet,
> The grizly King of Terrors sate,
> Discoursing with his Proserpine
> On things infernally divine.
> To him the winged Ambassador
> His message tells, then adds to her
> How much her mother Ceres mourns
> In Sicily, till she returns;
> That now she hoped (the long half-year
> Being ended) she would see her there,
> And that instead of shrieks and howls,
> The harmony of par-boiled souls,
> She'd now divert with tunes more gay,
> And go with her to see a play."

D'Urfey often introduces fresh and pleasing glimpses of country life. He is more happy in this direction than in his humour, which generally drifted away into maudlin and indelicate love-making between pseudo-Roman Corydons and Phyllises. The following effusion is very characteristic of the times,—

"One *April* morn, when from the sea
Phoebus was just appearing!
Damon and Celia young and gay,
Long settled Love indearing;
Met in a grove to vent their spleen,
On parents unrelenting;
He bred of *Tory* race had been,
She of the tribe *Dissenting.*

"Celia, whose eyes outshone the God,
Newly the hills adorning,
Told him mamma wou'd be stark mad,
She missing prayers that morning;
Damon, his arm around her waist,
Swore tho' nought should 'em sunder,
Shou'd my rough dad know how I'm blest,
T'would make him roar like thunder.

"Great ones whom proud ambition blinds,
By faction still support it,
Or where vile money taints the mind,
They for convenience court it;
But mighty Love, that scorns to show,
Party should raise his glory;
Swears he'll exalt a vassal true,
Let it be *Whig* or *Tory.*"

The following is a song from "The Country Miss and her
Furbelow."

"Celladon, when spring came on,
Woo'd Sylvia in a grove,
Both gay and young, and still he sung
The sweet Delights of Love.
Wedded joys in girls and boys,
And pretty chat of this and that,
The honey kiss, and charming bliss
That crowns the marriage bed;
He snatched her hand, she blushed and fanned
And seemed as if afraid,

'Forbear!' she crys, 'youre fawning lyes,
I've vowed to die a maid.'

"Celladon at that began
To talk of apes in hell,
And what was worse, the odious curse
Of growing old and stale.
Loss of bloom, when wrinkles come,
And offers kind when none will mind,
The rosie joy, and sparkling eye
Grown faded and decayed,
At which, when known, she changed her tone,
And to the shepherd said,
'Dear swain, give o'er, I'll think once more,
Before I'll die a maid.'"

D'Urfey was a disciple of the "gentle art." Addison says "I must not omit that my friend angles for a trout, the best of any man in England. Mayflies come in late this season, or I myself should have had one of his hooking." We can thus understand his enthusiastic commendation of fishing—

"Of all the world's enjoyments,
That ever valu'd were,
There's none of our employments,
With fishing can compare;
Some preach, some write,
Some swear, some fight,
All golden lucre courting,
But fishing still bears off the bell
For profit or for sporting.

"Chorus.—Then who a jolly fisherman, a fisherman will be?
His throat must wet,
Just like his net,
To keep out cold at sea.
"The country squire loves running
A pack of well-mouthed hounds,
Another fancies gunning
For wild ducks in his grounds;

This hunts, that fowls,
This hawks, Dick bowls,
No greater pleasure wishing,
But Tom that tells what sport excels,
Gives all the praise to fishing.
Then who, &c.

"A good *Westphalia gammon*
Is counted dainty fare;
But what is't to a salmon
Just taken from the Ware;
Wheat-ears and quailes,
Cocks, snipes and rayles,
Are prized while season's lasting,
But all must stoop to crawfish soup,
Or I've no skill in casting.
Then who, &c.

"And tho' some envious wranglers,
To jeer us will make bold,
And laugh at patient anglers,
Who stand so long i' th' cold;
They wait on Miss,
We wait on this,
And think it easie labour;
And if you know, fish profits too,
Consult our *Holland* neighbour.
Then who, &c."

D'Urfey was a favourite with Queen Anne, and many of his poems were written at Knole, Penshurst, and other seats of the nobility.

Up to the time we have now reached, we have not had the opportunity of enrolling the name of a lady among our humorists. Although in society so many of the fair sparkle and overflow with quick and graceful raillery, we find that when they come to impress their thoughts upon paper they are invariably sentimental. Authors are often a contrast to their writings, but no doubt the female mind is generally of a poetical complexion. Thus, in the early part of the last century we meet with only three lady humorists, Mrs. Manley, mostly noted for her scandalous stories: Mrs. Behn, whose humour was crude, chiefly that of rough harlequinade and gross immorality, and Mrs. Centlivre. Early opportunities of study were afforded to the last in a remarkable way. When flying from the anger of her stepmother, she met Anthony Hammond, then at Cambridge, and went to live with him at the University, disguised in boy's clothes. Remarkable for her beauty, she married, when only fifteen, a nephew of Sir Stephen Fox, and upon his death at sixteen, a Captain Carrol, who was killed in a duel. It was then partly owing to pecuniary embarrassments that she went on the stage and wrote plays—the first of her dramas appearing in her twentieth year. So great was the prejudice then against lady writers, that at her publisher's suggestion her first production was anonymous. But those, who began by deriding her pretensions, ended by acknowledging her merit; she became a great favourite and constant writer for the stage, and an intimate friend of Farquhar and Steele. There is an absence of indelicacy in her plays, but not a little farcical humour, especially in the character of "Marplot" in "The Busybody," and of rich "Mrs. Dowdy" with her vulgarity and admirers in "The Platonic Lady." She often adopts the tone of the day in ridiculing learned ladies. In one place she speaks as if even at that time the founding of a college for ladies was in contemplation—

Lady Reveller. Why in such haste, Cousin Valeria?

Valeria. Oh! dear Cousin, don't stop me; I shall lose the finest insect for dissection, a huge flesh fly, which Mr. Lovely sent me just now, and opening the box to try the experiment, away it flew.

Lady. I am glad the poor fly escaped; will you never be weary of these whimsies?

Val. Whimsies! Natural Philosophy a whimsy! Oh! the unlearned world!

Lady. Ridiculous learning!

Mrs. Alpiew. Ridiculous indeed for women. Philosophy suits our sex as jack-boots would do.

Val. Custom would bring them as much in fashion as furbelows, and practice would make us as valiant as e'er a hero of them all; the resolution is in the mind. Nothing can enslave that.

Lady. My stars! This girl will be mad—that's certain.

Val. Mad! So Nero banished philosophers from *Rome*, and the first discoverer of the *Antipodes* was condemned for a heretic.

Lady. In my conscience, Alpiew, this pretty creature's spoiled. Well, cousin, might I advise you should bestow your fortune in founding a college for the study of philosophy, where none but women should be admitted; and to immortalize your name, they should be called *Valerians*,—ha! ha! ha!

Val. What you make a jest of, I'd execute, were fortune in my power.

Her notices of married life are interesting, as she had great experience, having taken for her third husband Mr. Centlivre, cook to Queen Anne. In "The Wonder, a Woman keeps a Secret," we have the following dialogue upon this important subject:

Col. Britton. 'Egad, I think I must e'en marry, and sacrifice my body for the good of my soul; wilt thou recommend me to a wife, then—one that is willing to exchange her moydores for English Liberty—ha friend?

Fred. She must be very handsome, I suppose?

Col. The handsomer the better, but be sure she has a nose.

Fred. Ay! ay! and some gold.

Col. Oh, very much gold. I shall never be able to swallow the matrimonial pill, if it be not well gilded.

Fred. Puh, beauty will make it slide down nimbly.

Col. At first, perhaps it may, but the second or third dose will choke me. I confess, Frederick, women are the prettiest playthings in nature; but gold, substantial gold gives 'em the air, the mien, the shape, the grace and beauty of a goddess.

Fred. And has not gold the same divinity in their eyes, Colonel?

Col. Too often—money is the very god of marriage, the poets dress him in a saffron robe by which they figure out the golden

Deity, and his lighted torch blazons those mighty charms, which encourage us to list under his banner.

In "The Artifice" we have a matrimonial contention:

Lucy. If you two are one flesh, how come you to have different minds, pray, Sir?

Watchit. Because the mind has nothing to do with the flesh.

Mrs. W. That's your mistake, Sir; the body is governed by the mind. So much philosophy I know.

Wat. Yes, yes; I believe you understand natural philosophy very well, wife; I doubt not the flesh has got the better of the spirit in you. Look ye, madam! every man's wife is his vineyard; you are mine, therefore I wall you in. Ods budikins, ne'er a coxcomb in the kingdom shall plant as much as a primrose in my ground.

Mrs. W. I am sure your management will produce nothing but thorns.

Wat. Nay, every wife is a thorn in her husband's side. Your whole sex is a kind of sweet-briar, and he who meddles with it is sure to prick his fingers.

Lucy. That is when you handle us too roughly.

Mrs. W. You are a kind of rue: neither good for smell nor taste.

Wat. But very wholesome, wife.

Mrs. W. Ay, so they say of all bitters, yet I would not be obliged to feed on gentian and wormwood.

Some subjects are peculiarly suitable for light female humour. In "The Beau's Duel, or a Soldier for the Ladies," we have the following soliloquy by Sir William Mode, a fop, as he stands in his night-gown looking into his glass:

This rising early is the most confounded thing on earth, nothing so destructive to the complexion. Blister me, how I shall look in the side box to-night, wretchedly upon my soul. *[looking in the glass all the while.]* Yet it adds something of a languishing air, not altogether unbecoming, and by candle light may do mischief; but I must stay at home to recover some colour, and that may be as well laid on too; so 'tis resolved I will go. Oh 'tis unspeakable pleasure to be in the side box, or bow'd to from the stage, and be distinguished by the beaux of quality, to have a lord fly into one's arms, and kiss one as amorously as a mistress. Then tell me aloud, that he dined with his Grace and that he and the ladies were so fond of me, they talked of nothing else. Then says I, "My lord, his Grace does me too much honour." Then, my lord, "This play 'tis not worth seeing; we havn't been seen at t'other house to-night; and the ladies will be disappointed not to receive a bow from Sir William." "He, he, he," says I, "my lord, I wait upon your lordship." "Then," says my lord, "lead the way Sir William." "O, pray my lord, I beg your lordship's pardon." "Nay, Sir William." "Pray my lord," *(Enter La Riviere, Sir W's valet).* "Pray Sir William." "Pray my lord."

(As he says this several times La Riviere enters behind him, but as he designs to pass by him, is still prevented by his turning from one side to t'other, as he acts himself for the lord.)

La Riv. Hey! What the devil is he conjuring and talking with invisible lords? He's in his airs, some pleasing imagination hurries him out of his senses. But I must to my cue. Hem! hem! Sir, dere be one two gentlemen below come to wait upon you dis morning, sal I show dem up?

Sir. W. No, my lord, by no means, I know better things—

La Riv. What then am I a lord? Egad I never knew my quality before. *(Aside.)*

Sir W. Pshaw! this blockhead has rous'd me from the prettiest entertainment in the world *(Aside).* Well, what would you, Sir?

La Riv. I voo'd tell you, Sir, dere be one two gentlemen wait upon you.

Sir W. And let 'em wait till I have done. I had a thousand fine things to say on that occasion, but this rude fellow has frightened 'em all out of my head. *(Aside.)* Well, since my better diversion is over, show 'em up.

In "The Wonder" we have an amusing scene between Lissardo, servant to Felix, and Flora, maid to Violante. The former had been very sweet upon the latter—telling her that his "chaps watered for a kiss," and that "he would revenge himself on her lips;" but a change comes over him on his being presented by Violante with a ring to be worn for his master's sake.

> *Lissardo.* I shall, Madam, *(puts on the ring.)* Methinks a diamond ring is a vast addition to the little finger of a gentleman. *(Admiring his hand.)*
>
> *Flora.* That ring must be mine. Well, Lissardo, what haste you make to pay off arrears now? Look how the fellow stands!
>
> *Liss.* Egad! methinks I have a very pretty hand—and very white—and the shape! Faith! I never minded it so much before! In my opinion it is a very fine shaped hand, and becomes a diamond ring as well as the first grandee's in Portugal.
>
> *Flo.* The man's transported! Is this your love? This your impatience?
>
> *Liss. (Takes snuff.)* Now in my mind, I take snuff with a very jaunty air. Well, I am persuaded I want nothing but a coach and a title to make me a very fine gentleman.
>
> *(Struts about.)*
>
> *Flo.* Sweet Mr. Lissardo, *(curtseying,)* if I may presume to speak to you, without affronting your little finger—
>
> *Liss.* Do so, Madam, I ask your pardon. Is it to me or to the ring you direct your discourse, Madam?
>
> *Flo.* Madam! Good lack! how much a diamond ring improves one!
>
> *Liss.* Why, tho' I say it, I can carry myself as well as anybody. But what wert thou going to say, child?
>
> *Flo.* Why, I was going to say, that I fancy you had best let me keep that ring; it will be a very pretty wedding-ring.
>
> *Liss.* Would it not? Humph! Ah! But—but—but—I believe I shan't marry yet a while.
>
> *Flo.* You shan't, you say; very well! I suppose you design that ring for Inis?
>
> *Liss.* No, no, I never bribe an old acquaintance. Perhaps I might let it sparkle in the eyes of a stranger a little, till we come to a right understanding. But then, like all other mortal things, it would return from whence it came.
>
> *Flo.* Insolent! Is that your manner of dealing?

Liss. With all but thee—kiss me, you little rogue, you.
(Hugging her.)
Flo. Little rogue! Prithee, fellow, don't be so familiar,
(pushing him away,) if I mayn't keep your ring, I can keep my
    kisses.
Liss. You can, you say! Spoke with the air of a
    chambermaid.
Flo. Reply'd with the spirit of a serving-man.

D'Urfey is said to have been the first, and Carey the last
of those who at this period united the professions of musician,
dramatist and song writer. The latter was the natural son of the
Marquis of Halifax, who presented the crown to William III. He
wrote the popular song "Sally in our Alley," and ridiculed Ambrose
Philips in a poem called "Namby Pamby." Overcome either by
embarrassed circumstances, or the envy of rivals, he died by his own
hand in 1743. He has much that is clever mingled with extravagant
fancies. Most of his songs are amorous, though never indelicate.
Some are for drinking bouts.

"Come all ye jolly Bucchanals
That love to tope good wine,
Let's offer up a hogshead
Unto our master's shrine,
Come, let us drink and never shrink,
For I'll tell you the reason why,
It's a great sin to leave a house till we've drunk the cellar dry.
In times of old I was a fool,
I drank the water clear,
But Bacchus took me from that rule,
He thought 'twas too severe;
He filled a bumper to the brim
And bade me take a sup,
But had it been a gallon pot,
By Jove I'd tossed it up.
And ever since that happy time,
Good wine has been my cheer,
Now nothing puts me in a swoon
But water or small beer.
Then let us tope about, my lads,

And never flinch nor fly,
But fill our skins brimfull of wine,
And drain the bottles dry."

Many of his plays were burlesque operas, introducing songs. In one of them the "Dragon of Wantley," we have—

"Zeno, Plato, Aristotle,
All were lovers of the bottle;
Poets, Painters, and Musicians,
Churchmen, Lawyers, and Physicians;
All admire a pretty lass,
All require a cheerful glass,
Every pleasure has its season,
Love and drinking are no treason."
He was fond of jocose love-ditties, such as:
"Pigs shall not be
So fond as we;
We will out-coo the turtle-dove,
Fondly toying,
Still enjoying,
Sporting sparrows we'll outlove."

Among his successful farces is the well-known Chrononhotonthologos written to ridicule some bombastic tragedies of the day. Chrononhotonthologos is king of Queerummania, Bombardinian is his general, while his courtiers are Aldiborontiphoscophornio and Rigdum Funnidos. The following gives a good specimen of his ballad style.

"O! London is a dainty place,
A great and gallant city,
For all the streets are paved with gold,
And all the folks are witty.

"And there's your lords and ladies fine,
That ride in coach-and-six,
Who nothing drink but claret wine,
And talk of politicks.

"And there's your beauxs with powdered clothes,
Bedaubed from head to shin;
Their pocket-holes adorned with gold,
But not one sous within."

CHAPTER X.

Vanbrugh—Colley Cibber—Farquhar.

Vanbrugh—a man of Dutch extraction as his name suggests—was one of the few whom literature led, though indirectly, to fortune. He became first known as a playwriter, but also having studied architecture conceived the idea of combining his two arts by the construction of a grand theatre on the site of the present Haymarket Opera House. The enterprise was doomed to be one of the many failures from which that ill-starred spot has become remarkable, and Vanbrugh after vainly attempting to support his undertaking by the exertion of all his dramatic power, determined to quit literature altogether, and devoted himself to the more remunerative profession. In this he was successful—he built Blenheim, Castle Howard, and half-a-dozen of the stately halls of England. We may suppose that he acquired wealth, for he built several houses for himself, and in them seems to have exhibited his whimsical fancy. One which he built near Whitehall was called by Swift "a thing like a goose pie," and he called that which he built for himself, near Greenwich, "the mince pie."

There is a considerable amount of rough humour in Vanbrugh, and some indelicacy, more like that of Aristophanes than of English writers. We find one gentleman calling another "Old Satan," and fashionable ladies indulging freely in oaths. A nobleman tells a lady, before her husband, that he is desperately in love with her, "strike me speechless;" to which she replies by giving him a box on the ear, and her husband by drawing his sword. Everything bespeaks a low and primitive state of society; but we must also remember that while something strong was required, it was not then thought objectionable that the scenes of the drama should be very different from those of real life.

The following are from the "Relapse," the first play that made Vanbrugh known, and which we might therefore expect to be one of his most humorous comedies. Here we have a good caricature of the fops of the day. In the first, Lord Foppington in his fashionable twang, gives us his views, and sketches his mode of life.

Amanda. Well I must own I think books the best entertainment in the world.

Lord F. I am so much of your ladyship's mind, madam, that I have a private gallery where I walk sometimes, which is furnished with nothing but books and looking glasses. Madam, I have gilded 'em so prettily, before G—, it is the most entertaining thing in the world to walk and look upon 'em.

Amanda. Nay, I love a neat library too, but 'tis I think the inside of a book should recommend it most to us.

Lord F. That, I must confess, I am not altogether so fond of. For to my mind the inside of a book is to entertain oneself with the forced product of another man's brain. Now, I think a man of quality and breeding may be much better diverted with the natural sprouts of his own. But to say the truth, madam, let a man love reading never so well, when once he comes to know this town, he finds so many better ways of passing away the four-and-twenty hours that 'twere ten thousand pities he should consume his time in that. For example, madam, my life, my life, madam, is a perpetual stream of pleasure that glides through such a variety of entertainments, I believe the wisest of our ancestors never had the least conception of any of 'em. I rise, madam, about ten o'clock. I don't rise sooner because it is the worst thing in the world for the complexion, not that I pretend to be a beau, but a man must endeavour to look wholesome, lest he make so nauseous a figure in the side box, the ladies should be compelled to turn their eyes upon the play. So at ten o'clock I say I rise. Now, if I find it a good day I resolve to take a turn in the park, and see the fine women; so huddle on my clothes and get dressed by one. If it be nasty weather I take a turn in the chocolate house, where as you walk, madam, you have the prettiest prospect in the world; you have looking glasses all round you. But I'm afraid I tire the company.

Berinthia. Not at all; pray go on.

Lord F. Why then, ladies, from thence I go to dinner at Lacket's, where you are so nicely and delicately served that, stab my vitals! they shall compose you a dish no bigger than a saucer, shall come to fifty shillings. Between eating my dinner (and washing my mouth, ladies) I spend my time till I go to the play, when till nine o'clock I entertain myself with looking upon the company; and usually dispose of one hour more in leading them out. So there's twelve of the four-and-twenty pretty well over. The other twelve, madam, are disposed of in two articles, in the first four I toast myself drunk, and t'other eight I sleep myself sober again. Thus, ladies, you see my life is an eternal round O of delight.

Lord Foppington's interview with his Court artists is well described—

Tom Fashion. There's that fop now, has not by nature wherewithal to move a cook-maid, and by that time these fellows have done with him, egad he shall melt down a countess! But now for my reception; I'll engage it shall be as cold a one as a courtier's to his friend, who comes to put him in mind of his promise.

Lord F. (to his tailor.) Death and eternal tortures! Sir, I say the packet's too high by a foot.

Tailor. My lord, if it had been an inch lower it would not have held your lordship's packet-handkerchief.

Lord F. Rat my packet-handkerchief! have not I a page to carry it? You may make him a packet up to his chin a purpose for it; but I will not have mine come so near my face.

Tailor. 'Tis not for me to dispute your lordship's fancy.

Lord F. Look you, Sir, I shall never be reconciled to this nauseous packet, therefore pray get me another suit with all manner of expedition, for this is my eternal salvation. Mrs. Calico, are not you of my mind?

Mrs. Cal. O, directly, my lord! It can never be too low.

Lord F. You are positively in the right on't, for the packet becomes no part of the body but the knee.

(Exit tailor.)

Mrs. Cal. I hope your lordship is pleased with your steenkirk.

Lord F. In love with it, stap my vitals! bring your bill, you shall be paid to-morrow.

Mrs. C. I humbly thank your honour. *(Exit.)*

Lord F. Hark thee, shoemaker! these shoes an't ugly but they don't fit me.

Shoemaker. My lord, methinks they fit you very well.

Lord F. They hurt me just below the instep.

Shoe. (feeling his foot) My lord, they don't hurt you there.

Lord F. I tell thee they pinch me execrably.

Shoe. My lord, if they pinch you I'll be bound to be hanged, that's all.

Lord F. Why wilt thou undertake to persuade me that I cannot feel?

Shoe. Your lordship may please to feel what you think fit; but the shoe does not hurt you. I think I understand my trade.

Lord F. Now by all that's great and powerful thou art an incomprehensible coxcomb! but thou makest good shoes and so I'll bear with thee.

Tom Fashion personates his brother, Lord Foppington, and goes down to the country seat of Sir Tunbelly Clumpsey, in hope of marrying his rich daughter. The old Squire at first turns out to meet him with guns and pitchforks, but changes to the utmost servility on hearing that he is a lord. It is now Tom's object to have the marriage ceremony performed before he is discovered.

Fashion. Your father, I suppose you know, has resolved to make me happy in being your husband, and I hope I may depend upon your consent to perform what he desires.

Miss Hoyden. Sir, I never disobey my father in anything but eating of green gooseberries.

Fash. So good a daughter must needs be an admirable wife; I am therefore impatient till you are mine, and hope you will so far consider the violence of my love as not to defer my happiness so long as your father designs it.

Miss H. Pray, my lord, how long is that?

Fash. Madam, a thousand years—a whole week.

Miss H. A week! why I shall be an old woman by that time.

Fash. And I an old man.

Miss H. Why I thought it was to-morrow morning as soon as I was up, I am sure nurse told me so.

Fash. And it shall be to-morrow morning still, if you'll consent.

Miss H. If I'll consent! Why I thought I was to obey you as my husband.

Fash. That's when we're married, till then I am to obey you.

Miss H. Why then if we are to take it by turns it's the same thing. I'll obey you now, and when we are married you shall obey me.

Fash. With all my heart; but I doubt we must get nurse on our side, or we shall hardly prevail with the chaplain.

Miss H. O Lord, I can tell you a way how to persuade her to anything.

Fash. How's that?

Miss H. Why tell her she's a wholesome comely woman, and give her half-a-crown.

Fash. Nay, if that will do, she shall have half a score of them.

Miss H. O gemini! for half that she'd marry you herself. I'll run and call her.

Fash. So matters go swimmingly. This is a rare girl i' faith. I shall have a fine time on't with her in London, I'm much mistaken if she don't prove a March hare all the year round. What a scampering chase will she on't, when she finds the whole kennel of beaux at her tail! hey to the park, and the play, and the church and the devil; she'll show them sport, I'll warrant 'em. But no matter, she brings me an estate that will afford me a separate maintenance.

The following from "The Provoked Husband," gives a good specimen of social hypocrisy.

Servant. Madam, here's my Lady Fanciful to wait upon your ladyship.
Lady Brute. Shield me, kind heaven! what an inundation of impertinence is here coming upon us!

At the end of this unwelcome visit, we have the following hit at the ceremonious politeness then fashionable.

Lady B. What going already, madam.
Lady Fan. I must beg you excuse me this once, for really I have eighteen visits to return this afternoon. So you see I am importuned by the women as well as by the men.
Bel. (aside). And she's quits with 'em both.
Lady F. Nay, you shan't go one step out of the room.
Lady B. Indeed, I'll wait upon you down.
Lady F. No sweet, Lady Brute, you know I swoon at ceremony.
Lady B. Pray give me leave.
Lady F. You know I wont.
Lady B. Indeed I must.
Lady F. Indeed you shan't.
Lady B. Indeed I will.
Lady F. Indeed you shan't.
Lady B. Indeed I will.
Lady F. Indeed you shan't, indeed, indeed, indeed you shan't. *(Exit running.)*

The aversions and disputes of husbands and wives furnish the subject of some of his humour. Sir John Brute says:—

"Sure if women had been ready created, the devil instead of being kicked down in hell had been married."
Lady Brute. Are you afraid of being in love, Sir?

Heartfree. I should if there were any danger of it.

Lady B. Pray, why so?

Heart. Because I always had an aversion to being used like a dog.

Belinda. Why truly, men in love are seldom used much better.

Lady B. But were you never in love, Sir?

Heart. No, I thank heaven, madam.

Bel. Pray, where got you your learning then?

Heart. From other people's expense.

Bel. That's being a spunger, Sir, which is scarce honest. If you'd buy some experience with your own money, as 'twould be fairlier got, so 'twould stick longer by you.

* * * * *

Berinthia. Ah, Amanda, it's a delicious thing to be a young widow!

Aman. You'll hardly make me think so.

Ber. Phu! because you are in love with your husband; but that is not every woman's case.

Aman. I hope 'twas yours at least.

Ber. Mine, say ye? Now I have a great mind to tell you a lie, but I should do it so awkwardly you'd find me out.

Aman. Then e'en speak the truth.

Ber. Shall I? Then after all, I did love him, Amanda, as a man does penance.

Aman. Why did you not refuse to marry him, then?

Ber. Because my mother would have whipped me.

Aman. How did you live together?

Ber. Like man and wife—asunder. He loved the country, I the town. He hawks and hounds, I coaches and equipage. He eating and drinking, I carding and playing. He the sound of a horn, I the squeak of a fiddle. Whenever we met we gave one another the spleen.

Aman. But tell me one thing truly and sincerely.

Ber. What's that?

Aman. Notwithstanding all these jars, did not his death at last extremely trouble you?

Ber. O, yes. Not that my present pangs were so very violent, but the after pangs were intolerable. I was forced to wear a beastly widow's band a twelvemonth for 't.

In the "Journey to London," written at the end of Vanbrugh's life, and not finished, there is a very amusing account of the manner in which a country squire and family travelled up to London in the seventeenth century.

James. They have added two cart-horses to the four old mares, because my lady will have it said she came to town in her coach-and-six; and ha! ha! heavy George, the ploughman, rides postilion!

Uncle Richard. Very well; the journey begins as it should do—James!

James. Sir!

Uncle R. Dost know whether they bring all the children with them?

James. Only Squire Humphry and Miss Betty, Sir; the other six are put to board at half-a-crown a week a head with Joan Growse, at Smoke-dunghill Farm.

Uncle R. The Lord have mercy upon all good folks! What work will these people make! Dost know when they'll be here?

James. John says, Sir, they'd have been here last night, but that the old wheezy-belly horse tired, and the two fore-wheels came crash down at once in Waggon-rut Lane. Sir, they were cruelly loaden, as I understand. My lady herself, he says, laid on four mail trunks, besides the great deal-box, which fat Tom sat upon behind.

Uncle R. So.

James. Then within the coach there was Sir Francis, my lady, the great fat lap-dog, Squire Humphry, Miss Betty, my lady's maid, Mrs. Handy, and Doll Tripe, the cook— but she puked with sitting backward, so they mounted her into the coach-box.

Uncle R. Very well.

James. Then, Sir, for fear of a famine before they should get to the baiting-place, there was such baskets of plum-cake, Dutch gingerbread, Cheshire cheese,

> Naples biscuits, maccaroons, neats' tongues, and cold boiled beef; and in case of sickness, such bottles of usquebaugh, black-cherry brandy, cinnamon water, sack, tent, and strong beer, as made the old coach crack again.
>
> *Uncle R.* Well said!
>
> *James.* And for defence of this good cheer, and my lady's little pearl necklace, there was the family basket-hilt sword, the great Turkish cimiter, the old blunder-buss, a good bag of bullets, and a great horn of gunpowder.
>
> *Uncle R.* Admirable!

Vanbrugh's friend, Colley Cibber, was also of foreign origin. His father was a native of Holstein, and coming over to England before the Restoration, is known as having executed the two figures of lunatics, for the gates of Bethlehem Hospital. Colley commenced life as an actor and playwriter, and Vanbrugh was so pleased with his "Love's Last Shift, or the Fool of Fashion," that he wrote an improved version of it in "The Relapse." Thus Sir Novelty Fashion was developed into Lord Foppington, and Vanbrugh, who patronized Cibber, employed him to act the character. He was an exception to the rule that a good playwriter is not a good performer. In Cibber, we especially mark the Spanish element, which then tinged the drama, and although somewhat prosy and sententious, he is fertile and entertaining in his love intrigues. Of real humour, he seems to have no gift—some of his best attempts referring to such common failures as sometimes occur at hotels. We have in "She wou'd, and she wou'd not,"

> *Host.* Did you call, gentlemen?
>
> *Trapparti.* Yes, and bawl too, Sir. Here the gentlemen are almost famished, and nobody comes near 'em. What have you in the house now that will be ready presently?
>
> *Host.* You may have what you please, Sir.
>
> *Hypolita.* Can you get us a partridge?
>
> *Host.* We have no partridges; but we'll get you what you please in a moment. We have a very good neck of mutton, Sir, if you please, it shall be clapt down in a moment.

Hyp. Have you any pigeons or chickens?

Host. Truly, Sir, we have no fowl in the house at present; if you please, you may have anything else in a moment.

Hyp. Then, prithee, get us some young rabbits.

Host. Upon my word, Sir, rabbits are so scarce, they are not to be had for money.

Trap. Have you any fish?

Host. Fish! Sir; I dressed yesterday the finest dish that ever came upon a table; I am sorry we have none, Sir; but, if you please, you may have anything else in a moment.

Trap. Hast thou nothing but Anything else in the house?

Host. Very good mutton, Sir.

Hyp. Prithee, get us a breast, then.

Host. Breast! Don't you love the neck, Sir?

Hyp. Ha' ye nothing in the house but the neck?

Host. Really, Sir, we don't use to be so unprovided, but at present we have nothing else left.

Trap. Faith, Sir, I don't know but a Nothing else may be very good meat, when Anything else is not to be had.

Sometimes there is a little smartness in the dialogue, and in the "Careless Husband," Lord Foppington uses such strange expletives as "Sun burn me," "Stop my breath," "Set my blood." But the greater part of any amusement that there is, depends, as in the Roman Comedy, upon the tricks of low-minded mercenary servants.

Although neither of the two last-named writers was English by descent, they were both so by adoption, and the same may be said of the next author, Farquhar, who was born at Londonderry in 1678, but whose Irish characters want the charm of the pure national comicality. He was the son of a clergyman who sent him to the University, but his taste being averse to the prescribed course of study, he left it, and became an actor. Want of voice soon excluded him from the stage, and he entered the army—a profession which we might conclude, from the experiences of Wycherley and Vanbrugh, was somewhat favourable for the cultivation of dramatic talent. The constant companionship of men of wild and fanciful dispositions, the leisure for observing their talents and peculiarities, and the perpetual demand for the exercise of light repartee, would all tend to furnish effective materials for the stage. Farquhar soon married, and his poverty, with an increasing family, led to his producing a play nearly every year from 1703 to 1707. Finally he sold out, and was in deep distress. Speaking of his condition with his accustomed gaiety, he says:—

> "I have very little estate, but what is under the circumference of my hat, and should I by perchance come to lose my head, I should not be worth a groat."

He thus sketches his mental peculiarities:—

> "As to my mind, which in most men wears as many changes as their body, so in me 'tis generally drest like my person, in black. Melancholy is its every-day apparel; and it has hitherto found few holidays to make it change its clothes. In short, my constitution is very splenetic and yet very amorous, both which I endeavour to hide lest the former should offend others, and that the latter might incommode myself; and my reason is so vigilant in restraining these two failings, that I am taken for an easy-natured man with my own sex, and an ill-natured clown by yours."

Farquhar was very fond of jesting about his own misfortunes, and perhaps the following from "Love in a Bottle," exhibits a scene in which he had been himself an actor in real life.

> *Widow Bullfinch.* Mr. Lyric, what do you mean by all this? Here you have lodged two years in my house, promised me eighteen-pence a week for your lodging, and I have never received eighteen farthings, not the value of *that*, Mr. Lyric, *(snaps her fingers.)* You always put me off with telling me of your play, your play! Sir, you shall play no more with me: I'm in earnest.
> *Lyric.* There's more trouble in a play than you imagine, Madam.
> *Bull.* There's more trouble with a lodger than you think, Mr. Lyric.
> *Lyric.* First there's the decorum of time.

Bull. Which you never observe, for you keep the worst hours of any lodger in town.

Lyric. Then there's the exactness of characters.

Bull. And you have the most scandalous one I ever heard . . .

Lyric. *(Aside)* Was ever poor rogue so ridden. If ever the Muses had a horse, I am he. *(Aloud)* Faith! Madam, poor Pegasus is jaded.

Bull. Come, come, Sir; he shan't slip his neck out of collar for all that. Money I will have, and money I must have.

The above is taken from Farquhar's first play, and we generally find richer humour in the first attempts of genius than in their later and more elaborate productions. Widow Bullfinch says that "Champagne is a fine liquor, which all your beaux drink to make em' witty."

Mockmode. Witty! oh by the universe I must be witty! I'll drink nothing else. I never was witty in all my life. I love jokes dearly. Here, Club, bring us a bottle of what d'ye call it—the witty liquor.

Bull. But I thought that all you that were bred at the University would be wits naturally?

Mock. The quite contrary, Madam, there's no such thing there. We dare not have wit there for fear of being counted rakes. Your solid philosophy is all read there, which is clear another thing. But now I will be a wit, by the universe . . . Is that the witty liquor? Come fill the glasses. Now that I have found my mistress, I must next find my wits.

Club. So you had need, master, for those that find a mistress are generally out of their wits. *(Gives him a glass.)*

Mock. Come, fill for yourself. *(They jingle and drink.)* But where's the wit now, Club? Have you found it?

Club. Egad! master, I think 'tis a very good jest.

Mock. What?

Club. What? why drinking—you'll find, master, that this same gentleman in the straw doublet, this same will-i'-th'-wisp is a wit at the bottom. *(Fills.)* Here, here, master; how it puns and quibbles in the glass!

Mock. By the universe, now I have it!—the wit lies in the jingling. All wit consists most in jingling; hear how the glasses rhyme to one another.

Again:—

Mock. Could I but dance well, push well,[63] play upon the flute, and swear the most modish oaths, I would set up for quality with e'er a young nobleman of 'em all. Pray what are the most fashionable oaths in town? Zoons, I take it, is a very becoming one.

Rigadoon. *(a dancing-master.)* Zoons is only used by the disbanded officers and bullies, but zauns is the beaux pronunciation.

Mock. Zauns!

Rig. Yes, Sir; we swear as we dance; smooth and with a cadence—Zauns! 'Tis harmonious, and pleases the ladies, because it is soft. Zauns, Madam, is the only compliment our great beaux pass on a lady.

Mock. But suppose a lady speaks to me; what must I say?

Rig. Nothing, Sir; you must take snuff grin, and make her a humble cringe—thus: *(Bows foppishly and takes snuff; Mockmode imitates him awkwardly, and taking snuff, sneezes.)* O Lord, Sir! you must never sneeze; 'tis as unbecoming after orangery as grace after meat.

Mock. I thought people took it to clear the brain.

Rig. The beaux have no brains at all, Sir; their skull is a perfect snuff-box; and I heard a physician swear, who opened one of 'em, that the three divisions of his head were filled with orangery, bergamot, and plain Spanish.

Mock. Zauns! I must sneeze, *(sneezes.)* Bless me!

Rig. Oh, fy! Mr. Mockmode! what a rustical expression that is! 'Bless me!' You should upon all such occasions cry, Dem me! You would be as nauseous to the ladies as one of the old patriarchs, if you used that obsolete expression.

Sir Harry Wildair gives a good sketch of a lady's waiting-woman of the time.

> *Colonel Standard.* Here, here, Mrs. Parly; whither so fast?
>
> *Parly.* Oh Lord! my master! Sir, I was running to Mademoiselle Furbelow, the French milliner, for a new burgundy for my lady's head.
>
> *Col. S.* No, child; you're employed about an old-fashioned garniture for your master's head, if I mistake not your errand.
>
> *Parly.* Oh, Sir! there's the prettiest fashion lately come over! so airy, so French, and all that. The pinners are double ruffled with twelve plaits of a side, and open all from the face; the hair is frizzled all up round the head, and stands as stiff as a bodkin. Then the favourites hang loose on the temples, with a languishing lock in the middle. Then the caul is extremely wide, and over all is a coronet raised very high, and all the lappets behind.

This lady on being questioned, says that her wages are ten pounds a year, but she makes two hundred a year of her mistress's old clothes.

But Farquhar is best known as the author of the "Beaux Stratagem." Though not so full of humour, as "Love in a Bottle," it had more action and bolder sensational incidents. The play proved a great success, but one which will always have sad associations. It came too late. Farquhar died in destitution, while the plaudits resounded in his ears.

The following are specimens from his last play:—

(Aimwell (a gentleman of broken fortune looking for a rich wife) goes to church in the country to further his designs.)

> *Aimwell.* The appearance of a stranger in a country church draws as many gazers as a blazing star; no sooner he comes into the cathedral, but a train of whispers runs buzzing round the congregation in a moment: *Who is he? Whence comes he? Do you know him?* Then I, Sir, tips me the verger with half-a-crown; he pockets the simony, and inducts me into the best pew in the church; I pull out my snuff-box, turn myself round, bow to

the bishop, or the dean, if he be the commanding officer, single out a beauty, rivet both my eyes to hers, set my nose a bleeding by the strength of imagination, and show the whole church my concern—by my endeavouring to hide it; after the sermon the whole town gives me to her for a lover, and by persuading the lady that I am a-dying for her, the tables are turned, and she in good earnest falls in love with me.

Archer. There's nothing in this, Tom, without a precedent; but instead of rivetting your eyes to a beauty, try to fix 'em upon a fortune; that's our business at present.

Aim. Psha! no woman can be a beauty without a fortune. Let me alone, for I am a marksman.

Talking afterwards of Dorinda, whom he observes in church, he says,

Aimwell. Call me Oroondates, Cesario, Amadis, all that romance can in a lover paint, and then I'll answer:—O, Archer! I read her thousands in her looks, she looked like Ceres in her harvest; corn, wine and oil, milk and honey, gardens, groves, and purling streams played in her plenteous face.

CHAPTER XI.

Congreve—Lord Dorset.

The birthplace of Congreve is uncertain, but he was born about 1671, and was educated in Kilkenny and Dublin. He is an instance of that union of Irish versatility with English reflection, which has produced the most celebrated wits. We also mark in him a considerable improvement in delicacy. "The Old Batchelor" was his first play, the success of which was so great that Lord Halifax made him one of the commissioners for licensing hackney-coaches; he afterwards gave him a place in the Pipe Office and Custom House.

Belmour begins very suitably by saying—

"Come come, leave business to idlers, and wisdom to fools; they have need of 'em. Wit be my faculty, and pleasure my occupation; and let Father Time shake his glass."

Speaking of Belinda, he says—

"In my conscience I believe the baggage loves me, for she never speaks well of me herself, nor suffers anybody else to rail at me."

Heartwell, an old bachelor, says—

"Women's asses bear great burdens; are forced to undergo dressing, dancing, singing, sighing, whining, rhyming, flattery, lying, grinning, cringing, and the drudgery of loving to boot . . . Every man plays the fool once in his life, but to marry is to play the fool all one's life long."

In Belinda we have a specimen of one of the fast young ladies of the period, who certainly seems to have used strong language. She cries,

> Oh, that most inhuman, barbarous, hackney-coach! I am jolted to a jelly, am I not horridly touz'd?

She chides Belmour,

> Prithee hold thy tongue! Lord! he has so pestered me with flowers and stuff, I think I shan't endure the sight of a fire for a twelvemonth.
> *Belmour.* Yet all can't melt that cruel frozen heart.
> *Bel.* O, gad! I hate your hideous fancy—you said that once before—if you must talk impertinently, for Heaven's sake let it be with variety; don't come always like the devil wrapped in flames. I'll not hear a sentence more that begins with, "I burn," or an "I beseech you, Madam."

At last she exclaims,

> "O! my conscience! I could find in my heart to marry thee, purely to be rid of thee."

There is frequently a conflict of wit. Sharper tells Sir Joseph Willot that he lost many pounds, when he was defending him in a scuffle the night before. He hopes he will repay him.

> Money is but dirt, Sir Joseph; mere dirt, Sir Joseph.
> *Sir Joseph.* But I profess 'tis a dirt I have washed my hands of at present.

Lord Froth in "The Double Dealer" says,

There is nothing more unbecoming in a man of gravity than to laugh, to be pleased with what pleases the crowd. When I laugh, I always laugh alone.

Brisk. I suppose that's because you laugh at your own jests.

Sir Paul Plyant in great wroth expresses himself as follows:

The subjects of Congreve's Comedies would often be thought objectionable at the present day. The humour is not in the plot, but in the general dialogue. In "Love for Love," Ben Legend, a sailor, speaking of lawyers, says—

Lawyer, I believe there's many a cranny and leak unstopt in your conscience. If so be that one had a pump to your bosom, I believe we should discern a foul hold. They say a witch will sail in a sieve, but I believe the devil would not venture aboard your conscience.

The last play he wrote, which failed, was deficient in wit, but had plenty of inebriety in it. After singing a drinking song, Sir Wilful says in "The Way of the World."

The sun's a good pimple, an honest soaker, he has a cellar at your Antipodes. If I travel, Aunt, I touch at your Antipodes—your Antipodes are a good rascally sort of topsy-turvy fellows. If I had a bumper I'd stand on my head, and drink a health to them.

* * * * *

Scandal. Yes, mine *(pictures)* are not in black and white, and yet there are some set out in their true colours, both men and women. I can show you pride, folly, affectation, wantonness, inconstancy, covetousness, dissimulation, malice and ignorance all in one piece. Then I can show your lying, foppery, vanity, cowardice, bragging, incontinence, and ugliness in another piece, and yet one of them is a celebrated beauty, and t'other a professed beau. I have paintings, too, some pleasant enough.

Mrs. Frail. Come, let's hear 'em.

Scan. Why, I have a beau in a bagnio cupping for a complexion, and sweating for a shape.

Mrs. F. So—

Scan. Then I have a lady burning brandy in a cellar with a hackney coachman.

Mrs. F. Oh! well, but that story is not true.

Scan. I have some hieroglyphics, too; I have a lawyer with a hundred hands, two heads, and but one face; a divine with two faces and one head; and I have a soldier with his brains in his belly, and his heart where his head should be.

It has been said that Congreve retired on the appearance of Mrs. Centlivre, but so high was the opinion entertained of his genius that he was buried in Westminster Abbey, and his pall was supported by noblemen. Pope was one of his greatest admirers, and dedicated his translation of Homer to him.

Dryden writes on Congreve.

> "In easy dialogue is Fletcher's praise,
> He moved the mind, but had not power to raise,
> Great Jonson did by strength of judgment please,
> Yet doubling Fletcher's force, he wants his ease.
> In differing talents both adorned their age,
> One for the study, t'other for the stage,
> But both to Congreve justly shall submit,
> One matched in judgment, both over-matched in wit."

Macaulay says "the wit of Congreve far outshines that of every comic writer, except Sheridan, who has arisen within the last two centuries."

Lord Dorset of whom we have above spoken deserves some passing notice. He was high in the favour of Charles II., James, and William; and was one of the most accomplished of the courtiers of that day, who, notwithstanding their dissipation, were more or less scholars, and wrote poetry. What was better, he was a munificent supporter of real literary genius, and patronized Dryden, and to judge by their commendations was not neglectful of Congreve and Pope.

Most of his poems are in the pastoral strain, but do not show any great talent. Two or three of them have some humour—

> "Dorinda's sparkling wit and eyes
> United, cast too fierce a light,
> Which blazes high, but quickly dies,
> Pains not the heart, but hurts the sight;

* * * * *

> "Love is a calmer, gentler joy,
> Smooth are his looks, and soft his pace;
> Her cupid is a blackguard boy
> That runs his link right in your face."

Lord Dorset was at the battle of Opdam when the Dutch Admiral's fleet was destroyed in 1665. The night before the engagement he wrote the well known epistle

> "To all you ladies now on land,
> We men at sea indite,
> And first would have you understand
> How hard it is to write;
> The Muses now and Neptune too,
> We must implore to write to you.
> > With a fa la la la la.

> "For though the Muses should prove kind,
> And fill our empty brain,
> Yet if rough Neptune raise the wind,
> To wave the azure main,
> Our paper, pen and ink, and we,
> Roll up and down our ships at sea.
> > With a fa, la, &c.

> "Should foggy Opdam chance to throw
> Our sad and dismal story,
> The Dutch would scorn so weak a foe,
> And quit their fort at Goree;
> For what resistance can they find

From men who've left their hearts behind?
　　　　With a fa, la, &c.

"In justice you cannot refuse
To think of our distress,
When we for hope of honour lose
Our certain happiness;
All those designs are but to prove
Ourselves more worthy of your love.
　　　　With a fa, la, &c.

"And now we've told you all our loves,
And likewise all our fears,
In hopes this declaration moves,
Some pity from your tears;
Let's hear of no inconstancy,
We have too much of that at sea.
　　　　With a fa la la la la."

We can easily understand how the above lines were suggested, for in those times the same officers served both in army and navy, and many of the young sparks taken from the gaieties of London had not yet acquired their sea legs. Wycherley is said to have been present at some of the engagements with the Dutch.

END OF THE FIRST VOLUME.

* * * * *

FOOTNOTES:

1   Of course this will scarcely apply in those cases in which, by abstraction, we overlook the creative action of the mind, and regard its humorous productions as ludicrous. Nor does it hold good where from long exercise of ingenuity a habit has been formed and amusing fancies spring up, as it were naturally, and so involuntarily that, for the moment, we see them only as ludicrous. This view changes almost instantaneously, and beneath it we often find the best humour. It may be said that such cases should be placed entirely under the head of humour, but can we maintain that a man is unaware when he is humorous? The most telling effects are produced by the ludicrous, and where the creative action of the mind is scarcely discernible. Efforts to be humorous are seldom crowned with success; we require something that appears to be real or original, either as a close rendering of actual occurrences, or a spontaneous efflorescence of genius. Among the latter class we may reckon some of our most exquisite and permanent sayings.

2   A story is told of a Mr. Crispe, a merchant of London, who although deaf, when Sir Alexander Cary made a speech before his execution, followed the motion of his lips so as to be able to relate it to his friends.

3   Mrs. Barbauld had such a perpetual smile that one of her friends said it made her jaws ache to look at her.

4   St. Paul, who was brought up at the feet of Gamaliel, gives a different account in Rom. iv. 19. See also Heb. xi. 11.

5   Soame Jenyns strangely imagined that a portion of the happiness of Seraphim and of just men made perfect would be derived from an exquisite perception of the ludicrous; while Addison mentions that a learned monk laid it down as a doctrine that laughter was the effect of original sin, and that Adam could not laugh before the fall. Some of the early Christians felt so

strongly the incompatibility of strong human emotions with the divine nature that they expunged the words "Jesus wept."

6   Perhaps Solomon was amused by them, for in the catalogue of the valuable things brought in his ships are apes and peacocks.

7   I cannot see in Homer any of that philosophic satire on the condition of mortals, which some have found in those passages where men are represented as being deceived and tricked by the gods. Anything so deep would be beyond humour. He very probably conceived that the gods, whom he represented as similar to men, were sometimes not above playing severe practical jokes on them. The so-called irony of Sophocles in like manner, is too philosophical and bitter for humour.

8   Tom Brown, the humorist, says, Lycambes complimented the Iambics of Archilochus with the most convincing proof of their wit and goodness.

9   Archilochus could not have been called a satirist in the correct sense of the word. His observations were mostly personal or philosophical. He had evidently considerable power in illustrating the moral by the physical world, and one of his sayings "Speak not evil of the dead," has become proverbial.

10   Irony had previously been used in Asia. The only specimens of humour in the Old Testament are of this character, as in Job, "No doubt but ye are the people, and wisdom shall die with you;" where Elijah says to the prophets of Baal, "Cry aloud, for he is a god," and the children call after Elisha, "Go up, thou bald-head."

11   Magnes and others of the day used similar titles. We read that there were once three Homeric hymns extant, named "The Monkeys," "The seven-times-shorn Goat," and "The Song on the Thrushes."

12   After disposing of his daughters for a bunch of garlic and a little salt, he exclaims, "Oh, Mercury, God of Traffic, grant that I may sell my wife as profitably, and my mother too!"

13   So the pun may be represented.

14   Certainly not before 460 B.C.

15   Compare our "Billingsgate."

16   We sometimes speak of a seedy coat.

17   The answers to the above riddles are, thistledown, sleep, night and day, shade.

18   "Gugga" seems to have corresponded with our "Nigger."

19   About three and nine pence.

20   Roman mirrors made of silver.

21   *Scurra* originally meant a neighbour, then a gossip, then a pleasant fellow, and finally a jocose, and in those rude times a scurrilous man.

22   There is a story of Caligula having had an actor burnt alive for making an offensive pun in an Atellane play. Sometimes nicknames were thus made. Placidus was Acidus, Labienus, Rabienus; Claudius Tiberius Nero was Caldius Biberius Mero.

23   I have been obliged to omit some of the pungent indelicacy of the original. The Pope was the sacrificing priest.

24   We meet with such words as *verrucosus*, *sanna*, a grimace, and *stloppus*, the sound made by striking the inflated cheeks.

25   "A satirist is always to be suspected, who to make vice odious dwells upon all its acts and minutest circumstances with a sort of relish and retrospective fondness."—*Lamb.*

26   Palindromes, such as "Tibi subito motibus ibit." We have some in English, as where our forefather addresses his wife "Madam, I'm Adam."

27   Pyrogenes has a double meaning, "born of corn," and "born of fire," alluding to Bacchus' mother having been burnt. Bromos is a kind of cereal, Bromion a name for Bacchus.

28   A man of Capreæ, having caught an unusually large barbel, presented it to Tiberius, who was so enraged at his being able to find him in his retreat, that he ordered his face to be scrubbed with the fish.

29   Some of the pagans put off Christian baptism till the last moment under this idea.

30   There seems to me to be several reasons for drawing this conclusion.

31   "Semel minusne, an bis minus; non sat scio, An utrumque eorum, ut quondam audivi dicier Jovi ipsi regi noluit concedere."

32   The answers to these enigmas are rose, fleas, sea-mew, visions, wheels.

33   As late as the fourteenth century there were only four classical works in the Royal Library at Paris.

34   Ritson characteristically observes, "There is this distinction between the heathen deities and Christian saints, that the fables of the former were indebted for their existence to the flowing

inspiration of the sublime poet, and the legends of the latter to the gloomy fanaticism of a lazy monk or a stinking priest."

35   Sometimes anciently called "West Wales."

36   King Alfred advanced so far as to make a translation of a classical history written by Orosius in 416; but the object of the work was to show that Christianity was not the cause of the evils which had befallen the Roman Empire.

37   Two of them are mentioned as superior to Homer. One pretended to be derived from Dares, a Phrygian, who fought on the Trojan side, and another from Dictys, a Cretan, who was with the Greeks.

38   The kind of stories prevalent in these countries may be conjectured from the two related by John of Bromton, as believed by the natives. One relates that the head of a child lies at the bottom of the Gulf of Sataliah in Asia Minor, and that when the head is partly upright, such storms prevail in the gulf that no vessel can live, but when it is lying down there is a calm. The other asserts that once in every month a great black dragon comes in the clouds, plunges his head into the stream, but leaves his tail in the sky, and draws up the water, so that even ships are carried into the air. The only way for sailors to escape this monster, is to make a great noise by beating and shouting, so as to frighten him.

39   Originally an Arcadian superstition.

40   Pinnacles.

41   Tiles.

42   The following is the original.

> "Meum est propositum in taberna mori,
> Vinum sit appositum morientis ori,
> Ut dicant cum venerint angelorum chori,
> Deus sit propitius huic potatori."

43   An idea probably borrowed from the classical writers.

44   Or the "Amiable," a translation of his father's name.

45   Mr. Drummond in his Life of Erasmus.

46   Reprinted by Halliwell.

47   See "Art-Journal."

48   I remember to have seen such a procession at Como in the Holy Week. The various accessories of the Passion were borne along on the top of poles with appropriate mottoes, for example: Two ladders crossed, "He bowed the heavens and came down." A

stuffed cock, "The cock crew." A barber's basin, "Pilate washed his hands," &c. The effect was almost ludicrous.

49 Lucian makes the father of Cleanthis congratulate himself on having obtained a buffoon for his son's wedding feast. This individual was an ugly little fellow with close shaven head, except a few straggling hairs made up to resemble a cock. He began by dancing and contorting his body and spouting some Ægytian verses, then he launched all kinds of fooleries at the company. Most laughed, but on his calling Alcidamas a Maltese puppy, he was challenged to fight or have his brains dashed out.

50 But this may have been traditional, for the fools in classic times were sometimes shaven.

51 Wright's "History of the Grotesque."

52 Such as the Wife of Bath's tale, and in "January and May," or the "Marchante's Tale."

53 She was roasting a pig.

54 Most of the ridiculous answers said to have been made at examinations are mere humorous inventions. We almost think there must be a slight improvement made in the following, though they are upon the authority of an examiner,

> What are the great Jewish Feasts?
> Purim, Urim, and Thummin.
> What bounded Samaria on the East?
> The Jordan.
> What on the West?
> The other side of Jordan.
> Derive an English word from the Latin *necto?*
> Necktie.

Nor can we doubt that a slight humorous colouring has been introduced into the following from the "Memorials of Archibald Constable," recently published by his son.—An old deaf relation said on her death-bed to her attendant, "Ann, if I should be spared, I hope my nephew will get the doctor to open my head, and see whether anything can be done for my hearing."

55 One of Anne Boleyn's principal favourites was Sir Thomas Wyatt, who was celebrated at that day as a man of humour, though at present we see nothing in his poems but a few poetical conceits. The titles of them are suggestive: "The Lover sending

sighs to move his suit." "Of his Love who pricked her finger with a needle." "The Lover praiseth the beauty of his Lady's hand." He wrote the following upon the Queen's name:—

> "What word is that, that changeth not,
> Though it be turned and made in twain?
> It is mine Anna, God it wot,
> The only causer of my pain;
> My love that meedeth with disdain;
> Yet is it loved, what will you more?
> It is my salve and eke my sore."

56 Christina of Sweden made a similar remark when the Order of the Garter was sent to Charles Gustavus.

57 Pace had said the same to Queen Elizabeth, and from such strokes jesters were called 'honest,' as 'Honest Jo,' &c.

58 There is little humour in Shadwell's works; he succeeded Dryden as Poet Laureate, which was perhaps the cause of the above lines.

Rochester said, "If Shadwell had burnt all he wrote, and printed all he spoke, he would have had more wit and humour than any poet." Probably his wit would have been like Rochester's. Whether Shadwell were himself a good poet or not, he made a hit at the poetasters of his day, in which he showed some genius.

> *Poet.*   O, very loftily!
> The winged vallance of your eyes advance
> Shake off your canopied and downie trance:
> Phoebus already quaffs the morning dew,
> Each does his daily lease of life renew.
> Now you shall hear description, 'tis the very life of poetry.
> He darts his beams on the lark's mossy house,
> And from his quiet tenement doth rouse
> The little charming and harmonious fowl
> Which sings its lump of body to a soul.
> Swiftly it clambers up in the steep air
> With warbling notes, and makes each note a stair.

59 Sir Roger L'Estrange gives the names of the people attacked.

60   One of Cromwell's principal officers.

61   Thus familiarly called, no doubt owing to the custom of giving
      pet names to jesters.

62   Guardian, Vol. I. No. 2.

63   Fence.

BIBLIOBAZAAR

The essential book market!

Did you know that you can get any of our titles in large print?

Did you know that we have an ever-growing collection of books in many languages?

Order online:
www.bibliobazaar.com

Find all of your favorite classic books!

Stay up to date with the latest government reports!

At BiblioBazaar, we aim to make knowledge more accessible by making thousands of titles available to you- *quickly and affordably*.

Contact us:
BiblioBazaar
PO Box 21206
Charleston, SC 29413